Published in 1981 by Grisewood and Dempsey Ltd.
Elsley Court, 20-22 Great Titchfield Street, London W1P 7AD

Reprinted 1984

Printed in Spain by Gráficas Reunidas, S. A., Madrid.

ISBN 0 906279 08 9

RAINBOW

Prehistoric Life

Encyclopedia

This edition produced exclusively for

WHSMITH

Contents

AUTHOR
Mark Lambert

EDITOR
Adrian Sington

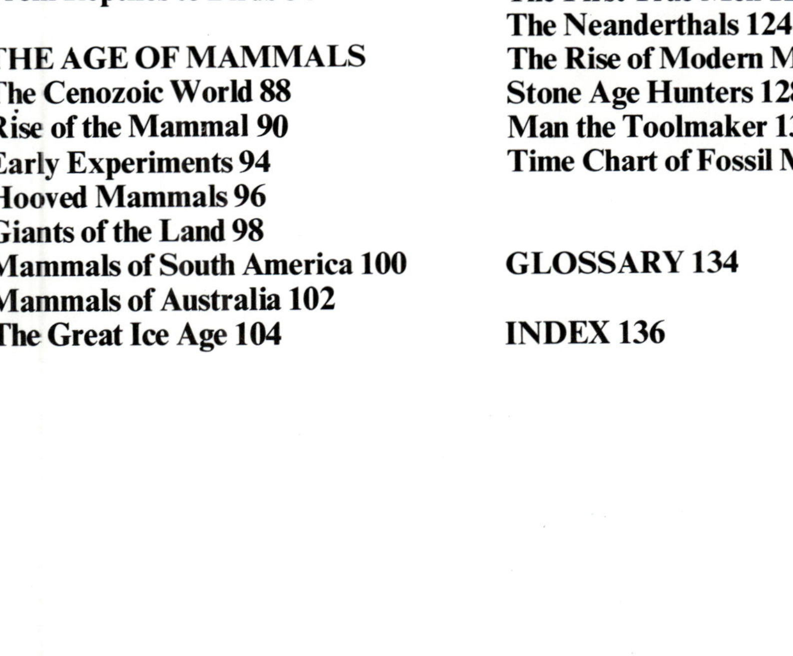

IN THE BEGINNING

The Creation of Earth

No one knows for certain how the Universe and the Solar System began. Over the years many scientists have suggested theories. Today, however, we believe that the Universe began about 18,000 million years ago with an enormous explosion, known as the Big Bang. After the explosion matter was hurled out into space. There it condensed into galaxies. Inside the galaxies, stars began to form.

As long ago as 1775 Immanuel Kant, a German philosopher, suggested that the Solar System was formed from a spinning disc of dust and gas. The centre of the disc became a star, the Sun and the outer parts became the planets. Other scientists had similar ideas. But in 1916 Sir James Jeans, an English astronomer, put forward a completely different theory. He suggested that another star passed close to the Sun and drew off a cigar-shaped filament of material. This broke up into the planets. Yet another theory was put forward by the Russian scientist Otto Schmidt in 1944. He suggested that the Sun passed through a cloud of gas and dust and gathered up a disc of material that later became the planets.

Today scientists believe that the ideas of Immanuel Kant were correct. According to the modern Cold Gas Disc Theory, the Sun formed at the centre of a whirling disc of dust and gas. As gravity pulled the particles together, vast amounts of energy were released and the Sun began to heat up. Eventually it became so hot that hydrogen atoms fused together to form helium. This reaction is called *thermonuclear fusion*. It gives out an enormous amount of heat and light. The Sun began to shine brightly about 5,000 million years ago and will continue to burn for at least another 5,000 million years, before it starts to cool down.

According to Sir James Jeans' theory (the tidal theory) of how the planets formed, a passing star dragged out a tongue of hot gas from the Sun's surface. This broke up and the pieces cooled and condensed into the planets. If this theory were true, then the sun and planets should be made of the same chemicals. But in fact their composition is very different. Scientists now believe that such a tongue of gas would have drifted out into space rather than form planets.

From earliest times people have had many fanciful ideas about the Earth, planets and stars. This idea of the Earth carried by three elephants standing on the back of a tortoise comes from an ancient Indian tribe.

Several stages in the formation of the earth from the cold disc of gas around the Sun. The Earth gathered material and heated up into a molten ball. As it cooled and became more solid, water vapour formed dense clouds. These eventually released a deluge of water that formed the oceans.

Meanwhile the outer parts of the spinning disc froze. The particles began to join up to form lumps. These gathered up more particles and gradually the planets formed. As they grew the planets also became hot. But because they were smaller than the Sun not enough heat energy was released for thermonuclear fusion to occur. So, gradually they cooled down. Among the cooling planets was Earth, so far the only planet on which it has been possible for life to develop.

The Young World

From a molten ball of fire Earth cooled and became solid. Clouds formed, rains fell, the seas grew and Earth was ready for life to begin.

The Earth began to form about 5,000 million years ago. It started as a fiery ball of molten material. This gradually cooled down and as it cooled it began to shrink. Soon the various layers of the Earth began to appear. The crust began to form on the surface. At first this just consisted of vast rafts of rock floating on the molten material below. But soon these rafts joined up and the Earth became enclosed in a solid case.

Meanwhile, inside the ball of molten material, the heaviest elements, such as iron and nickel, sank to the centre of the planet. There they eventually formed the Earth's core. Today the centre of the core is solid, but the outer part still remains molten and liquid. Movements in the liquid outer core generate electric currents and cause the Earth's magnetic field. The whole core extends 3,470 kilometres from the planet's centre.

Outside the core the lighter elements formed the mantle. This now consists of very dense rock and is 2,900 kilometres thick. The relatively thin crust lies on the outside of the mantle. There are two kinds of crust—oceanic crust and continental crust. Oceanic crust is thin, with a thickness of about 6 kilometres. Continental crust is much thicker, having an average thickness of about 35 kilometres.

If you could travel back in time, you would be ill-advised to try and visit Earth during this period. Conditions on the surface were not pleasant. The crust heaved and buckled under the colossal strains and stresses produced as the Earth cooled and shrank. Volcanoes spouted forth thousands of tons of molten rock. Gases, such as ammonia, methane and carbon monoxide hissed from every crack in the surface. All are extremely poisonous.

At the same time water vapour, forced out of the shrinking planet, steamed out into the poisonous atmosphere. Dark clouds covered the whole Earth. Eventually the quantity of water vapour became too great for the atmosphere to hold. Then, about 3,500 million years ago, the rains began. Torrential rain poured down, probably for thousands of years. Steam rose from the hot rocks, only to condense in the atmosphere and fall as rain again. Rushing torrents of water poured down from the mountains into the valleys and plains. In this way the Earth's first seas were formed. Water probably covered over three quarters of the Earth's surface.

Meanwhile, the Earth's atmosphere was developing. At first this consisted mostly of hydrogen and helium, the two most common gases in the Universe. But because these are light gases, they quickly escaped into space.

Even after the young Earth cooled, many volcanoes still erupted on the surface. The fountains of lava they spouted forth cooled to form rocks. The gases released at the same time helped to form Earth's primitive atmosphere.

The next atmosphere to form came from the Earth itself, as it cooled. It consisted mostly of water vapour, ammonia and methane, together with small amounts of other gases. This atmosphere was bombarded with ultra-violet rays from the Sun. Much of the ammonia and methane was broken down into simpler chemicals. The new atmosphere that formed consisted mostly of these simpler chemicals—hydrogen, nitrogen and probably carbon dioxide. The hydrogen escaped into space, but the heavier gases remained. These were the chemicals that fell with the rains into the newly forming seas. Together with chemicals washed from the rocks, they formed the 'primeval soup' in which life would begin.

All of this took many millions of years to happen and occurred millions of years ago. But such vast periods of time are difficult to understand. On page 108 there is a time scale on which the whole of the history of life on Earth has been condensed into a single year. On this time scale the first backboned animals appeared in early October, mammals appeared in late November and man appeared only in the evening of December 31st.

On the same time scale the Big Bang occurred five whole years before life began. The Sun began to shine brightly only during the last of these five years, at about the end of April. By mid-June of the same year Earth's crust had formed and the seas first covered the land in mid-October. Sometime between then and January of the following year life on Earth finally began.

Above: The oldest known rocks in the world are in Greenland. They have been dated at between 3,700 and 3,750 million years old. However, they are metamorphic rocks (see page 16). So even older rocks must have existed. The actual age of the Earth is taken from meteorite remains, dated at 4,600 million years old.

Below: In 1650 Archbishop Ussher added up the ages of the generations of people mentioned in the Old Testament. He concluded that the Earth was formed at 9.00 AM on October 2nd, 4004 BC.

Continents Adrift

Over millions of years Earth's continents have gradually drifted across the planet's surface.

Scientists used to believe that Earth's continents had always been where they are now. A few people, however, began to notice evidence which suggested that the continents had moved. In 1620 Francis Bacon, an English philosopher, pointed out that the coastlines of Africa and South America are remarkably similar. In the early 1800s Alexander von Humboldt, a German naturalist, suggested that these continents could once have fitted together. Later, other scientists worked out that all the continents could be fitted together in a kind of jigsaw puzzle. Fossils of the same plants and animals were found on different continents. This suggested that these continents had once been joined.

These and other pieces of evidence helped the German meteorologist Alfred Wegener to produce his theory of continental drift, which he published in 1915. It was only accepted in the early 1950s. Until then scientists could not explain how the continents could drift across Earth's apparently solid surface.

Today, however, we can explain Wegener's theory because geologists have learned more about the structure of the Earth's surface. The crust and the upper layer of the mantle are solid. Together they are called the *lithosphere*. But 75 kilometres below the surface of the Earth, there is a layer of semi-solid mantle called the *asthenosphere*. The lithosphere floats on the asthenosphere.

The modern theory of continental drift is based on the idea that the lithosphere is made up of a number of rigid plates. These plates are continually moving and as they move they carry the continents along. The plates move because they are carried by powerful currents in the semi-solid asthenosphere below.

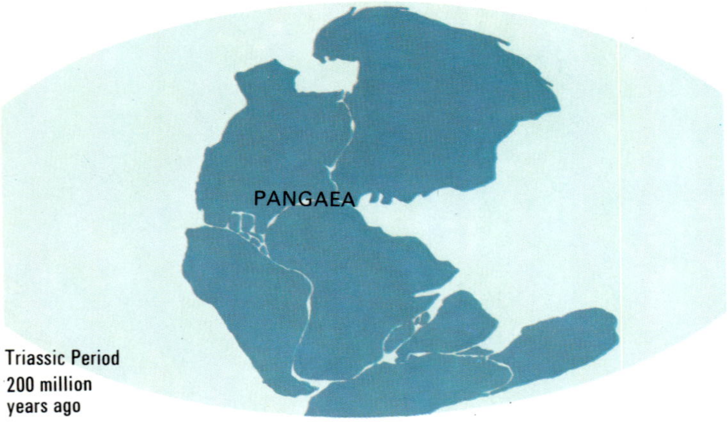

Triassic Period
200 million years ago

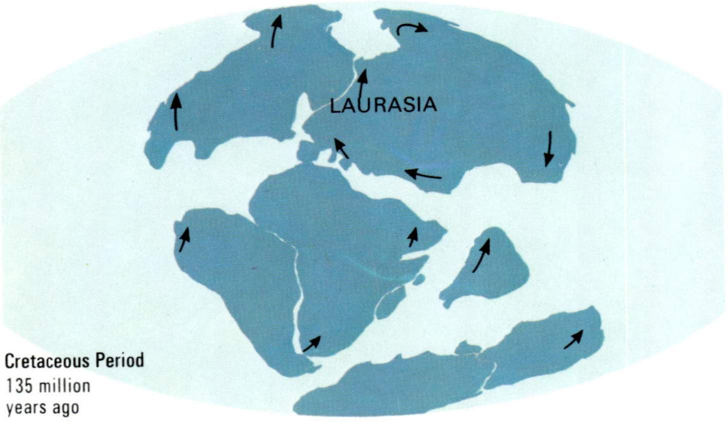

Cretaceous Period
135 million years ago

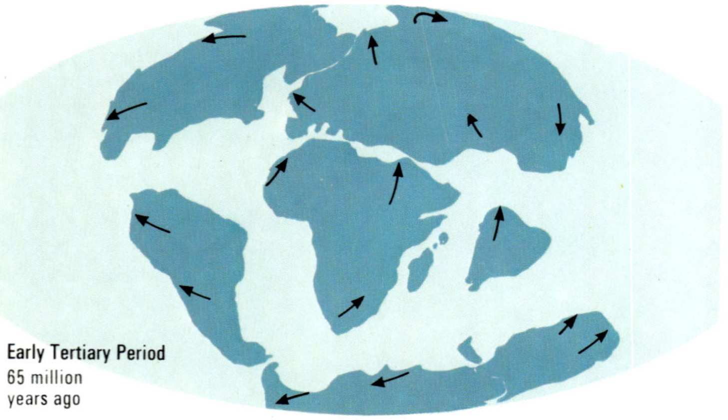

Early Tertiary Period
65 million years ago

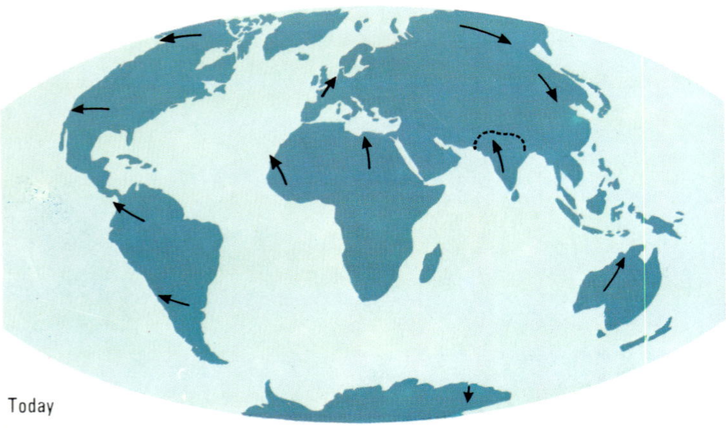

Today

During the Triassic period (see the Geological Time Scale on page 22) all the continents came together to form one large landmass, known today as Pangaea. This split up into two smaller landmasses, Laurasia and Gondwanaland. By the start of the Tertiary period the continents were drifting towards their present positions.

Above: Evidence for continental drift comes from fossil animals and plants. Similar fossils have been found in South America, Africa, India and Australia. This suggests that these continents were once joined together. Evidence from the rocks shows that, before these animals and plants existed, these continents were at the South Pole. The blue area shows the land that was once covered by ice.

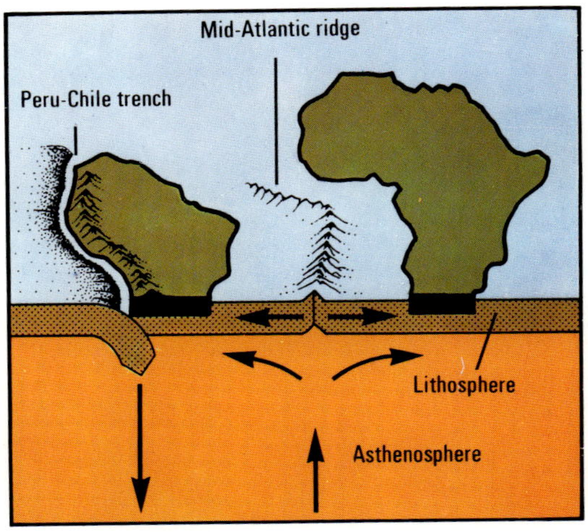

Right: Where hot magma rises in the asthenosphere, the Earth's plates are pushed apart and new material is added to their edges. Where two plates meet, one is forced down beneath the other.

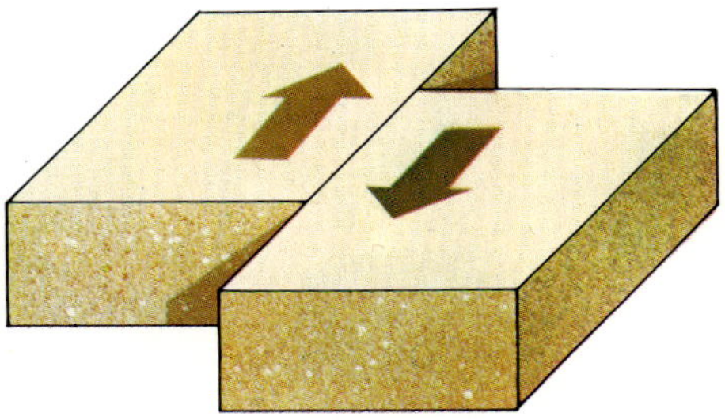

Above: Where two plates slide against each other a transform fault forms.

Below: A satellite picture of the Sinai Peninsular. On the eastern side the Dead Sea and the Gulf of Aqaba lie on a spreading ridge that extends down the Red Sea. Gradually Africa and the Sinai Peninsular are moving away from Asia.

Underneath the edges of some plates there are rising convection currents in the asthenosphere. These currents spread outwards when they reach the lithosphere and push the plates apart. As the plates separate, new rock is added to the lithosphere from the molten rock below. Such places are called *constructive plate margins* and they form ridges, usually in the middle of oceans, such as the mid-Atlantic ridge.

In other places, of course, the opposite happens and two plates push against each other. Where this occurs one of the plates is forced downwards. A deep trench forms and the descending plate melts in the asthenosphere below. Such places are called *destructive plate margins.* An example is the Peru-Chile trench which runs down the west coast of South America.

Shaping the Earth

Throughout its history Earth has been continuously shaped and reshaped by the plate movement, volcanic action and the weather.

The Earth's crust is on the move. Slowly but surely the plates are inching their way across the surface, changing the appearance of the world. The Atlantic Ocean, for example, is slowly widening by a few centimetres every year. Iceland, which lies on the Mid-Atlantic ridge, is getting larger at the rate of two centimetres every year.

When two plates collide, one is forced under the other. But when two continents meet, neither of them can be forced down. As a result the edges of the continents buckle and fold and mountains form. The Himalayas formed in this way when India collided with Asia 50 million years ago. All over the world mountains are formed as the Earth's plates are pushed together; and rift valleys are formed as the plates are pulled apart.

Mountain formation is often helped by volcanic action. When one plate is forced beneath another, the disturbance that occurs in the asthenosphere below causes volcanoes to erupt on the surface. The Andes of South America were formed partly by folding and partly by volcanic action.

Above: Carbon dioxide in the air dissolves in falling rain. When it reaches the ground, therefore, rain water is slightly acid. It acts chemically on certain rocks, such as limestone. It seeps into joints and cracks, eating the rock away. In some places the surface breaks up, creating the bleak scenery known as *karst* (named after a region in Yugoslavia).

Below: Where magma wells up in the asthenosphere, plates move apart, forming an oceanic ridge with a rift valley in the centre (1). Volcanic islands are also found near oceanic ridges. When two continents meet, they begin to buckle, forming fold mountains (2). When one plate is forced beneath another, there is considerable volcanic activity and fold mountains form on any overlying continent (3). Transform faults, formed where two plates slide against each other, cause earthquakes (4).

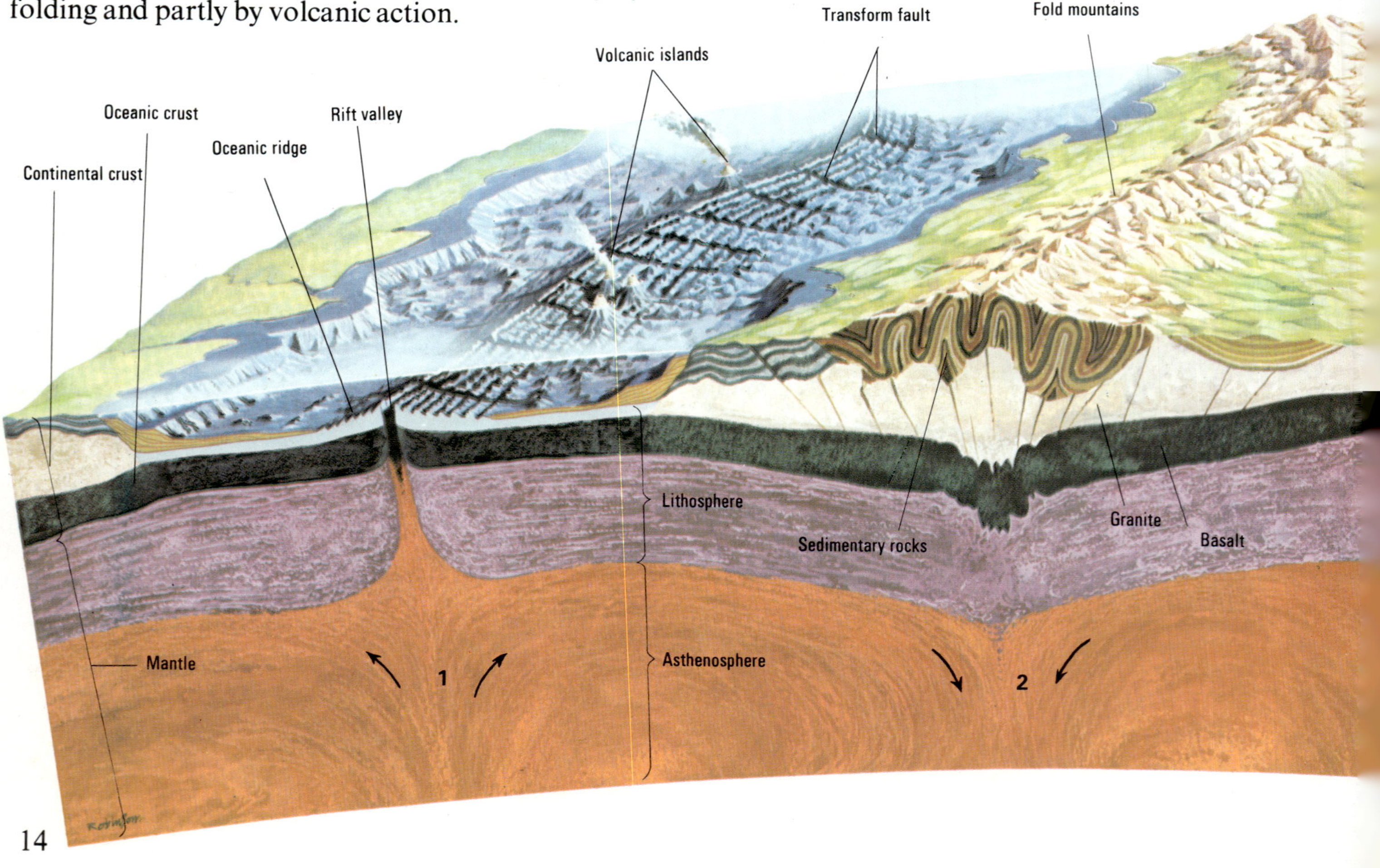

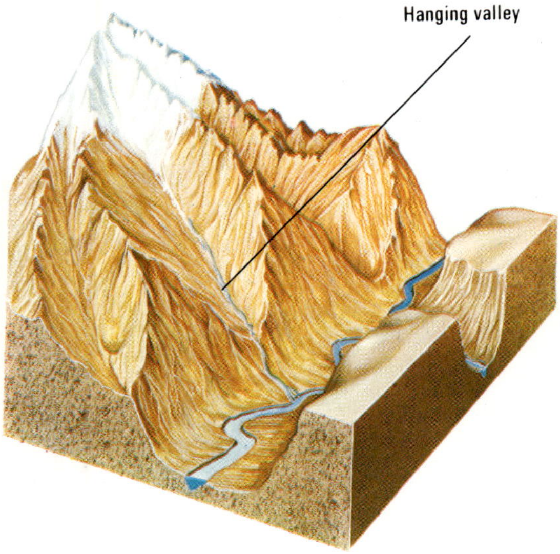

Glaciers (right) are moving sheets of ice. Jagged rocks, called *moraine,* are pushed along underneath the glacier and wear away the rock below. In high mountains (left) glaciers gouge out deep U-shaped valleys, leaving other valleys, hanging above. Sharp, jagged edges and peaks are also features of glaciated mountains. Glaciers end in lowlands (right, below), leaving carved-out rock basins, worn hillocks, scratched rocks and piles of moraine.

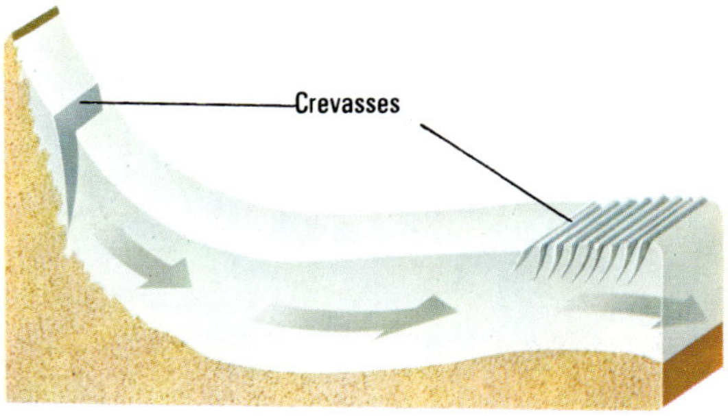

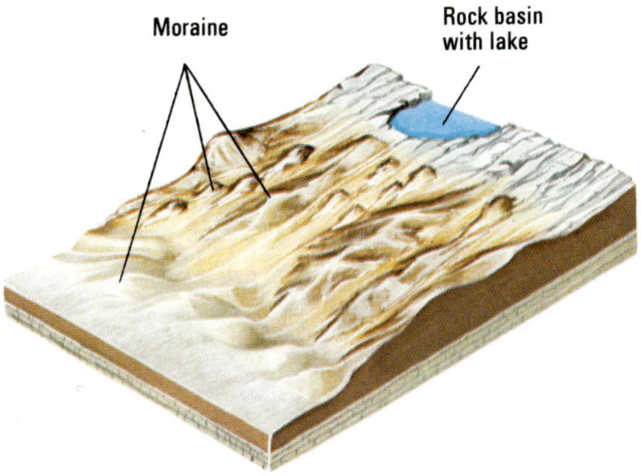

Further upheavals in the Earth's crust are caused when two plates slide against each other. This kind of plate edge is called a *transform fault*. The world's earthquake zones follow the edges of plates. Sudden, jerky movements of the plates trigger off earthquakes.

Once mountains are formed they are not permanent. Immediately, the weather begins to erode them away. Water seeps into the rock and freezes. This shatters the rock into lumps which tumble downhill. Rainwater is slightly acid and dissolves some of the chemicals in rocks, causing them to break up.

Large pieces of rock are carried down by glaciers. These scrape out huge valleys in the sides of mountains. Further down, rivers carry the smaller particles. These act like sandpaper, wearing away the rocks over which the rivers flow. Eventually, fine particles are carried into the valleys and plains. Some of this remains as soil, but much of it is carried into the sea. There it lies as a sediment on the bottom.

Reading the Rocks

The rocks we find today were formed millions of years ago. Scientists can now find out exactly how old the rocks are.

When the Earth cooled, 4,600 million years ago, the first rocks were formed. But today no one has yet discovered any of these rocks. On the surface they have been eroded away and replaced by younger rocks.

There are three main types of rock that can be found on the Earth's surface. First, there are rocks that have formed from molten material, or *magma,* pushed up from below. Such rocks are called *igneous rocks.* Examples include granite and basalt.

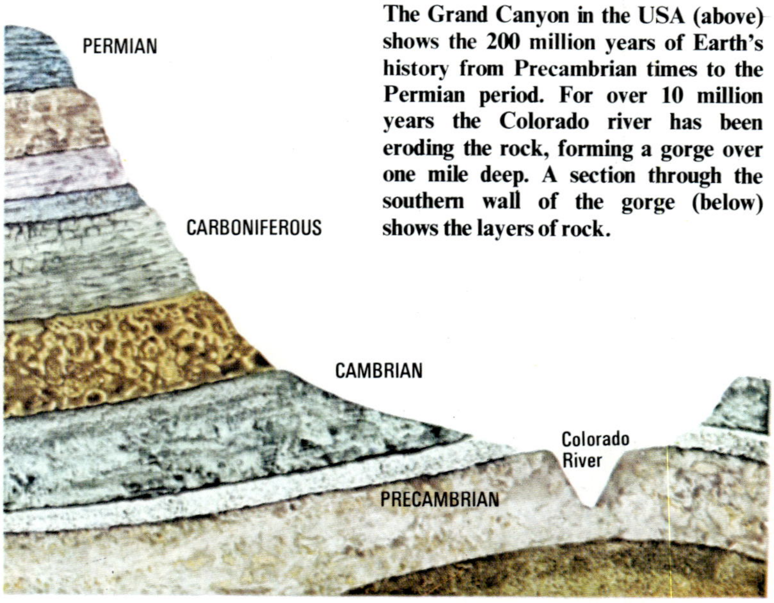

The Grand Canyon in the USA (above) shows the 200 million years of Earth's history from Precambrian times to the Permian period. For over 10 million years the Colorado river has been eroding the rock, forming a gorge over one mile deep. A section through the southern wall of the gorge (below) shows the layers of rock.

When igneous rocks are eroded away and washed into the sea, sediments form. Gradually, sediments build up in layers and the weight of the upper layers compresses the lower layers into new rocks. Rocks of this type are called *sedimentary rocks.* Examples include sandstone, mudstone and shale. Sedimentary rock can be formed in other ways too. Limestone was not formed from particles of igneous rocks. Instead it was formed in the seas from compressed chalk or calcium carbonate, the remains of once-living sea animals. Coal is another sedimentary rock. It is formed from the remains of swamp plants.

The third type of rock is called *metamorphic rock.* Metamorphic means 'changed' and this type of rock is formed when a sedimentary rock is reheated or squeezed under great pressure. Metamorphic rocks include slate (formed from mudstone or shale) and marble (from limestone).

The rocks that interest scientists who study fossils (palaeontologists) are sedimentary rocks. No fossils are found in the other two types of rock. Igneous rock burns everything as it forms. Any fossils present when metamorphic rocks form are destroyed in the process.

The first scientist to understand the importance of sedimentary rock was the Scottish geologist James Hutton. In the late 1700s he realized that such rocks were formed in water. He came to the conclusion that sedimentary rocks must have taken a long time to form and that the Earth must therefore be extremely old.

In the early 1800s William Smith, an English engineer and geologist, was working on the building of canals in England. He earned the nickname 'Strata' Smith because of his interest in the layers, or *strata,* of rock that were exposed as the canals were excavated. He quickly realized that, as sediments form one on top of the other, the younger rocks should lie on top.

But it is not always that simple. Often the rocks near the Earth's surface have been twisted, tilted or folded by movements in the crust. But then Smith discovered another way of dating rocks.

By this time fossils (see page 18) were recognized as being the remains of once-living animals and plants. William Smith discovered that some fossils could be found only in one layer of rock. Therefore such fossils were the remains of creatures that

Above: A mountainside cliff showing the layers of rock laid down millions of years ago. The vertical lines are breaks in the rock that have been widened by water.

Above right: An *unconformity* is the name given to a break in the sequence of rocks. Here, the Devonian rocks at the bottom have been tilted and then eroded away. No Carboniferous or Permian rocks were formed. The upper rocks were laid down in the Triassic period.

had existed only for a short time during Earth's history. Smith realized that these fossils, now known as index fossils, could be used to date rocks. If identical index fossils occur in two different layers of rock, then those layers must be the same age.

Using Smith's ideas, geologists in the 1800s studied rocks all over the world. Gradually they were able to place all the sedimentary rocks in order and build up a calendar of Earth's history—the Geological Time Scale (see page 22). On this scale the fossil-bearing sedimentary rocks are divided into three main groups. Each group represents a long era in the history of life on Earth. The eras are divided into periods and some periods, mostly the more recent ones, are divided into epochs.

In the 1800s geologists could only give the ages of rocks relative to each other. But in the early 1900s scientists discovered that igneous and metamorphic rocks can be dated more accurately by measuring the amounts of radioactive substances they contain. Using the ages of igneous rocks given by radioactive dating, scientists can work out the actual ages of fossil-bearing sedimentary rocks.

Rock sequences on the surface are often very complicated. Usually, however, the rocks can be identified and dated by the index fossils they contain. Unusual rock sequences are caused by movements in the Earth's crust after the rocks formed. For example, if faults occur, blocks of rock may slip against each other. Later erosion of the surface leaves rocks of varying ages exposed (above). Or the rocks may have been lifted, folded and then eroded (below).

Key

ROCK		FOSSIL
A	Cambrian	Trilobite
B	Ordovician	Crinoid
C	Silurian	Brachiopod
D	Devonian	Eurypterid
E	Carboniferous	Blastoid
F	Permian	Brachiopod
G	Triassic	Ammonite

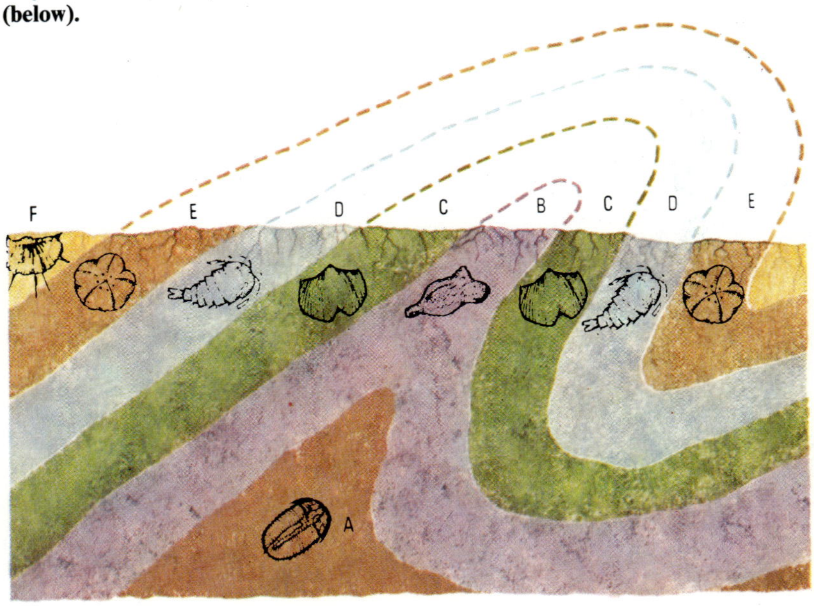

Below: A fine example of a fossil sea-lily, or crinoid, in limestone. Sea-lilies still exist today. They are primitive animals that have changed little from their Palaeozoic ancestors. The largest numbers existed in the Silurian, Carboniferous and Permian periods. In Britain and North America there are limestones almost entirely made up of fossil sea-lilies. Some species are good index fossils.

Above: Permineralized teeth are common fossils. The eating habits of extinct animals can be deduced from their fossil teeth.

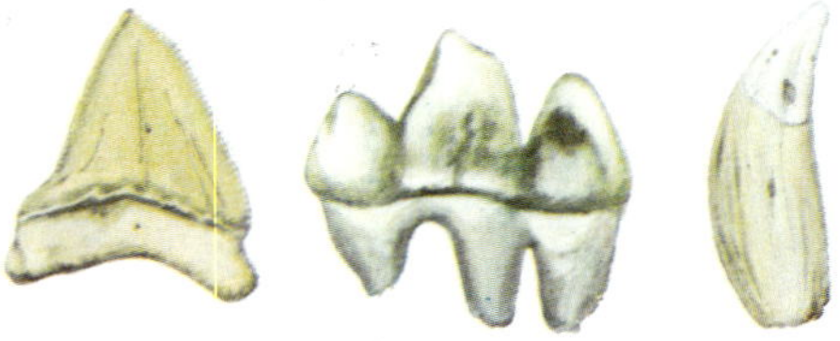

Above: A petrified (turned to stone) tree trunk. The original wood has been slowly replaced by minerals, preserving every detail.

The Fossil Story

From the study of fossils and how they were formed we can learn a great deal about the animals and plants of the distant past.

People have been finding fossils for over 2,000 years. Some Ancient Greek scholars realized what fossils were, but their ideas were soon forgotten. In Europe in the 1500s people believed that fossils were God's practice creations or stone creatures made by the devil himself.

But in the mid-1600s Nicolaus Steno, a Danish anatomist, realized that fossils resemble living animals and plants in almost every detail. They must therefore be the remains of creatures that once lived on Earth.

There are about four and a half million species of plants and animals living today. But this is only a tiny fraction of those that have lived in the past. Scientists have estimated that the number of species that have existed since life began totals over 9,800 million. This is only an estimate because very few species, about 300,000, have survived in the fossil record.

There are two main reasons why we have so few fossils. First, most fossils are formed from the hard parts of animals, such as bones, shells and teeth. Soft parts usually decay too quickly to become fossilized. Occasionally, however, we do find some fossilized soft parts of animals. Second, for a fossil to form the animal must be buried rapidly in a sediment. Only then can the process of fossilization begin. Most sediments are formed in water. Therefore the most common fossils are those of water animals, particularly sea animals. Fossils of land animals are less common. Those that do form are nearly always the result of animal remains falling into rivers, lakes or swamps.

The next stage of fossilization depends on the

Above: A fossil trilobite mould (left) and cast (right). The mould formed, as sediment hardened into rock around the skeleton of the dead animal. Then the material of the skeleton was replaced by minerals, forming the cast.

Above: Under very special conditions soft parts, such as the leaves of plants, have been preserved as thin films of carbon. Even though only the carbon content of the leaves remains, extremely fine detail can be seen in such fossils.

chemicals present in the sediment and the nature of the hard part that will form the fossil. Most hard parts of animals contain tiny holes, or pores. Minerals from the sediment may enter these pores and fill the spaces. The fossil may then have a slightly stony appearance, but it is basically unchanged from the original. This type of fossilization is called *Permineralization.*

A bone or shell that is buried for a long time becomes included in the rock as the sediment hardens. The shell may then be dissolved, leaving a space, or mould, in the rock. Sometimes, as it dissolves, the material of the shell may be replaced by minerals from the sediment. In this way a cast of the original shell is formed inside the mould and is known as a *replacement fossil.* Replacement often takes place very slowly and even the tiniest details of the original animal are preserved. Both permineralized and replacement fossils can be found inside their moulds in the rocks.

Occasionally, the softer parts of animals and plants can also become fossilized. They are often preserved as thin films of carbon or as impressions in the rock.

Below: A line of dinosaur footprints in the rock. Millions of years ago these footprints were made in mud. This was later baked hard by the Sun and then covered by sediment.

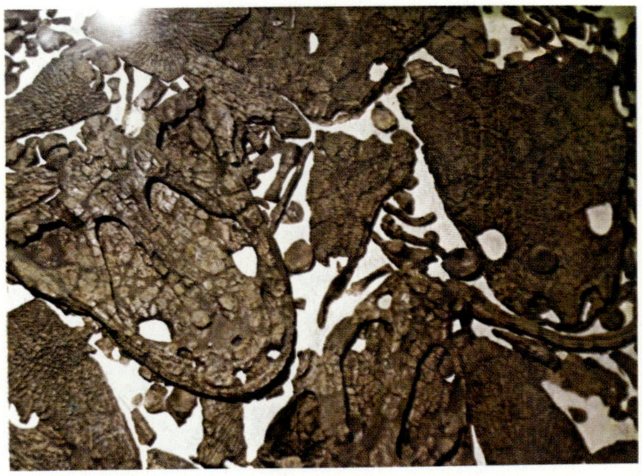

Above: The fossil of a group of Triassic amphibians. They probably all died together when their pond dried up.

Left: The history of a fossil. 1. A sea reptile dies and its body sinks to the bottom. 2. The flesh decays and the skeleton is buried in sediment. 3. The sediment is covered by other sediments and hardens into rock. At the same time the bones of the skeleton become fossilized. 4. Millions of years later, movements in the Earth's crust cause the rocks to rise out of the sea. The rocks are eroded away and eventually the fossil is exposed.

In the colder regions of the world mammoths and woolly rhinoceroses have been found preserved in the frozen ground. Some substances act as natural preservatives. Even whole animals have been found in ancient tar pits. Insects are often found trapped in lumps of amber. Mummified dinosaur eggs have been discovered in ancient desert sands.

Another group of fossils are called *trace fossils*. These are not fossils of animal parts, but they provide evidence that certain animals once existed. Such fossils include footprints, burrows and droppings.

You can find many fossils yourself. The best places to look are in quarries, road-cuttings and cliffs. In such places the sedimentary rocks that carry fossils are exposed. If you buy a geological map, this will tell you the locations and ages of the rocks in your area.

Always ask permission from the landowner before going onto private land. Also remember that some cliffs are dangerous and must not be climbed. Always tell someone where you are going.

You will need a basic kit for finding and extracting fossils. This should include geological hammers, stone chisels and brushes. Take plenty of containers, such as tobacco tins and plastic bags, to hold small fossils. Newspaper and string can be used to wrap larger finds. Other useful items include a notebook, for recording your finds, and a camera for taking pictures of fossils before you extract them.

At your fossil site there may be fossils all around you, if only you can find them. Small rocks that have fallen from the sides of quarries or from cliff-faces may contain fossils. Nodules (rounded lumps of rock) are also worth examining. Ironstone nodules from the waste heaps of coalmines often contain fish or insect fossils. Split open any large

Above: Some of the types of index fossil that are used to identify the relative ages of rocks. Many species of these kinds of animal existed for only a short period of time. Therefore their fossils are found only in rocks of a particular age.

Above left: About 30 million years ago this insect became trapped in the sticky resin oozing from a coniferous tree, such as a pine. The resin hardened into a pebble of amber and the insect remained preserved inside.

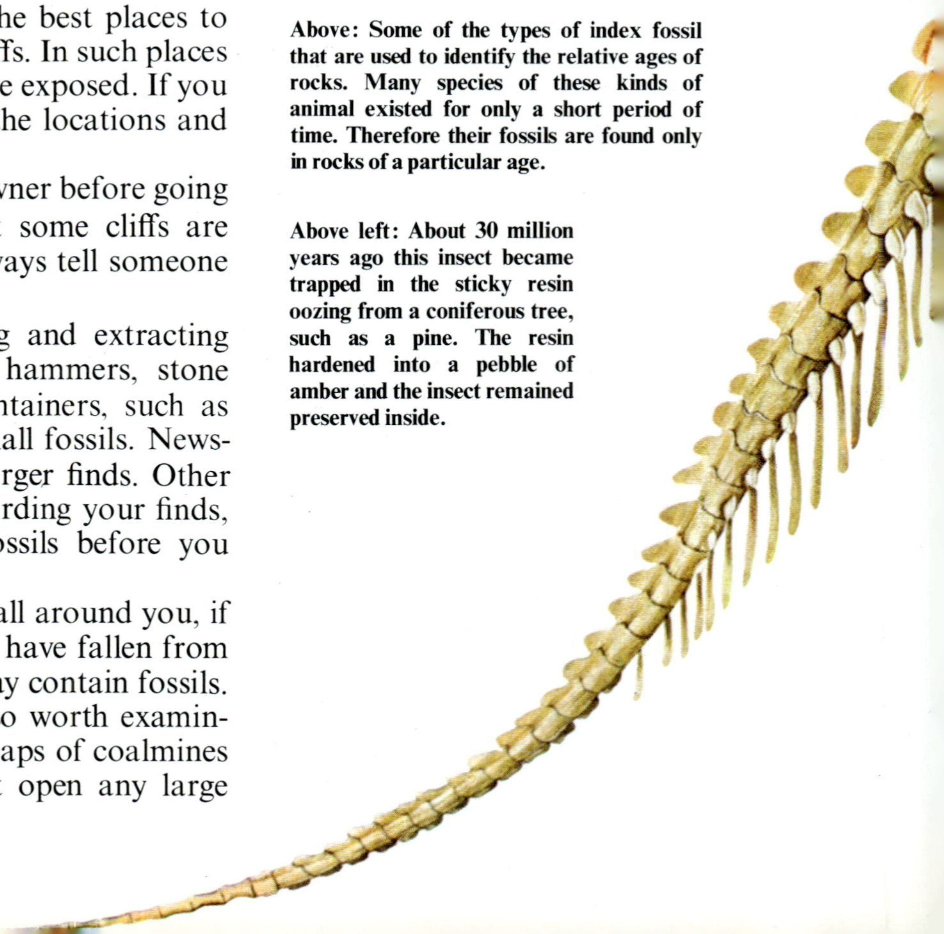

Above: The Dinosaur National Monument, Utah, USA, covers about 80,000 hectares (200,000 acres). Here, huge dinosaur bones are on display still embedded in the rocks where they were found.

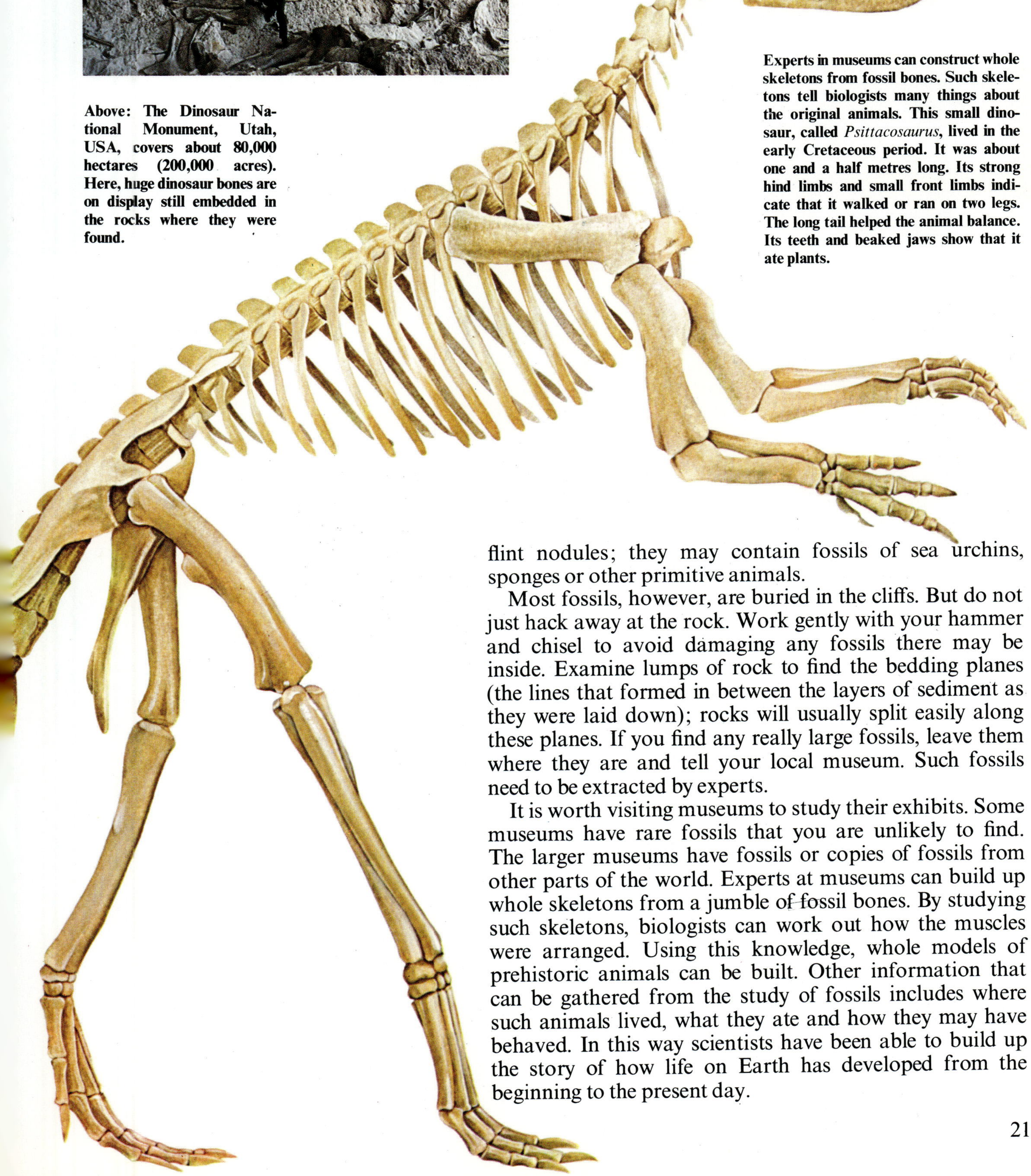

Experts in museums can construct whole skeletons from fossil bones. Such skeletons tell biologists many things about the original animals. This small dinosaur, called *Psittacosaurus*, lived in the early Cretaceous period. It was about one and a half metres long. Its strong hind limbs and small front limbs indicate that it walked or ran on two legs. The long tail helped the animal balance. Its teeth and beaked jaws show that it ate plants.

flint nodules; they may contain fossils of sea urchins, sponges or other primitive animals.

Most fossils, however, are buried in the cliffs. But do not just hack away at the rock. Work gently with your hammer and chisel to avoid damaging any fossils there may be inside. Examine lumps of rock to find the bedding planes (the lines that formed in between the layers of sediment as they were laid down); rocks will usually split easily along these planes. If you find any really large fossils, leave them where they are and tell your local museum. Such fossils need to be extracted by experts.

It is worth visiting museums to study their exhibits. Some museums have rare fossils that you are unlikely to find. The larger museums have fossils or copies of fossils from other parts of the world. Experts at museums can build up whole skeletons from a jumble of fossil bones. By studying such skeletons, biologists can work out how the muscles were arranged. Using this knowledge, whole models of prehistoric animals can be built. Other information that can be gathered from the study of fossils includes where such animals lived, what they ate and how they may have behaved. In this way scientists have been able to build up the story of how life on Earth has developed from the beginning to the present day.

GEOLOGICAL TIME SCALE

ERA	PERIOD	EPOCH	YEARS AGO (MILLIONS)	CLIMATE	MAJOR GEOLOGICAL EVENTS AND ROCKS
CENOZOIC	QUATERNARY	Recent (Holocene)	0.01	Rather cool with long glacial periods. Large areas of northern hemisphere covered with ice	Sea level fell because so much water was locked up in glaciers. The land rose in many places, causing rivers to cut down again. Grand Canyon formed. Vast sheets of boulder clay deposited by glaciers. Ice finally retreated about 11,000 years ago
		Pleistocene	1.8		
	TERTIARY	Pliocene	7	Cooling down all over the world: tropical forests converted to grassland in many places	Uplift of the land continued, raising mountains even higher and causing rivers to cut more deeply into their beds. Raised beaches formed around coasts where they were lifted clear of the sea
		Miocene	26	Continuing warm	Volcanic activity and uplift increased, ending in the Alpine Revolution at the end of the epoch. The Alps and Himalayas were formed, and the Rockies and Appalachians were lifted up yet again
		Oligocene	38	Continuing warm	The land continued to rise, and the sea withdrew from large areas. Extensive lake and estuary deposits formed. More lava flows
		Eocene	54	Rather warm in Europe and North America	Uplift of the land continued with more volcanic activity. Final break between Greenland and Europe, and between Australia and Antarctica. India collides with Asia. Disappearance of Turgai Sea east of Ural Mountains
		Paleocene	65	Becoming cooler, especially near the poles. Temperate in Europe	Slow-down of continental drift and withdrawal of seas from much of the continents
MESOZOIC	CRETACEOUS		135	Warm, with rainfall similar to that of today	Continued continental drift activity and higher sea levels. Beginning of North and South Atlantic. Isolation of Africa, Australia and South America. The Laramide Revolution pushed up the Rockies and Andes at the end of the period
	JURASSIC		190	Warm, sometimes as far north as Alaska. Becoming increasingly humid as seas spread over land	Renewed continental drift activity caused sea to spread over land and deposit thick clays and limestones. Formation of Central Atlantic. Some volcanic activity and mountain-building in western North America
	TRIASSIC		225	Mainly warm and dry. Extensive deserts	Extensive salt and gypsum deposits formed in drying seas. Red sandstones deposited on land from eroded mountains. Much volcanic activity in North America
PALAEOZOIC	PERMIAN		280	Mainly warm and dry, but Ice Age continued in southern hemisphere	Meeting of Euramerica with Asia and Gondwanaland to form single world supercontinent. This caused extensive mountain-building – the Appalachians were further uplifted, together with the Urals and Austrian Alps
	CARBONIFEROUS	Pennsylvanian	300	Warm and very humid in Europe and North America, with tropical swamps. Ice Age in southern hemisphere	Thick limestones deposited in Mississippian times. Coal seams in Pennsylvanian in northern hemisphere formed as a result of continual marine flooding of the forests
		Mississippian	345		
	DEVONIAN		395	Warm and often very dry	Continued uplift of land in N.W. Europe produced the Old Red Sandstone Continent, in which great thicknesses of red sandstone were deposited. Marine deposits in North America
	SILURIAN		440	Becoming warmer: desert conditions in some places	Meeting of Europe and North America at the end of the Silurian caused the Caledonian Mountains to rise in Newfoundland and N.W. Europe. Extensive salt deposits in inland seas of North America
	ORDOVICIAN		530	Temperatures about normal, becoming warmer	Seas still widespread. More sediment filled troughs. Much volcanic activity produced beds of ash and lava. Appalachians rose up
	CAMBRIAN		570	Cold at first, with arctic conditions in North America, but gradually becoming normal	Widespread shallow seas. Sea bed sank in many places and troughs filled with sediment. Troughs started to buckle up later
PRECAMBRIAN TIME Time extending back to the formation of the earth			4600+	Atmosphere with little oxygen, especially in early stages. Often cold, with glacial periods. Some warmer periods	Great thicknesses of sedimentary rocks accumulated, but most of those surviving have been greatly altered by folding and pressure. Much volcanic activity

MOUNTAIN BUILDING	MAJOR FEATURES OF PLANT LIFE	MAJOR FEATURES OF ANIMAL LIFE	PERIOD/SYSTEM
	Development of arctic floras able to withstand harsh climates. These floras later left as relict floras on tops of mountains when glaciers retreated	Java and Peking Man evolved from early hominids and eventually gave rise to modern man. Woolly rhinoceroses and mammoths coped with Arctic conditions	QUATERNARY
	Development of modern temperate floras as climate cooled down. Coniferous forests in north. Further spread of grasslands around tropics	Ape-man *(Australopithecus)* in Africa towards end of epoch. Numerous kinds of elephants and other large mammals, but most of the larger ones died out as the climate cooled	TERTIARY
	Grasslands began to appear, and rapidly increased	Numerous apes in Africa. The ancestors of modern man diverged from the apes. Herds of grazing animals appearing on the grasslands	
	Continued increase in flowering plants	Early apes appeared. Many other modern mammals beginning to evolve	
	Plants of very modern appearance were spreading all over the world. Flowering trees dominated large areas	Many strange herbivorous mammals appeared. Early horses and elephants	
	Rapid increase in flowering plants. Cycads declined	Mammals evolved rapidly and filled niches left by reptiles	
	First appearance of flowering plants. Conifers, ferns and cycads still common	Dinosaurs and pterosaurs continued to dominate the land at first, but became extinct later. Many birds and small mammals. Extinction of ammonites and many other marine creatures	CRETACEOUS
	Cycads abundant. Maidenhair trees *(Ginkgo)* common. Widespread thickets of large ferns	Ammonites abundant in sea, together with new kinds of coral and sea urchins. Dinosaurs abundant on land. Flying reptiles (pterosaurs) and the first birds. Small mammals	JURASSIC
	First appearance of cycads and bennettitaleans. Conifers continued to dominate the land	Continued evolution of reptiles produced the first dinosaurs and the large marine reptiles. End of the mammal-like reptiles; evolution of the first mammals. Ammonites flourished in sea	TRIASSIC
	Giant clubmosses and horsetails became extinct in the face of drier conditions. Smaller seed ferns replaced large types. Great increase in conifers.	Rapid increase and spread of reptiles. Amphibians less important and mostly in the water. Widespread extinctions in the sea: trilobites became extinct, along with many fish and corals	PERMIAN
	Giant clubmosses, ferns and horsetails in the coal swamps of northern hemisphere. Seed ferns and first conifers.	Amphibians increased and spread; soon gave rise to reptiles. Insects became very common. Corals, brachiopods and fishes, very common in the seas	CARBONIFEROUS
	Land plants became common and widespread. Several new types appeared, including ferns, clubmosses, and the earliest seed plants	The age of fishes – many kinds in fresh and salt water. Graptolites died out. Goniatites – ancestors of ammonites – appeared. Amphibians evolved from fishes and moved on to land	DEVONIAN
	Algae continued to thrive in the water. The first known land plants appeared – leafless and rootless plants known as *Cooksonia*	Graptolites decreased. Jawless, armoured fishes abundant. First jawed fishes appeared. Large sea scorpions (eurypterids). Coral reefs and abundant brachiopods	SILURIAN
	Lime-secreting algae abundant, often forming small reefs. No known land plants, although simple mosses and lichens may have lived on land	Graptolites and trilobites abundant. Corals and brachiopods spread rapidly. Earliest vertebrates – jawless fishes	ORDOVICIAN
	Lime-secreting algae contributed to rock formation in Upper Cambrian	Fossils abundant in rocks. All major groups of invertebrates represented. Graptolites, primitive shellfish, corals, echinoderms, crustaceans and other arthropods. Trilobites especially common	CAMBRIAN
	Algae, fungi and bacteria. Blue green algae well-preserved in ancient rocks	Rare traces of animal life in later Precambrian rocks – less than 1000 million years old. Forerunners of trilobites, worms and jellyfishes	PRECAMBRIAN

Sabre-toothed tiger from the Pleistocene.

An ammonite from the Jurassic seas.

Annularia, a plant fossil from the Carboniferous.

A trilobite from the early Palaeozoic Era.

Evolution

According to the theory of evolution modern plants and animals have evolved from very simple organisms.

In the early 1800s most people believed in the description of the Creation given in the Bible. Earth and its plants and animals had all been created at the same time—a few thousand years ago. Fossils were supposed to be the remains of past catastrophes, such as the Biblical flood and Egyptian plagues.

However, some scientists were beginning to form new theories. The idea that rocks form very slowly, first suggested by James Hutton (see page 16), was made popular by Charles Lyall, a Scottish geologist. Scientists also began to notice that fossils of some animals showed slight changes from one period to another. In France Jean Lamarck suggested that animal characteristics could change from one generation to the next. He thought that if an animal acquired a new and useful characteristic during its lifetime, it could pass that characteristic on to its offspring. But in 1859 Charles Darwin and Alfred Wallace, two British naturalists, both published their ideas for a more convincing theory of evolution, proving Lamarck wrong.

During the 1830s Darwin, voyaging on the *Beagle,* had visited South America and the Galapagos islands. From what he observed there and from his later studies he became convinced that animals and plants change gradually over many generations. The process by which they change he called *natural selection.* Darwin suggested that some individuals are born with new characteristics that give them an advantage over their

Right: Charles Darwin (1809-1882). During the 1830s he visited the Galapagos Islands. Over twenty-five years later he published *The Origin of Species.* This work set out the theory of evolution.

Below: The front limbs of vertebrates (animals with backbones) are adapted for grasping, swimming, flying, walking or digging. But they are all based on the same structure—the five digit, or *pentadactyl,* limb. This suggests that these animals have evolved from the same ancestor.

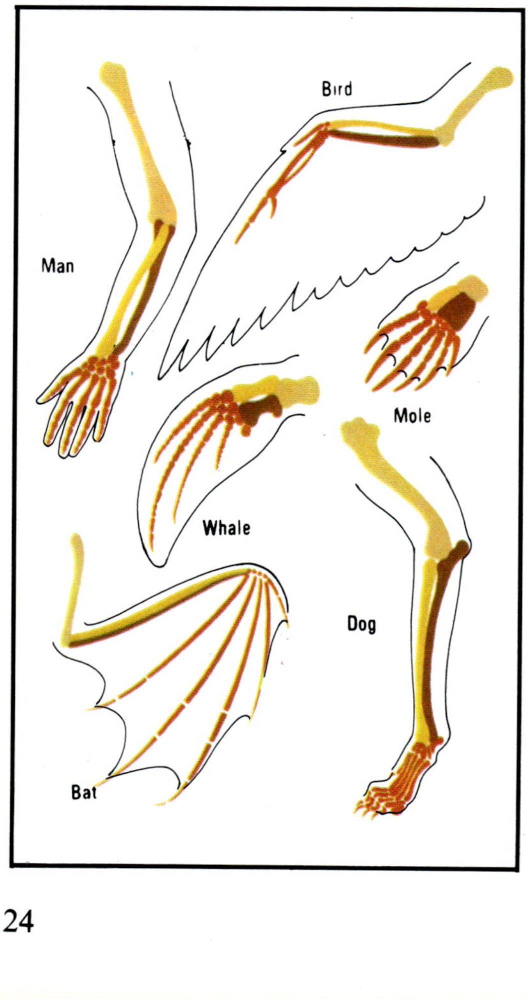

Below: A 'family tree' of the animal kingdom, showing the relative abundance of animal groups during the course of Earth's history. Their possible origins are shown by the thin lines.

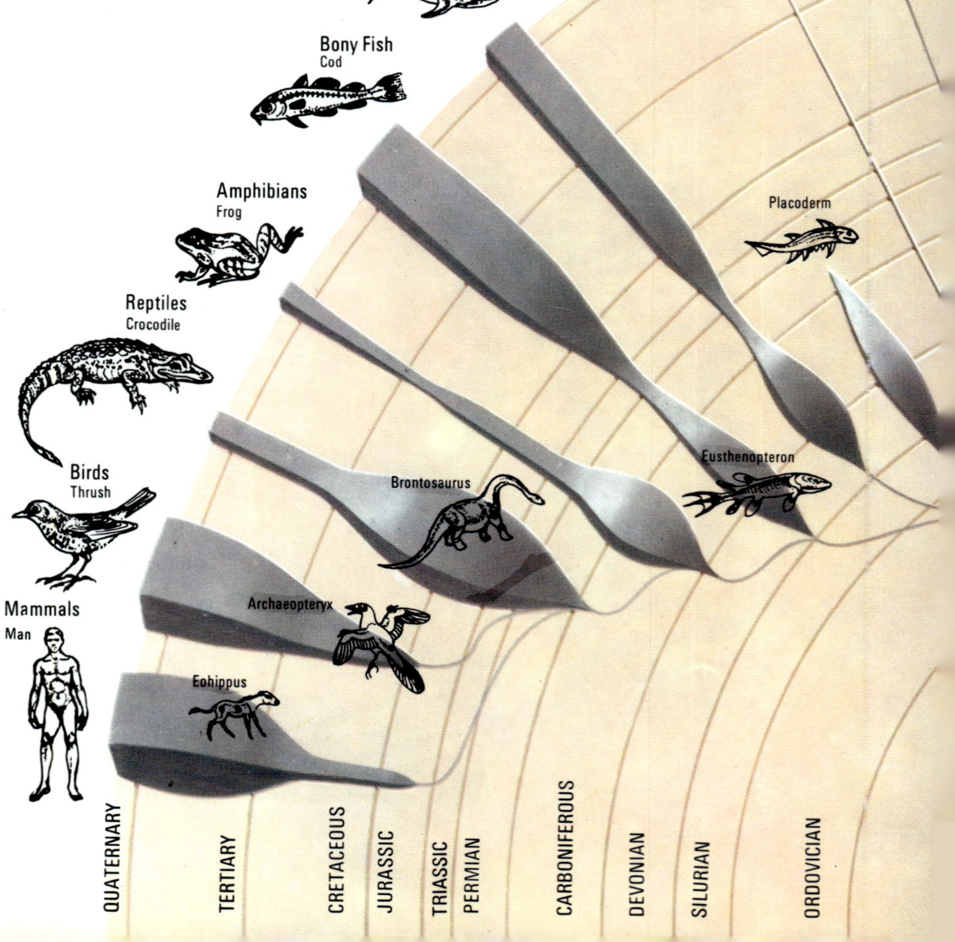

fellows. They are more suited to their environment and so stand a better chance of being able to survive and breed. In this way useful characteristics are passed on to the next generation. Poor characteristics die out because they reduce an individual's chances of survival. In other words, nature selects the good characteristics for survival and discards the poor ones.

Darwin believed that all life on Earth evolved in this way. When conditions changed, only those animals best suited to the new environment remained. Others died out; sometimes whole groups of animals became extinct. But new groups evolved from those that survived.

The study of both modern and fossil animals has produced much evidence to support the theory of evolution. Modern animals often have very similar features. These indicate that such animals may have had a common ancestor. Series of fossils have been found that show how some kinds of animals evolved over millions of years.

Today we have an outline story of how life has evolved since the formation of the Earth. However, there are many gaps in the story and much remains to be discovered.

Above: The peppered moths show natural selection in action today. The white moths are common in unpolluted areas. There they are well-camouflaged on lichen-covered trees. However, in industrial areas, where the trees are covered in soot, they are easily seen and eaten by birds. But the dark variety is camouflaged and has become common in such areas. So nature selects the variety that is most suited to the environment.

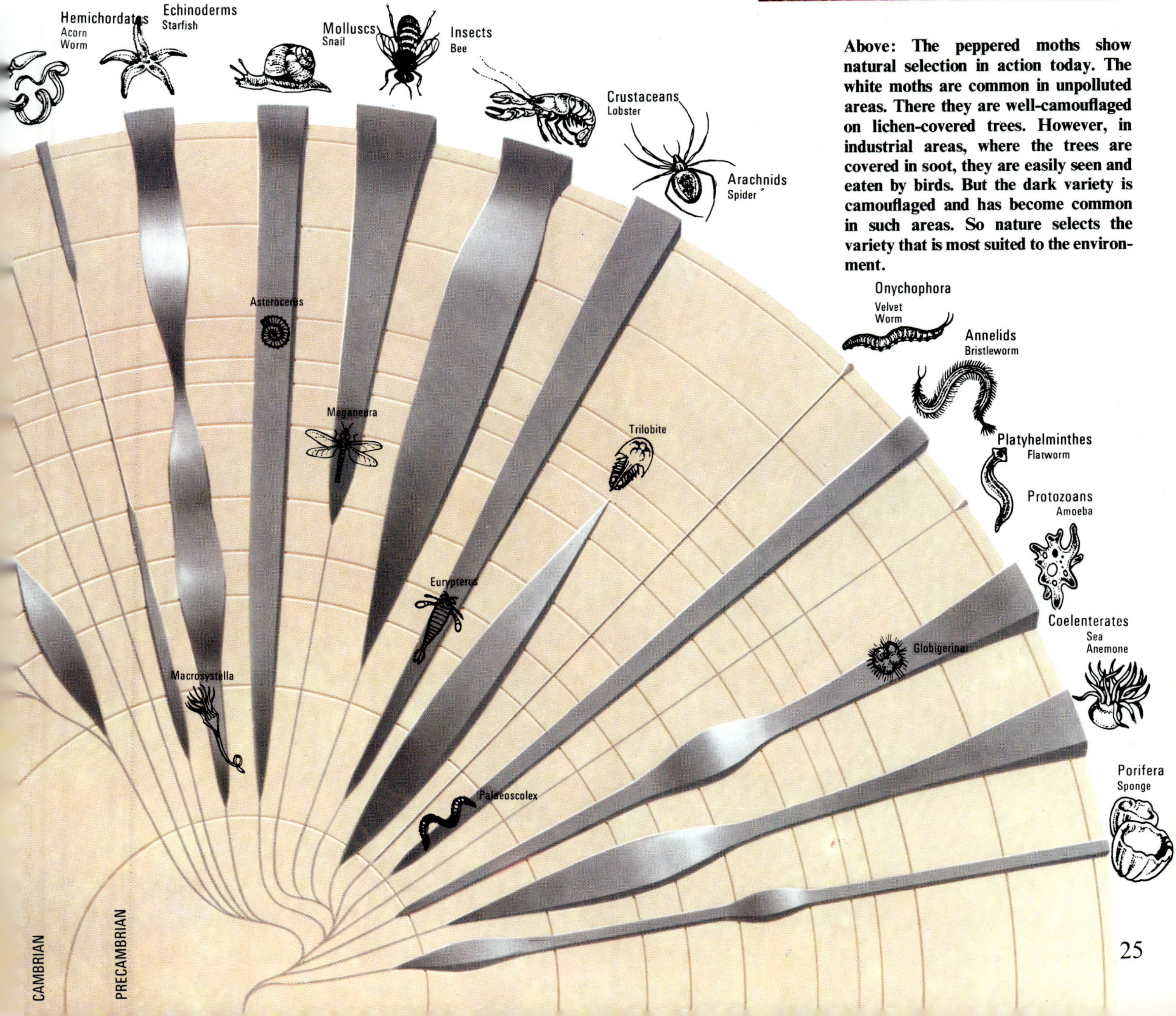

THE BIRTH OF LIFE

Origins of Life

We do not know exactly when life on Earth began. But the oldest known fossils are 3,400 million years old. So life must have started before then. From fossil evidence we also know that life on Earth began in the seas. But at the moment we can only guess at the processes that produced living organisms.

By living organisms we mean organisms that could reproduce themselves. To begin with these were probably little more than chemical compounds with complicated molecules. Somehow these complex chemicals were built up from simple ones.

A recent theory suggests that this process began in outer space, as the Sun and planets were forming from a cloud of dust and gas. After the Earth was formed, complicated molecules that were able to reproduce themselves were carried to Earth by the meteorites that bombarded the planet's surface. However, this theory is not widely accepted. Most scientists believe that life began on Earth itself.

About 3,500 million years ago the Earth's seas were a warm, rich 'soup' of chemicals. Ammonia, methane, hydrogen, nitrogen, hydrogen cyanide, hydrogen sulphide and perhaps a little oxygen, were all dissolved in the water, together with many other chemicals washed from the rocks. Violent storms were raging in the atmosphere above and lightning flashed almost continuously. At the same time the Sun was bombarding the young world with vast amounts of energy, in the form of ultra-violet radiation.

The poisonous chemicals and lethal radiation would have meant death to modern life as we know it. But it was probably in this stormy environment that the first steps towards life occurred. Small molecules were built up into larger ones and the first organic (carbon-based) chemicals appeared. Among these were amino acids, which are the building blocks of proteins—the essential ingredient of life.

Gradually the storms died down and the Earth's seas became quieter. The Sun shone and water evaporated from the seas, concentrating the organic chemicals. Underwater, perhaps in rock pools of highly concentrated chemicals, molecules began to join together to form chains. This process may have occurred round the particles of clay that lay in the pools. The particles could have acted as catalysts (materials that speed up and help chemical reactions). Some of the long-chain molecules were *nucleic acids.* These chemicals were capable of replicating themselves and building up proteins from amino acids. They grew by reacting or linking up with smaller molecules. Life on Earth had begun.

At first the nucleic acids were easily destroyed and the proteins they made were very unstable. But in the water there were also molecules of fat. Fatty substances do not mix easily with water and so the fat molecules probably collected together in flat sheets on the surface. When the surface was splashed, droplets of water became enclosed by a skin of fat molecules. Sometimes nucleic acids and proteins were included in the droplets. Thus they became wrapped in a fatty skin, or *membrane,* that protected them from the poisonous chemicals in the seas and enabled the nucleic acids to survive.

In this way the first primitive cells were formed. Successful cells grew and multiplied and true cell membranes were developed. For several million years the seas were inhabited by these bacteria-like organisms—the ancestors of all later life on Earth had been formed.

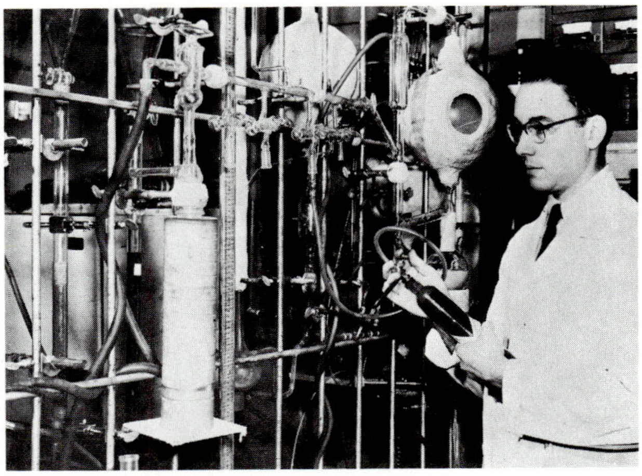

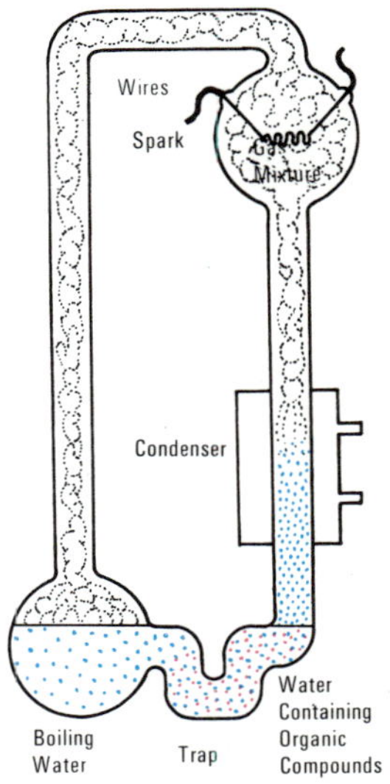

Above and left: Some of our ideas about the origins of life are supported by the results of experiments. In 1953 two American scientists, Stanley Miller and Harold Urey, built a piece of apparatus in which they could recreate the conditions that existed on Earth 3,500 million years ago. Inside the apparatus they put a mixture of gases consisting of methane, ammonia and hydrogen. Boiling water provided water vapour. Then they sent sparks across two wires inside the apparatus to simulate lightning. After some time they found that they had made complicated organic chemicals, such as amino acids and sugars.

Below: An artist's idea of the Earth before life began. Volcanoes poured forth smoke, fumes and lava, causing the water around them to heat up. Rain poured down from the dense clouds and lightning flashed across the poisonous atmosphere. At the same time, the Earth was being bombarded with energy from the Sun, in the form of strong ultra-violet radiation. Such were the conditions that Miller and Urey tried to recreate. From their experiments we now know that the first steps towards the formation of living organisms could have occurred in this hostile environment.

From Cells to Seaweed

The development of chlorophyll —the green secret of life— set the scene for the evolution of plants and animals.

The first living organisms on Earth were probably very like some bacteria that exist today. They lived in the mud at the bottom of the sea. The murky water above protected them from the Sun's harmful ultra-violet rays. They needed no air and their chemical processes were carried out without the aid of oxygen.

While there was food in the sea, these bacteria flourished. But the food

Above: Stromatolites are the remains of blue-green algae that secreted limestone. It was formed in layers. The oldest known stromatolites are about 2,800 million years old.

Below: The long chain molecules of nucleic acids formed in the seas from the organic chemicals that were present.

Below: As the nucleic acids became enclosed by membranes, simple bacteria-like cells formed. From these, evolved organisms with chlorophyll that could create their own food by photosynthesis.

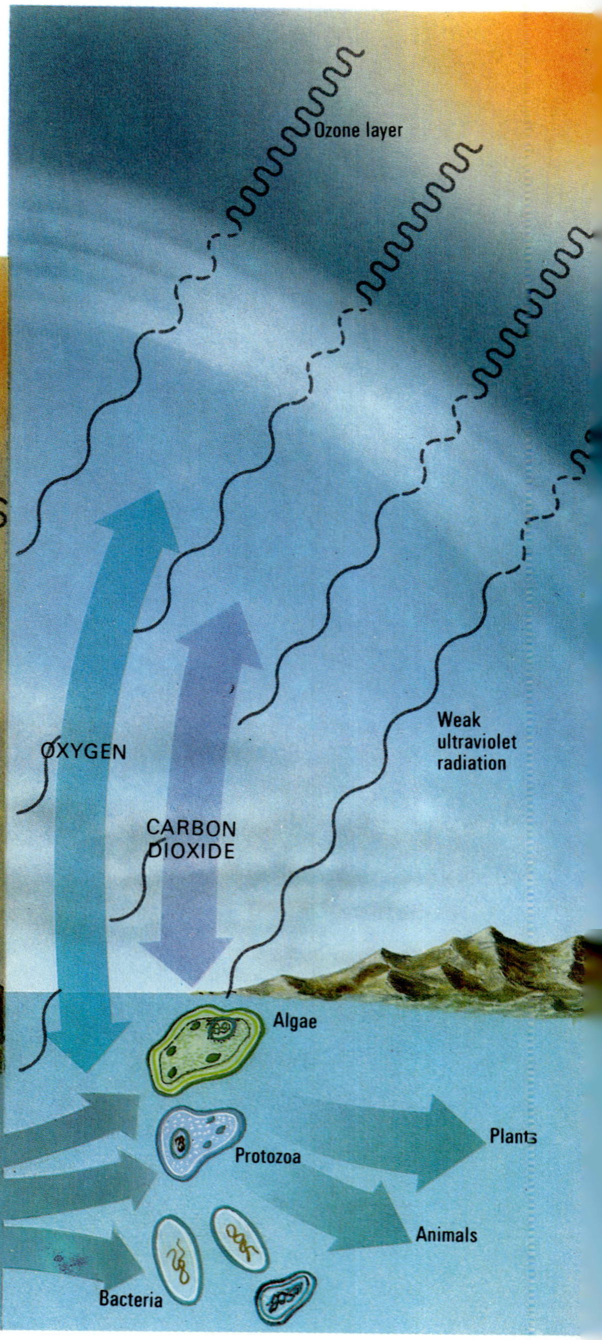

Below: Photosynthetic algae changed the atmosphere by removing carbon dioxide and making oxygen. The strong ultra-violet radiation was cut off by the new ozone layer.

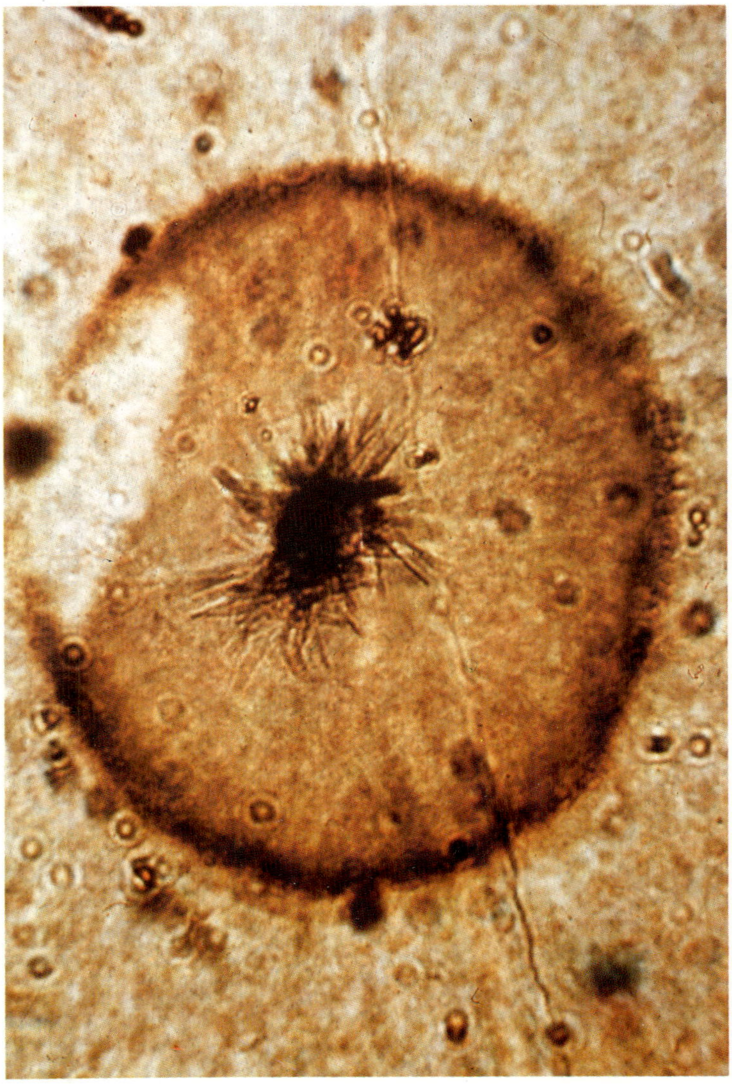

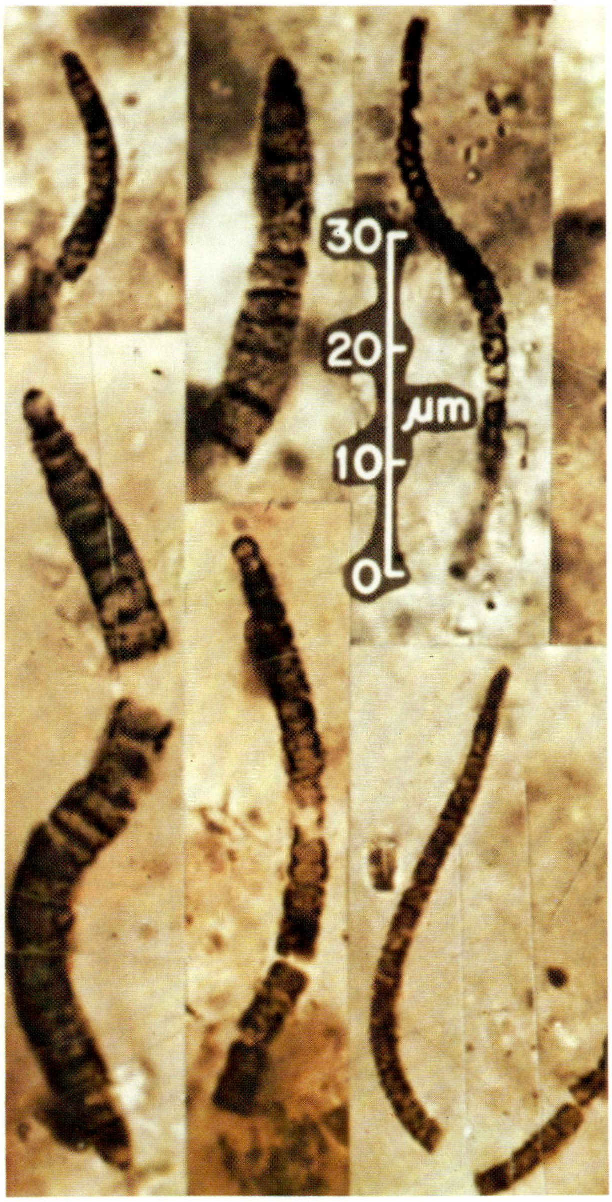

Above: A fossil of a single-celled blue-green alga that lived 2,000 million years ago.

Right: Fossils of filamentous (strings of cells) algae found in rocks 1,000 million years old.

supply eventually became scarcer. Then some of the bacteria developed a 'magic' ingredient called *chlorophyll*. In fact this substance is the secret of all life on Earth. Using chlorophyll and light the bacteria could convert the atmosphere's carbon dioxide into food materials. At the same time they released oxygen, a process called *photosynthesis*.

Photosynthetic bacteria began to change the world's atmosphere with the oxygen they released. Over millions of years, the amount of oxygen increased. High up in the atmosphere some of this oxygen was converted into ozone by the ultra-violet radiation from the Sun. The layer of ozone formed a barrier, 25 km above the Earth, through which the strongest and most harmful ultra-violet rays could not pass.

Conditions on Earth's surface were now ideal for life. New, more advanced forms of life began to evolve which took advantage of these conditions. Simple plants, called *blue-green algae*, were the first to appear. The oldest known fossil is a blue-green alga called *Aphanocapsa*. It was found in rocks 3,400 million years old. Blue-green algae still exist today.

More advanced plants and animals also began to evolve, probably soon after the blue-green algae. The simplest of these plants were single-celled algae. They were followed by larger, many-celled algae, such as seaweeds. At the same time, using the oxygen to breathe, primitive animals evolved. Again, the first to appear were single-celled animals, or protozoans. These may have evolved from photosynthetic bacteria that had lost their chlorophyll.

The story of how life began is mostly guesswork. Only a few fossils have been found in the oldest—Precambrian—rocks, so we know very little about what was happening during that time. We know that many different kinds of animals were evolving because some of them left fossil trails and burrows. But these animals were all soft-bodied and so fossils are very rare indeed.

The Palaeozoic World

About 250 million years ago, during the Permian period, this area lay under the sea. Limestone sediments were laid down and these gradually hardened into rock. Millions of years later the seas retreated and these rocks were pushed up by movements in the Earth's crust. Later erosion left this towering mass of limestone. From the study of such rocks scientists can learn much about life and conditions in the Palaeozoic era.

At the dawn of the Palaeozoic era the seas were filled with many different forms of life. Hard-shelled sea creatures were followed by animals with backbones that colonized the land.

Palaeozoic means 'ancient life'. The Palaeozoic era began 470 million years ago with the Cambrian period and it is in Cambrian rocks that the first good record of life appears. So geologists chose these rocks as the beginning of the three eras on the Geological Time Scale.

There were two main reasons for this sudden change in the rocks and fossils. First, there was a great change in the climate. At the end of Precambrian times the world was in the grip of a tremendous Ice Age. But at the start of the Palaeozoic era the air warmed up and the ice melted. Water flooded much of the land and there were vast shallow seas around the continents. Living things began to flourish and evolve rapidly in these seas.

Second, many animals developed hard shells, which make very good fossils. This was possible because there was a great deal of lime in the water. Since Precambrian times certain algae had been producing large amounts of lime (calcium carbonate), using the carbon dioxide they took from the air. Somehow animals evolved a way of using this lime to make shells. This gave them a distinct advantage as their soft bodies were now protected from predators.

By the end of the Cambrian period most of the groups of invertebrates (animals without backbones) had evolved. As the Ordovician and Silurian periods progressed, the climate became warmer. Primitive plants appeared in a few places on the land. The first vertebrates (animals with backbones), jawless fishes and armoured fishes, evolved in the seas.

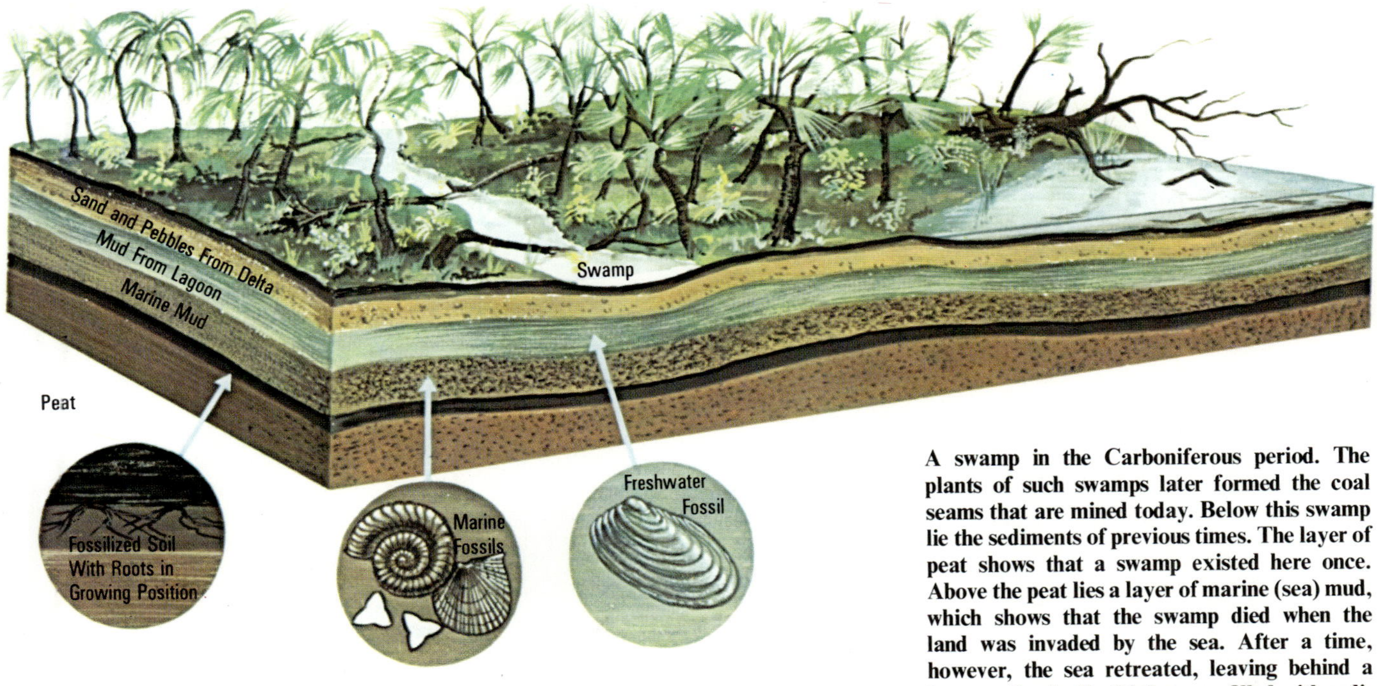

A swamp in the Carboniferous period. The plants of such swamps later formed the coal seams that are mined today. Below this swamp lie the sediments of previous times. The layer of peat shows that a swamp existed here once. Above the peat lies a layer of marine (sea) mud, which shows that the swamp died when the land was invaded by the sea. After a time, however, the sea retreated, leaving behind a lagoon. Gradually this became filled with sediments from a river, thus creating the right conditions for a new swamp.

True fishes evolved in the warm Devonian seas. On land there were now many different kinds of plants. Insects appeared to take advantage of this food supply. Fishes also emerged from the water and the first amphibians evolved.

During the Carboniferous period the southern continents were covered by ice. But in the north the environment was ideal for amphibians. Shallow seas covered much of the land and quickly receded, leaving swamps. The moist, warm air encouraged the growth of many plants and luxuriant forests grew up.

During the Permian period, the southern Ice Age continued. In the north the land dried out and many amphibians became extinct. But by this time reptiles had appeared. With their tough, waterproof skins, they could survive in the dry Permian deserts.

Meanwhile the continents had been on the move throughout the Palaeozoic era. Occasionally, two continents had collided, throwing up mountain chains. During the Carboniferous period all the continents began to move together. Gondwanaland formed in the southern hemisphere. By the end of the Permian period the northern continents had joined Gondwanaland to form the vast supercontinent of Pangaea.

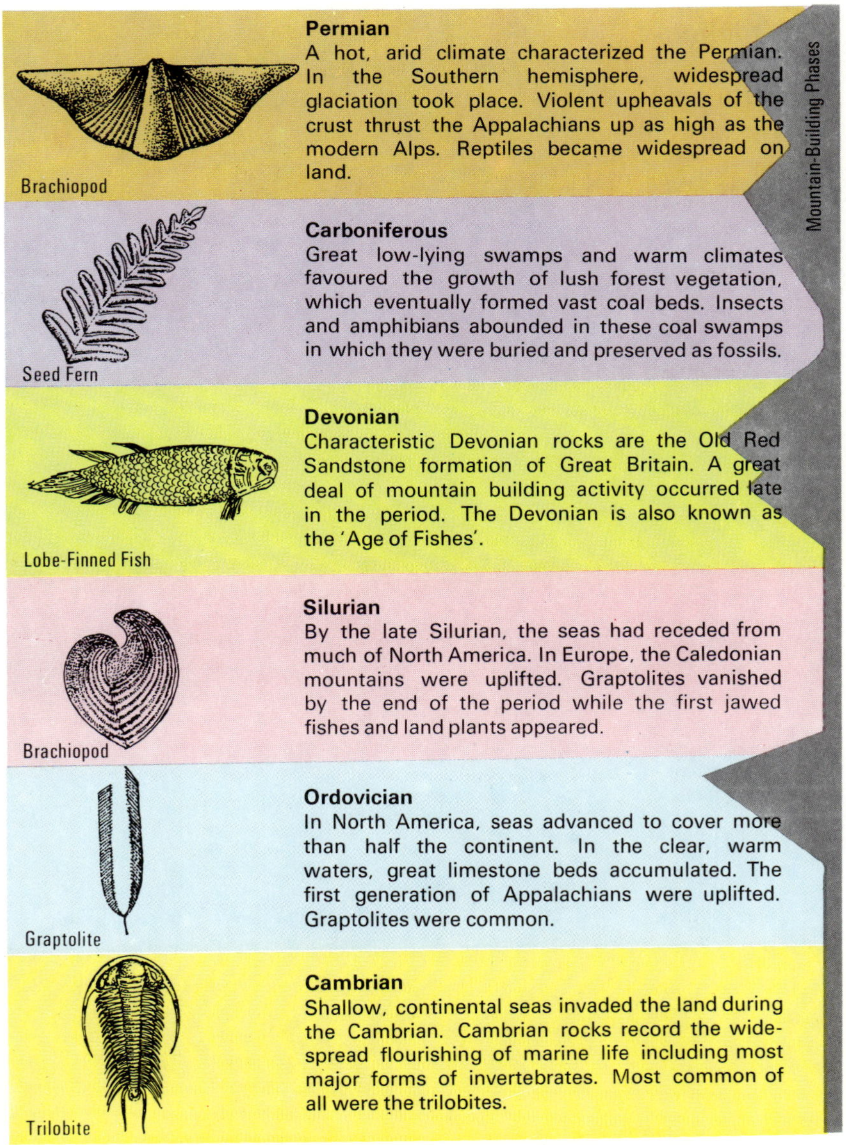

Life in Ancient Seas

Animals without backbones dominated the seas for millions of years. Trilobites and sea scorpions were the largest invertebrates that ever lived.

As Precambrian times came to an end, the seas contained many soft-bodied animals. Worm-like animals and jelly fish existed then, together with the ancestors of later shelled animals.

Over a period of 20-30 million years animals developed shells. The Cambrian seas abounded with such creatures. To begin with they were small. There were brachiopods, or lamp-shells, so called because the shells of some kinds looked like Roman lamps. Gastropods (sea-snails) and bivalves appeared. Cambrian echinoderms (spiny-skinned animals) were the ancestors of sea-lilies, sea-urchins and starfish. Two other important Cambrian groups were the trilobites and graptolites.

Trilobites were arthropods, the group to which modern insects belong. Their remains formed useful index fossils. Most trilobites were between two centimetres and ten centimetres long. Their bodies were flat and they had a number of pairs of two-branched legs. The upper branch of each leg was probably a gill, used for taking in oxygen. The lower branches of the legs were for walking. The animals probably cruised around the sea bed, feeding on worms

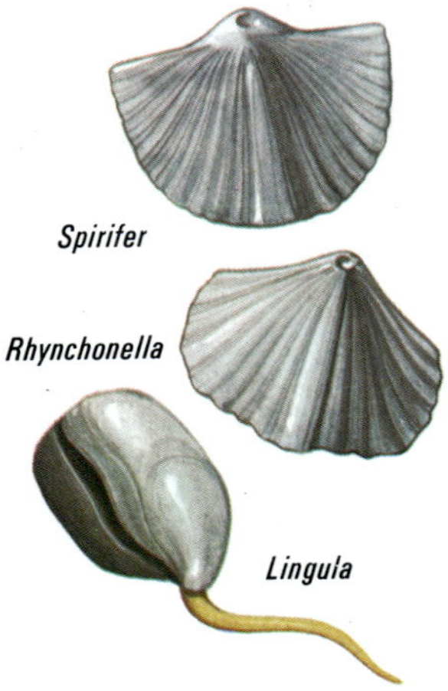

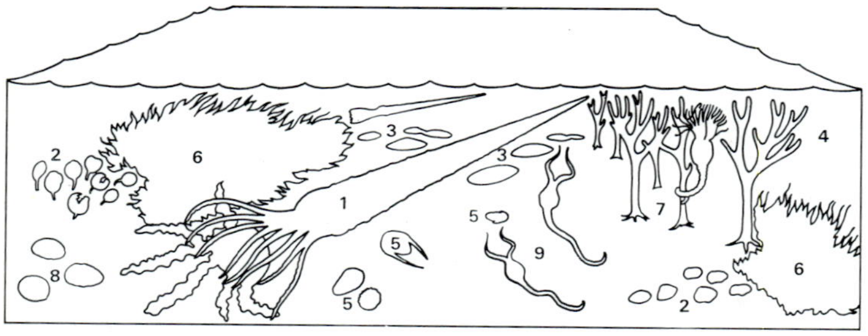

Below: The Ordovician seas were inhabited by more advanced kinds of animals than the seas of the earlier Cambrian period. Large, straight nautiloids (1) were common. They preyed on other sea-creatures, such as jellyfish. Also there were brachiopods (2), corals (3), colonies of animals called bryozoans (4), trilobites (5) and algae (6). Among the echinoderms present were cystoids (7), edrioasteroids (8) and homalozoans, or calcichordates (9)—the possible ancestors of backboned animals.

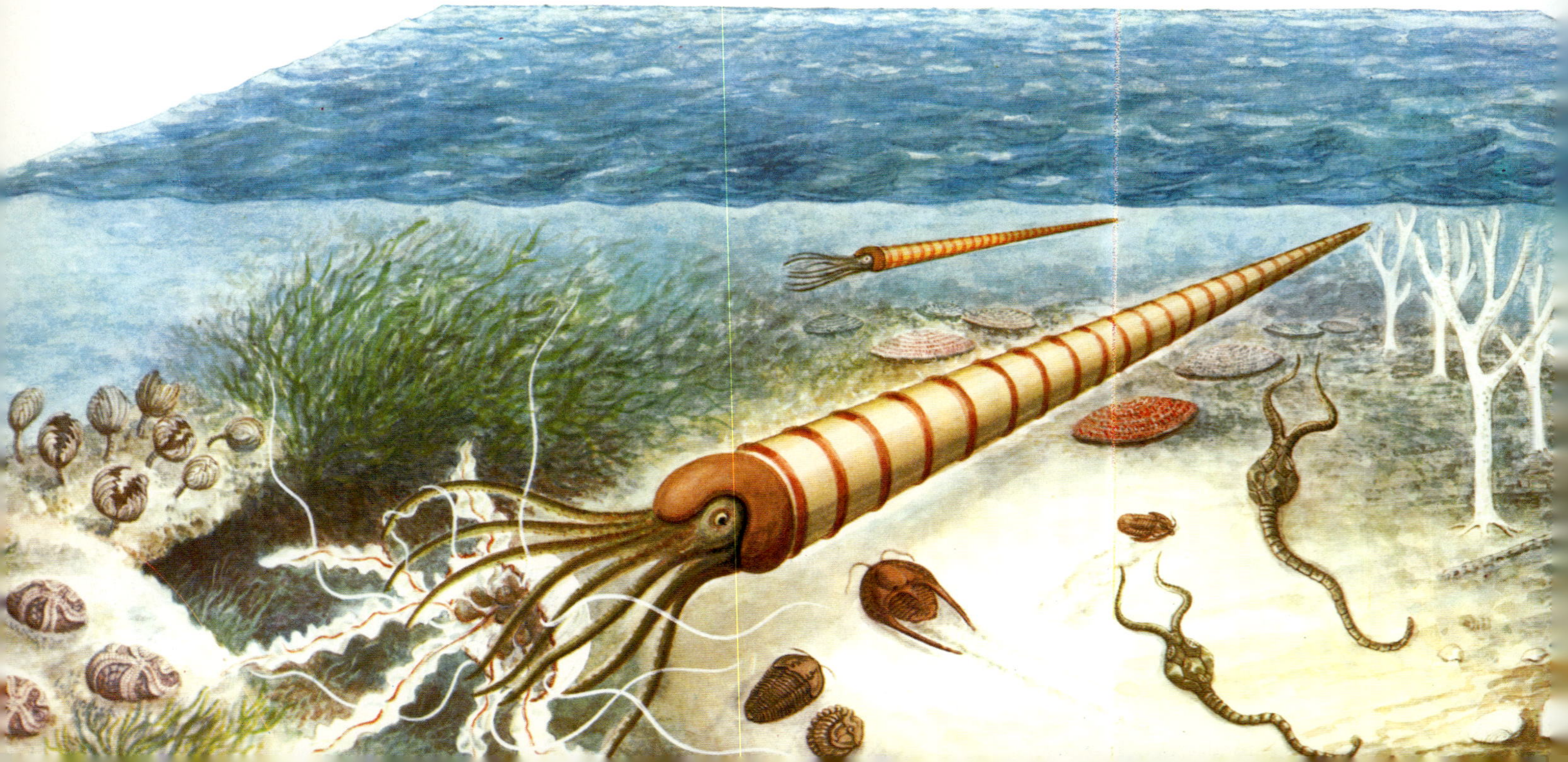

Above: A few of the many life-forms that lived in the Cambrian seas. Some were confined to the early, middle or late Cambrian, but others existed throughout the period. Here, several trilobites (1) are shown, together with sponges (2), jellyfish (3), a red alga (4), brachiopods (5), corals (6), crinoids (7) and other primitive echinoderms (8), a ragworm (9), a green alga (10) and several primitive arthropods (11).

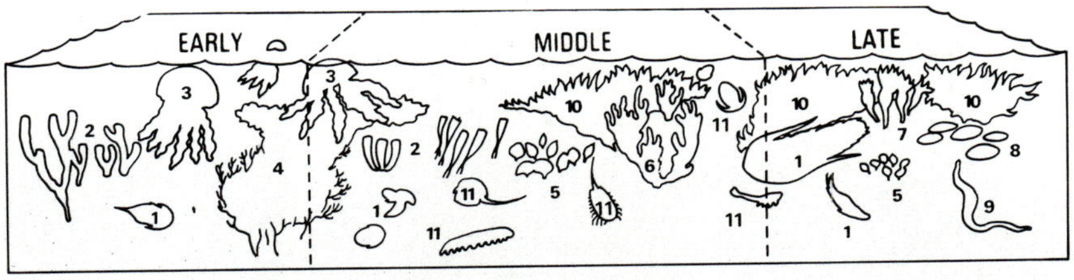

Left: Three of the many kinds of brachiopods that have existed since the Cambrian period. About 2,000 fossil species are known, but only 250 species exist today. *Lingula* is one of the living species. In fact it is an example of a 'living fossil'. Its form and way of life have remained unchanged for over 500 million years.

Right: The fossil remains of a shrimp-like Cambrian animal called *Waptia*. A reconstruction of this animal can be seen in the drawing above, just below the head of the large trilobite.

and other soft-bodied creatures. Towards the end of the Cambrian period new types of trilobites appeared. Some were the giants of the seas, reaching lengths of up to 60 centimetres. Others became adapted for burrowing or swimming. Some could roll themselves into a ball for protection.

Graptolites are also important index fossils (see page 16). Their fossil remains look like tiny saw-blades printed on the rocks. Scientists know very little about these animals. But graptolites may have been the ancestors of a modern group of animals called pterobranchs. These are tiny tube-dwelling animals that live in deep seas. Their name, pterobranch, means 'winged gill' and derives from the fact that these animals push out from their tubes feathery winged gills to 'catch' food and oxygen.

All the Cambrian groups continued into the Ordovician and Silurian periods. Trilobites, brachiopods and graptolites were common. Gastropods and bivalves also spread. And they were joined by another mollusc group called the cephalopods (squids and their relatives). The early cephalopods were straight-shelled nautiloids. These were the ancestors of the coiled-shelled ammonites and the modern coiled-shelled *Nautilus*. During this time corals and sea-lilies (types of echinoderm) were also abundant. There were so many in some places that their remains formed limestone rocks. In the Silurian period a group of fierce predators appeared. These were the giant eurypterids, or sea-scorpions. One kind was over two metres long.

Pterygotus was the largest of the Silurian sea scorpions. Some fossil specimens measure over two metres. It swam using its two largest limbs, which were paddle-like. It probably ate fish and other sea scorpions.

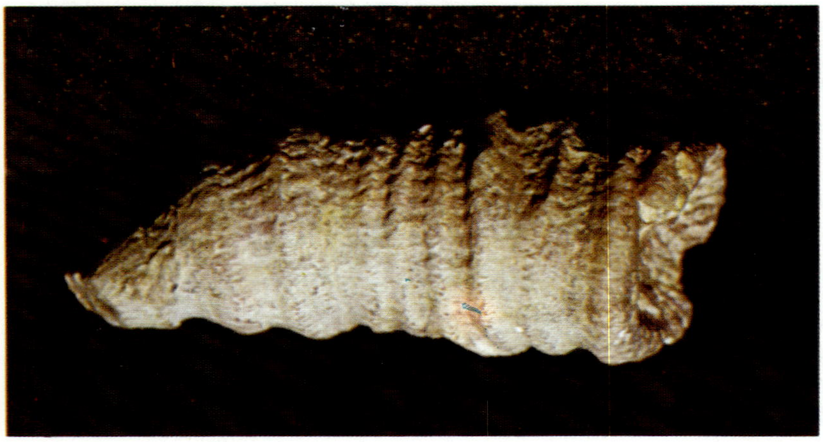

There were several other groups of echinoderms—including the edrioasteroids (early sea-urchin relatives) and homalozoans. The homalozoans were an early Ordovician group. Some scientists call them calcichordates. This is because they could be the ancestors of the chordates (sea-squirts, lancelets and vertebrates).

Towards the end of the Palaeozoic era the invertebrate life of the seas began to change dramatically. Goniatites appeared in the Devonian period and flourished during the Carboniferous period. But by the end of the Permian period they were extinct. They were probably the ancestors of the ammonites.

Above: A fossil coral *(Tryplasma)* **from the Silurian period.**

Below: A fossil trilobite *(Dalmanites)*. **This species existed during the Silurian and Devonian periods.**

Other groups also died out at this time. The graptolites disappeared during the Carboniferous period. Trilobites died out during the Permian period, together with many corals and brachiopods. Of the echinoderms, all except one group of sea-lilies and one type of sea-urchin became extinct. However, these echinoderms became very successful during the Mesozoic era. All the later sea-lilies and sea-urchins evolved from them.

On the Geological Time Scale it looks as if the mass extinctions of the Permian period occurred suddenly. Actually, they happened slowly over millions of years— the Permian period lasted 55 million years. The extinctions were probably due to the changing geography of the time. The continents were moving together. As they did so the shallow seas between them became smaller and finally disappeared. By the end of the Permian period only a narrow continental shelf remained around the supercontinent of Pangaea. At the same time the movements of the continents would have caused great changes in climate. Animals that could not tolerate or adapt to the new conditions died out.

THE EVOLUTION OF AMMONITES

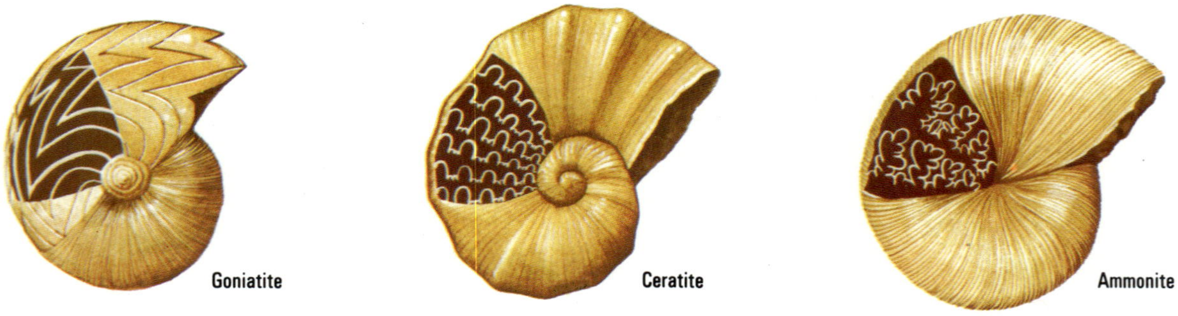

Ammonoids evolved in the Devonian period. The chambers in their shells were divided by partitions called septa. In fossils there are often lines, called sutures, that mark where the septa joined the shell. Ammonoids can sometimes be identified by their sutures. The goniatites were Devonian ammonoids with jagged sutures. The ceratites appeared in the Carboniferous period. They had lobed sutures. Ammonites, the most familiar type of ammonoid, appeared in the Permian period. Their sutures were often elaborate and frilled. Goniatites and ceratites were extinct by the end of the Permian period. But ammonites flourished throughout the Mesozoic era. Many of them had ornate ribs and markings on the outsides of their shells (right). However, by the end of the Cretaceous period the ammonites too were extinct.

During the Mesozoic era two important groups of invertebrates, the ammonites and belemnites, flourished in the seas. Ammonites were squid-like creatures that lived inside coiled, chambered shells. Belemnites were also squid-like animals. But they had internal shells. They were the ancestors of modern squids and octopuses.

At the end of the Cretaceous period there were more mass extinctions. The ammonites, for example, were completely wiped out. Again, the causes were changes in geography and climate. At the beginning of the Cenozoic era the invertebrate animals of the seas were very similar to those of today.

Trepospira

Schizodus

Left: A fossil sea-snail, or gastropod (top) and a fossil bivalve (bottom). These two kinds of mollusc first appeared in the Cambrian period and their numbers increased rapidly in the Ordovician period. *Trepospira* **existed during the Devonian and Permian periods.** *Schizodus* **was a Carboniferous and Permian bivalve. Bivalves are so-called because their shells are in two halves, or valves. Modern bivalves include mussels, cockles and oysters.**

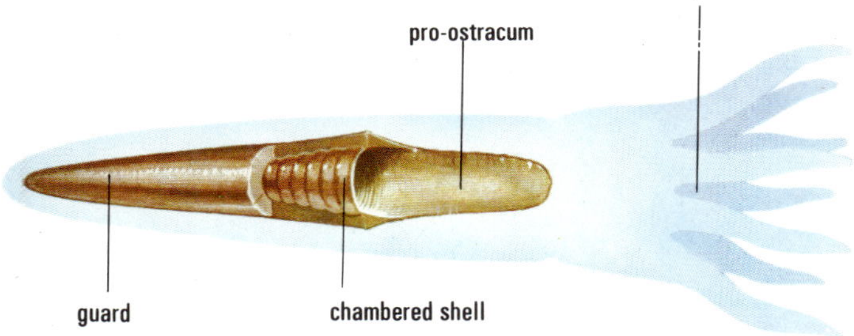

Above: A diagram of a belemnite. These animals were Mesozoic relatives of modern squids. They had internal shells. The bullet-like fossil that is commonly found is the remains of the guard. This protected a chambered shell inside. A horny projection, called the pro-ostracum, supported the rest of the animal's soft body.

Right: A fossil starfish *(Palasterina)* **from the early Devonian period.**

Below: A fossil sea-urchin *(Stomechinus)* **from the Jurassic period.**

Jawless fishes, such as the anaspid *Jamoytius* and the cephalaspid *Hemicyclaspis*, were the first backboned animals on Earth. Modern lampreys (left) are also jawless fishes. They are parasites that attach themselves to their prey with a sucker round the mouth. They may be descendants of the Ordovician anaspids.

The Age of Fishes

During the Devonian period (395–345 million years ago) the seas swarmed with many strange fishes.

The first vertebrates to inhabit the world were fishes. Sometime during the Ordovician period one group of invertebrates—possibly a type of calcichordate (see pages 33-34)—began to evolve backbones. By the end of the period jawless fishes had appeared. One group of jawless fishes are called cephalaspids. These had heavy, flattened shields covering their heads. They probably heaved themselves along the seabed sucking up mud and food. Modern jawless fishes include the lampreys. These could be descended from the anaspids, another Ordovician group.

During the Silurian period, the first jawed fishes appeared. These were heavily armoured fishes known as placoderms. Their jaws consisted of two hinged pieces of armour that covered their heads. The armour probably gave them protection from sea-scorpions. The early placoderms were all quite small. But by the Devonian period they were armoured giants. *Dunkleosteus* was over nine metres long. A man could have stood inside its open jaws.

Jawless fishes and placoderms existed throughout the Devonian period. But at the same time more advanced fishes were evolving. First there were those with skeletons made of cartilage—the sharks and rays. *Cladoselache* was a Devonian shark. Its jaws were formed from parts of skeleton inside its head—the arrangement found in nearly all vertebrates. *Cladoselache* also had razor-sharp teeth that pointed inwards, like those of modern sharks.

The Devonian seas were dominated by giant placoderms, such as *Dunkleosteus* (also known as *Dinichthys*). But by the end of the Carboniferous period they were extinct. Their place was taken by sharks and rays, which had evolved from early placoderms in the Devonian period (*Cladoselache* was a Devonian shark). However, many Palaeozoic types died out in the Permian period. Modern sharks and rays evolved in the Mesozoic era, during the Jurassic period. *Aellopos* was a Jurassic fish that may have been the ancestor of modern skates and rays.

These sharks and rays nearly became extinct at the end of the Permian period. Modern sharks are descended from a different group of sharks that ate shellfish.

Most modern fish, however, are bony fish and this type first appeared in the Devonian period. They may have evolved from a group known as spiny sharks, or acanthodians, which lived in the Silurian and Devonian periods. The first bony fishes were chondrosteans. These were snub-nosed fishes with asymmetrical tails. Their bodies were covered with hard scales. Modern relatives of these ancient fish include the sturgeon.

In the Mesozoic era chondrosteans were largely replaced by holosteans, streamlined fish with symmetrical tails. In the Jurassic period the last group of fishes, the teleosts, appeared. Most modern fishes belong to this group.

All these bony fishes belong to the major group known as ray-fins. However, another group, the lobe-fins also appeared in the Devonian period. Their fins were carried on fleshy lobes. Members of this group were the first vertebrates to emerge onto the land (see page 44).

Climatius was a spiny shark, or acanthodian. It existed during the late Silurian and early Devonian periods. Scientists believe that such fishes evolved from the jawless fishes and were the ancestors of all bony fishes

Cheirolepis was a Devonian fish. It is the earliest known ray-fin and it belonged to the group known as chondrosteans. From this group of fishes evolved all the later ray-fins, the holosteans and teleosts.

Caturus, a ray-fin, was a Jurassic holostean. Notice that it was much more streamlined than _Cheirolepis_ and its tail was symmetrical.

The coelacanth is a lobe-finned fish. It is a 'living fossil', because it has remained almost unchanged since the Devonian period. Until 1938, when the first living specimen was caught and identified, everyone thought it was extinct.

The Progression of Plants

As life evolved in the Cambrian and Ordovician periods, the only plants that we know of were algae that lived in the water. There may have been some mosses and lichens on land, but they left no fossils. The first plants to enter the fossil record were a group known as psilophytes. For plants to become established on land, they had to develop a method of obtaining water. Most algae live in water. So they absorb the water they need through the walls of their plant bodies. But land plants have to draw water up from the soil in which they are growing. So they developed water-vascular systems—plumbing systems using tube-like cells, which, like a 'siphon', draw up water.

Above: A reconstruction of *Cooksonia,* the oldest known psilophyte. It had no leaves and it produced spores in capsules on the ends of its branched stems. It was a tiny plant (its spore capsules were only two millimetres across) that grew on the banks of pools in the late Silurian period.

Below: A diagram of a coal forest, showing some of the plants that grew there (top) and the fossils they left behind them in the coal seams (bottom). From left to right the fossils are *Alethopteris, Sphenophyllum, Neuropteris, Asterotheca, Annularia* and *Lepidodendron.* Most of these are form genera; that is, scientific names given to fossil parts of plants (see text on page 40).

Left: *Drephanophycus* was an early Devonian clubmoss. Its stems were up to 5 centimetres thick and it had small spiky leaves. Some of the leaves bore spore capsules.

Above: The few clubmosses left today are much smaller than their Devonian ancestors.

Below: *Medullosa* was a common seed fern in the coal forests. Its thick, woody stems reached 12 centimetres in diameter and its roots penetrated deep into the ground.

Below: Beside a pool in the coal forest, a small, low-growing seed fern overhangs the water. Behind it, growing higher up the bank is the small horsetail *Sphenophyllum.*

Psilophytes had simple vascular systems. Each upright stem had a column of water-carrying cells up the middle. Psilophytes were very primitive plants. They had long, slender stems, but no true leaves or roots. They grew from horizontal stems, or rhizomes, in the ground. And they collected water through root-like hairs that grew out from the rhizomes. The stems were covered in a cuticle—a layer of waxy material that helped to prevent the plant from losing too much water.

Psilophytes, like modern ferns, reproduced by means of spores. These were produced in spore-containers, or sporangia, at the tips of the stems. When ripe, the sporangia burst open, scattering spores into the wind. Psilophytes may be the ancestors of a modern group of plants known as psilotes. Psilophytes probably grew around the edges of pools and lakes, so that the seeds had a suitably soggy terrain in which to germinate.

Right: *Lepidodendron* **was the largest of all the clubmosses, growing to a height of about 30 metres. Some specimens may have reached 40 metres. Its leaves grew directly out of the stems and branches. On older plants the leaves on the main stem fell off, leaving a pattern of diamond-shaped scars where the leaf bases had been. The underground organs of** *Lepidodendron* **formed four horizontal main roots that branched repeatedly.**

Psaronius **was a tree fern. A crown of leaves sprouted from the top of its stem. The stem appeared large, but most of it consisted of a thick covering of fibrous roots.**

The giant horsetail *Calamites* **grew to a height of about 18 metres. It grew from a large underground rhizome.**

Until the early Carboniferous period the rest of the land remained bare. Then more advanced plants appeared and spread rapidly. By the middle of the period the land was covered by clubmosses, horsetails and ferns. Some of these were giants. *Lepidodendron* was a tree-like clubmoss that could grow to heights of over 30 metres.

The Carboniferous period is sometimes called The Age of Ferns. But this is not strictly true. Most of the fern-like plants that existed then were not true ferns. Instead they were seed ferns—plants that reproduced by means of seeds instead of spores.

The remains of all these Carboniferous plants have been preserved in the coal measures. But the fossils that we find are only of bits of plants. Fossil stems are common and so are fossil leaves. But it is often difficult to say which leaves belonged to which stems. So these parts of plants are given names called form-genera. For example, the names *Lepidodendron* and *Calamites* (a horsetail) refer to certain fossil stems. At the same time scientists found fossil leaves and called them *Lepidophyllum* and *Annularia*. *Lepidophyllum* leaves are now thought to belong to *Lepidodendron* stems and *Annularia* leaves are thought to be those of *Calamites*. There are similar form-genera among the seed-ferns. For example, certain stems are called *Sutcliffia* and *Medullosa*; names for related leaves include *Neuropteris* and *Alethopteris* (see page 38).

Above: Dominating this Jurassic scene are ferns and several conifers, such as the tall swamp cypress on the left. On the small headland to the left are two tree ferns and the bennettitalean *Williamsonia*. On the opposite headland a cycad is growing in the shade of a ginkgo. Large horsetails grow in the shallow water.

Another group of seed-bearing plants also existed during the Carboniferous period. These were the Cordaitales—tall trees that produced their seeds on cone-like structures. They formed large forests. This group had died out by the end of the Permian period. But they were probably the ancestors of three Mesozoic groups—the conifers the ginkgos and the bennettitaleans. The large clubmosses, horsetails and seed-ferns also died out and were replaced by smaller types. The seed ferns continued until the Triassic period and they were probably the ancestors of cycads and flowering plants.

Conifers and other gymnosperms (plants with exposed seeds) dominated the Mesozoic era. By the Jurassic period there were many conifers that still exist today. The ginkgos were also flourishing. With their fan-like leaves they resembled flowering trees. Today all except one species are extinct.

The cycads and bennettitaleans were palm-like plants. The bennettitaleans became extinct by the end of the Cretaceous period. The cycads were considerably reduced in numbers but a few still survive today.

Meanwhile, some seed ferns were evolving a more efficient way of producing seeds. The first flowering plants appeared in the Cretaceous period. By the end of the period they completely dominated the world. They were very adaptable plants. This, together with their highly efficient method of seed formation, ensured their success. They have now colonized almost every kind of living area in the world. Some flowering plants can tolerate the harsh conditions found in deserts and polar regions. Some have even returned to the water.

Above: The maidenhair tree *(Ginkgo biloba)* is the only living representative of the ginkgos that flourished in the Mesozoic era. Male and female cones are borne on separate trees. This tree has pollen-bearing male cones.

Right: A reconstruction of the Cretaceous bennettitalean *Cycadaoides,* with its curious spherical trunk.

Below: Magnolias are believed to be the most primitive of modern flowering plants. The insides of the large flowers are very cone-like in appearance.

Insects, Spiders and Scorpions

As plants spread across the land, insects and other plant-eating animals spread with them. Carnivorous animals preyed on the plant-eaters.

It is never long before animals take advantage of a new source of food. So, during the Silurian period, over 400 million years ago, plant-eating animals appeared on land. They browsed on the psilophytes and any mosses that were present.

These first land animals were all arthropods—animals with hard outer skeletons and jointed legs. By the late Silurian period there were several kinds of arthropod. The myriapods—centipedes and millipedes were very successful. They pushed their way through the decaying plant material that lay on the ground, eating as they went.

Nowadays, arthropods are small creatures. Their heavy outer skeletons and the way in which they breathe limit their size. In addition, large insects are more easily spotted by predators and eaten. In Silurian and Devonian times, however, there were no predators and by the Carboniferous period some myriapods were giants. One kind, called *Arthropleura* grew to about 1.8 metres long. Its only enemies were a few amphibians large enough to eat them.

The first insects also probably appeared during the Silurian period. But the earliest known insect fossil, a springtail called *Rhyniella,* comes from Devonian rocks. This was a flightless insect which crawled among the dead leaves on the ground using its feelers to find a way.

But there was fierce competition for food on the ground. So the insects that evolved wings had an advantage because they could reach the leaves of even the tallest trees. By the Carboniferous period there were many flying insects — dragonflies, cockroaches, grasshoppers and mayflies. Again, because there were few large predators, some of them grew to enormous sizes.

Above: A reconstruction of the giant myriapod *Arthropleura.* This man-sized creature must have been an awe-inspiring sight as it ploughed through the coal forest undergrowth.

Insects adapted to many different kinds of food, including pollen and seeds. Some insects probably helped to pollinate the seed ferns. Later, in the Mesozoic and Cenozoic eras, many new types of pollinating insect—such as bees—evolved as the flowering plants spread.

After the plant-eaters came the predators. Early scorpions all lived in water. The bodies of some of them were so large that they needed the support given by water. *Brontoscorpio,* a Devonian scorpion, was about 80 centimetres long. However, by the Carboniferous period land scorpions had appeared. There were primitive spiders too. With their poisonous fangs they preyed on the insects, such as *Rhyniella,* and myriapods in the leaf-litter.

When insects developed wings, they could escape from such predators. But the spiders developed a new trick. At some stage, perhaps during the Carboniferous period, they began to build webs to catch the insects.

Below: A piece of this fossil leaf of the seed fern *Glossopteris* was nibbled away by an insect.

The giant carboniferous dragonfly *Meganeura* about to land on a *Lepidodendron* branch. Its wingspan was 70 centimetres. Like modern dragonflies, it could not fold its wings when at rest. This was also the case with other early flying insects. There were probably two reasons for its large size. First, there were no predators in the branches of the trees. Second, there were no cold seasons. The constant hot, tropical climate allowed insects to grow continuously.

Right: *Lemmatophora* was a primitive stone-fly. It had an extra pair of wing flaps in front of its normal wings.

Left: Two Carboniferous spiders, *Arthrocylosa* (left) and *Plesiosiro* (right) on the foliage of a seed fern. Early spiders may have used silk to build retreats or line burrows. When insects began to fly, some spiders began to build silk webs to catch them.

Below: The centipede *Latzelia* (top) and the millipede *Euphoberia* (bottom). Both were Carboniferous myriapods. *Euphoberia* was particularly common and may have been a burrower. *Latzelia* hunted its prey among the leaf litter.

Above: Large numbers of cockroaches scavenged in the coal forests.

Below: The late Silurian scorpion *Palaeophonus* is the oldest known scorpion. It probably lived in water.

From Fins to Feet

Above: The first invaders of the land may have been young rhipidistians. Adult rhipidistians, such as the Devonian type *Eusthenopteron* (left) would have been too large and heavy. But the young would have been able to shelter from predators in the shallow waters near the bank. From there, tempted by insects on the land, some of them may have crawled out. Their descendants could have evolved into the first amphibians, such as *Ichthyostega* (right).

The first backboned animals appeared on the land about 350 million years ago. These were the amphibians—animals that could live both on land and in water.

During the Devonian period there was abundant food in the seas. But there was also food available on land. Insects were there in large numbers—an excellent source of food for any animal that could reach them. For most fishes this was impossible. Their bodies were designed for swimming rather than walking. And they could not breathe air. Their gills were designed for taking dissolved oxygen from the water. But one group of fishes, the lobe-fins, were built slightly differently.

Below: Drawings to show how the lobed fin of a rhipidistian (1) could have evolved into the leg of an amphibian (4). The major bones of the amphibian leg were all present in the rhipidistian lobe. The intermediate stages shown here (2 and 3) are imaginary, but they show what probably happened. The bones of the lobe enlarged and the lower part of the limb turned downwards, so that it touched the ground. The smaller bones enlarged and divided to form the bones of the toes.

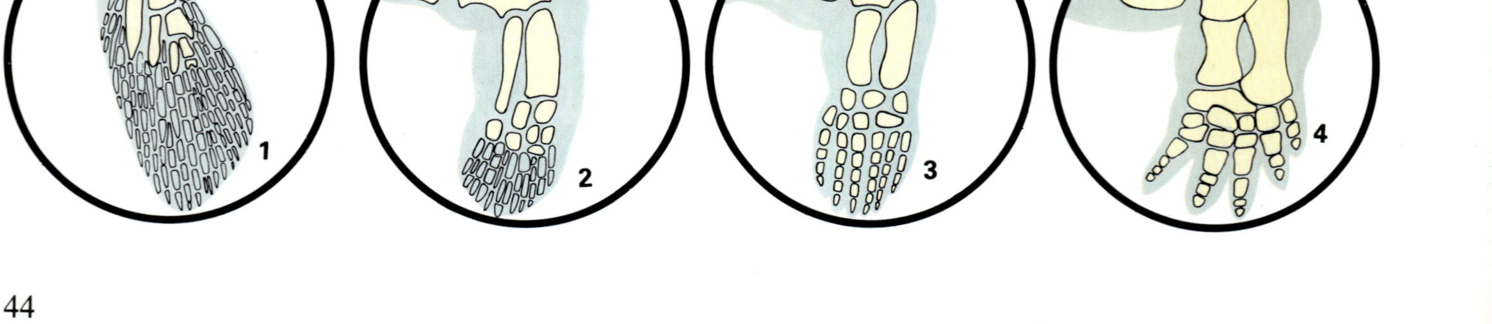

The name 'lobe-fin' comes from the fact that the fins of these fishes were supported on fleshy lobes. Some lobe-fins also had lungs. There were three groups. First, there were the coelacanths. In the Devonian period there were a number of coelacanths. Until recently scientists believed that they had become extinct during the Mesozoic era. But it is now known that one species still survives today (see page 37). Second, there were the lungfishes, so called because they could breathe air into their lungs if the water became foul. However, if a lungfish's pond dried up, it did not try to crawl out onto the land. Instead it buried itself in a mud burrow and waited for the waters to return. Six species of lungfish exist today (see page 46).

Third, there were the rhipidistians. This group became extinct during the Permian period. But scientists believe that early rhipidistians were the ancestors of all back-boned land animals.

Rhipidistians were fishes, but they were certainly equipped for crawling. They had large, fleshy lobes at the bases of their fins. When necessary, these could have been used as primitive limbs. They would have been helpful to a fish crawling along the bottom of a shallow pool. And they could have been used to help a fish heave itself out onto a muddy bank. So, tempted by the insect food available, some rhipidistians probably tried to crawl out of the water. Those with the strongest limbs succeeded. They could breathe in air because they had simple lungs. At first, these amphibious fishes probably spent very little time on the land. But, gradually, the descendants of the successful land-invaders evolved stronger and better developed limbs.

Above: Is prehistory being repeated? Mudskippers are amphibious fish that spend much of their time out of water. Are they, therefore, copying what the rhipidistians did 350 million years ago? Probably not; mudskippers are too specialized to evolve much further. But they do show how some of the problems of moving from water to land can be solved. A mudskipper moves across the mud by using its front fins as crutches. It can breathe air—taking in oxygen through membranes at the back of its mouth. And it can keep its eyes moist—by pulling them back into its head. Some mudskippers feed on small organisms in the mud. Others feed on insects.

Above: Most modern amphibians go through a water-living tadpole, or larval stage. The frog tadpole shown here (left) is about to lose its tail and become an adult. However, some amphibians never grow up. They keep their tadpole characteristics as adults. The axolotl (right) is a large salamander with gills. Creatures that keep their larval characteristics as adults are described as being *neotenous.* In the late 1800s scientists found a number of fossil amphibians with gills in some late Carboniferous and early Permian rocks. For some time it was thought that these were a new group of neotenous amphibians and they were called branchiosaurs (centre). However, we now know that most of them were actually the tadpoles of small water-living labyrinthodonts. Only *Branchiosaurus* itself was truly neotenous.

Amphibians could live and feed in the swamps, but they were not true conquerers of the land. Nearly all modern amphibians, such as frogs, toads, newts and salamanders, need water. For example, they must return to water to breed. There they lay soft, jelly-like eggs that hatch out into tadpoles. These spend all their time in water, taking in oxygen through gills. Eventually, they change into adults and leave the water. Scientists have found fossil amphibians with gills—tadpoles. Such fossils are called branchiosaurs because they were once thought to be a new group of prehistoric amphibians. But it is now known that most of these fossils are the remains of tadpoles. They show that early amphibians also had to lay their eggs in water.

The first amphibians were very different from modern types. There were two main groups, the labyrinthodonts and the lepospondyls. The labyrinthodonts were the first to appear. These were large, fish-like creatures, sometimes up to 4 metres long.

Among the most primitive labyrinthodonts was *Ichthyostega* (see page 45). This late Devonian amphibian looked like a giant salamander. It was about a metre long, with a broad snout and a long, fish-like tail. It could walk on land, but its movements were probably slow and clumsy. The upper parts of its limbs were held out horizontally from its body, which made walking rather difficult. It was much better at swimming and it must have spent most of its life in water. There it preyed on fish and other, smaller amphibians.

Large amphibia of this type continued into the Carboniferous and Permian periods. *Eryops,* a Permian labyrinthodont (see page 51), was similar in general appearance to *Ichthyostega*. It, too, spent much of its time in water. Perhaps it lay in wait for fish, like a crocodile.

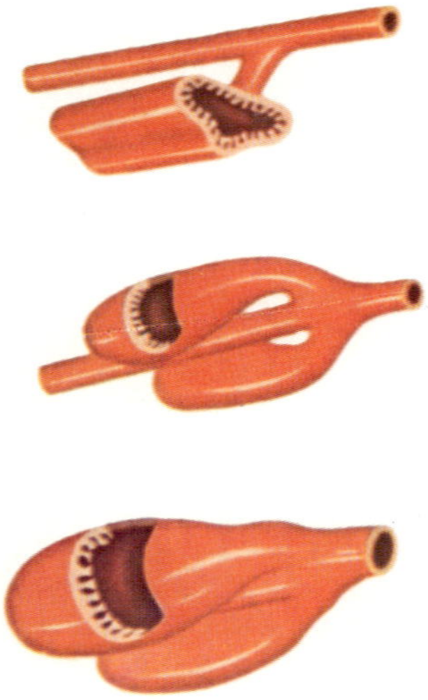

Lungs were first evolved by the early bony fishes. Such fishes often lived in stagnant waters where oxygen was in short supply. Those fishes with lungs could rise to the surface and gulp air to get the oxygen they needed. The first lungs were probably simple sac-like structures that opened into the bottom of the throat (top left). This sac evolved into a pair of lungs. Most lungfishes have a pair of lungs (middle left), although the Australian lungfish (right) has only one. Rhipidistians also had two lungs. The efficient lungs of amphibians (bottom left) evolved from those of rhipidistians.

As the holostean and teleost bony fishes moved into clearer waters the oxygen content increased and lungs became unnessary. So such fishes evolved a different purpose for the sac. The opening to the throat closed and the sac became a buoyancy bag, or swim bladder. The swim bladders of modern bony fish help them to float in the water.

Despite their fish-like appearance, these amphibians had developed some important features for living on land. They had sturdy limbs and strong backbones that could support their weight. They also developed eardrums that were sensitive enough to hear sound in air (sounds are much fainter in air than in water). And their eyes were protected by eyelids and kept moist by tear glands.

Nearly all amphibians depend on water for breeding. However, when the rhipidistians left the water, they took the first step towards conquering the land. Therefore, we might expect to find that amphibians gradually became less dependant on water. However, quite the opposite happened. Throughout the early history of amphibians, many kinds actually returned to the water.

For example, many anthracosaurs (a sub-group of the labyrinthodonts) were land dwellers. But later types, such as *Eogyrinus* (see page 49) lived in water. Many of the Triassic labrynthodonts (see page 50) lived entirely in water. Similarly, many of the second main group of early amphibians, the lepospondyls, were water-living. Some of them even did without limbs altogether.

The first amphibians would have had no competition from other animals. It is curious, therefore, that they seem to have been so reluctant to remain on land. One explanation is that they were carnivores. They ate fish—or at least other amphibians that ate fish. Therefore they had to remain in or near water.

However, the fossil record is not complete. Our knowledge of Carboniferous and Permian land animals comes from fossils found in coal measures—the remains of swamps. There may have been animals living on drier ground that did not leave fossils which would reveal a large group of land-dwelling amphibians.

Whatever the case, one group of amphibians did evolve—into the reptiles. When these animals became established, the amphibians could not compete. Many became extinct and the rest retreated back to the water.

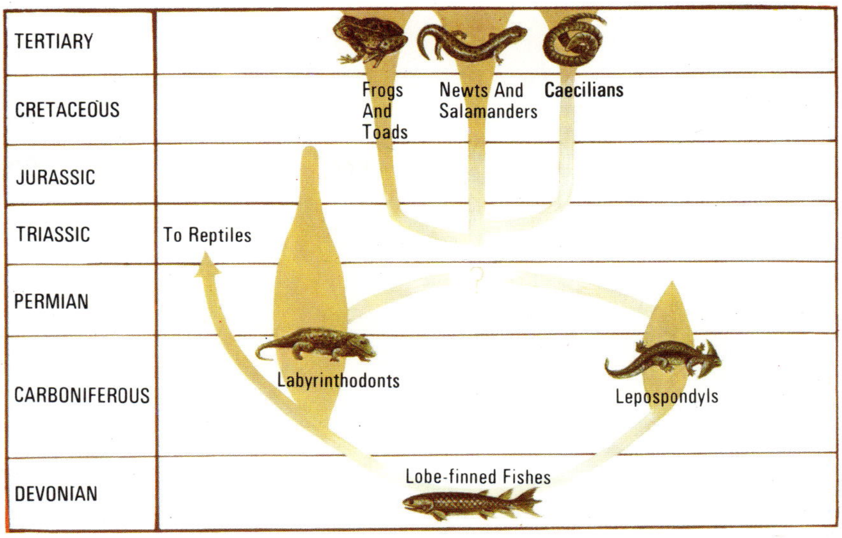

Above: Early amphibians are divided into two groups, the labyrinthodonts and the lepospondyls. The reptiles probably arose from early labyrinthodonts, but the origin of modern amphibians is not known. Some scientists suggest that they arose directly from lobe-finned fishes.

Below: Some Carboniferous lepospondyls. ***Phlegethontia*** **(left) and** ***Ophiderpeton*** **(centre) were legless and snake-like.** ***Microbrachis*** **(right) was a salamander-like amphibian. Some scientists suggest that** ***Microbrachis*** **and its relatives could be the ancestors of modern salamanders and caecilians. Frogs and toads may have evolved from labyrinthodonts.**

The Coal Swamps

Today's coal measures are the remains of swamp forests that existed 300 million years ago.

During the Carboniferous period the northern hemisphere had a tropical climate. Plants grew rapidly and luxuriant forests appeared. There were ferns (including tall tree ferns), seed ferns, giant horsetails, clubmosses and cone-bearing cordaitales. Frequently these forests grew in swamps and this hot, steaming environment supported a rich variety of life at every level.

Insects and spiders crawled among the branches and in the leaf litter on the ground. The first flying insects appeared, including giant dragonflies. Many kinds of large amphibians wallowed and hunted in the swamp pools. We know a lot about life in these forests because the plants formed coal and many forms of life were preserved as fossils.

After the plants died, their remains fell into the stagnant pools below, but lack of oxygen prevented them from decaying completely. Instead, bacteria caused partial decay, leaving a slimy material. This was gradually compressed into, what we know today as, peat.

As millions of years passed, the seas covered and uncovered the land, leaving behind sediments that hardened into rock. Under the weight of such rocks, the peat was compressed into low-grade coal, or lignite. In some places there was greater pressure and bituminous coal was formed. The highest grade of coal, anthracite, was formed by extreme pressure, caused by buckling and folding of the rocks.

Below left: In the hot, steamy climate of the Carboniferous period, coal swamps abounded with many kinds of amphibians, insects, spiders and scorpions.

Above, top: Some Carboniferous labyrinthodonts were long-bodied, water-living types. *Eogyrinus* was about 4 metres long. It probably ate fish and swam by waving its body from side to side.

Above, bottom: *Diplocaulus* was a lepospondyl that lived in ponds during the late Carboniferous and early Permian periods. It was about 60 centimetres long and its skull was widened into a strange head-shield, shaped like a Napoleonic hat. The shield was about 30 centimetres wide. Its function is not known, but it may have given the animal some protection against predators.

Below right: During the early Permian period the climate began to change. Periods of dry conditions alternated with periods of wet conditions. Gradually, the forests began to disappear. During this time there were large, land-living labyrinthodonts, such as *Edops* and *Eryops*.

Above: Towards the end of the Permian period many labyrinthodonts returned to the water and in many cases their legs became feeble and useless. During the Triassic period there were several highly specialized types. *Gerrothorax* **(left) was a long-nosed amphibian, with a total length of about one metre. It may have hunted fish in deep waters.** *Aphaneramma* **(right) was a strange, broad skulled amphibian, about 70 centimetres long. It probably lived on the bottom and swam by using vertical wave movements of its body.**

Amphibians and Reptiles

As the climate became drier during the Permian period, amphibians began to die out and the land was taken over by a new group—the reptiles.

Below: A scene in North America during the middle of the Permian period. By then the climate was becoming much drier and the forests had disappeared. However, large land-living labyrinthodonts still survived. *Eryops* **(foreground right and background left) was about 1.5 metres long. It ate fish and probably spent much of its time in water.** *Cacops* **(foreground left) was smaller and its back was armoured. This probably gave it some protection against predators, such as cotylosaurs (island, left). The seymouriamorphs (island, centre) were the most reptile-like of all the labyrinthodont amphibians.** *Diadectes* **(island, right) may have been a cotylosaur, but it was probably a seymouriamorph.**

Amphibians prefer wet environments. So they found it difficult to survive in the desert-like conditions that existed in the second half of the Permian period. The lepospondyls were all extinct by the end of the period. Many labyrinthodonts also disappeared. A few large labyrinthodonts survived into the Triassic period. Some lived in water and others lived sluggish crocodile-like lives in order to conserve energy in the hot Triassic sun.

No one knows how modern amphibians evolved. The earliest frog-like amphibian, *Triadobatrachus,* lived in the Triassic period. True frogs and salamanders only appeared in the Jurassic period. But there is no real evidence to link these types with earlier amphibians.

Meanwhile, as the early amphibians died out, the reptiles were beginning to evolve. They had developed a distinct advantage over

Left: An Oligocene frog with impressions of its skin preserved in the rock around its fossilized bones.

Right: The oldest known fossil egg was found in Permian rocks in North America. It was a large egg, about 6 centimetres long. Therefore it must have belonged to one of the larger cotylosaurs or mammal-like reptiles.

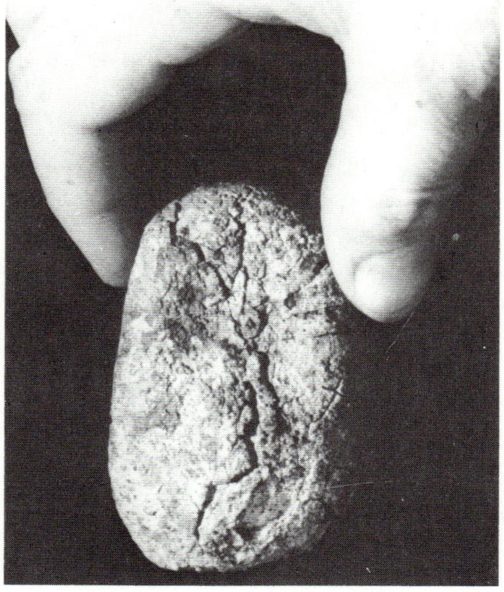

Below: *Hylonomus,* the oldest known reptile. Fossils of this cotylosaur have been found in the fossilized stumps of coal forest trees in North America. Apparently, it made its home in such tree stumps.

the amphibians—they did not have to return to water to breed. Instead the young developed in eggs with hard shells that could be laid on land without breaking.

Again, no one is sure about the origin of the reptiles. But they evolved in the Carboniferous period, probably from early labyrinthodonts. The oldest known reptile is *Hylonomus*. This was a small reptile, about one metre long. It lived in the late Carboniferous period about 300 million years ago.

Hylonomus belonged to a group known as the cotylosaurs, or stem reptiles. These animals were common during the Permian period and among them were the ancestors of all later reptiles. Most were lizard-like in appearance. Some were very small; *Nyctiphruretus* was only 2.5 centimetres long. Other carnivores were larger, ranging up to about 1.5 metres in length. The pareiasaurs were massive; *Scutosaurus* was 2.5 metres long. They were probably herbivores.

By the end of the Permian period the cotylosaurs were nearly all extinct. But they had never been the dominant animals of the Permian period. The top predators of these times were mammal-like reptiles—the group that would eventually give rise to the mammals 20 million years later.

Mammal-like Reptiles

Below: Two middle Permian therapsids. The dinocephalian *Moschops* (right) was a peaceful herbivore. But its carnivorous relative *Titanosuchus* was a fierce predator.

The dominant reptiles of the Permian period were strange and often fierce. Over 160 million years later their descendants, the mammals, took over the world.

Mammal-like reptiles first appeared in the Carboniferous period, having evolved from early cotylosaurs. They are known as mammal-like reptiles because they had several characteristics found in true mammals. Some of them may even have been warm-blooded and had some internal method of controlling their body temperature.

The earliest mammal-like reptiles were the pelycosaurs. *Varanops* was an early Permian type. It was about one metre long and was a fierce predator. *Dimetrodon* was a later relative. This large predator—it was 3.5 metres long—had long, pointed teeth and carried an enormous 'sail' along its back. The 'sail' may have helped the animal to control its temperature. When it was turned sideways onto the Sun, the 'sail' heated up. To cool down, the animal faced the Sun or found some shade.

Some of the pelycosaurs were the first truly land-based herbivores. *Edaphosaurus*, another 'sail-back', had blunt teeth suitable for crushing plant material. One of the largest herbivores was *Cotylorhynchus*, which measured 3.75 metres in length.

During the early part of the Permian period the reptiles were confined to North America. But as the continents closed up, they spread all over the world. One of the best known fossil areas is the Karoo Basin in Africa.

The pelycosaurs were the dominant reptiles until the middle of the Permian period. Then a new group appeared. These were the therapsids, of which there were two main groups, the dicynodonts and the theriodonts.

The dicynodonts were extremely common. Among the most primitive types were the dinocephalians ('big-heads'), such as *Moschops*. These were slow-moving herbivores. However, they could walk more easily than earlier reptiles, as their legs were turned in under their bodies. Later dicynodonts, such as *Dicynodon* itself, were more active. Many of them had a pair of tusks in the upper jaw. And their cheek teeth were replaced with horny pads, giving them turtle-like jaws.

Lystrosaurus was a Triassic dicynodont that appears to have lived in water. Fossils of this reptile have provided evidence for continental drift. They have been

Right: *Edaphosaurus* **was an early Permian 'sail-back'. This pelycosaur was about 3.3 metres long. It was a plant-eater and had powerful teeth for crushing tough plant material. Its 'sail' was supported by a number of spines that extended out of its backbone. The spines carried many small cross bars, rather like the spars across the masts of a tall sailing ship. Therefore the 'sail' must have been quite thick. Like** *Dimetrodon, Edaphosaurus* **probably used its 'sail' to help control its body temperature (see text).**

found in India, southern Africa and Antarctica. This indicates that these continents were joined together in Permian times (see page 13).

The theriodonts were the most mammal-like of all the reptiles. Their teeth were like those of mammals, with incisors (cutting teeth) at the front, canines (pointed 'dog-teeth') and cheek teeth. Parts of their skeletons were also mammal-like.

The most primitive types were the gorgonopsians. These were large, fearsome carnivores with dagger-like teeth. *Lycaenops* lived in southern Africa during the late Permian period.

By the end of the Permian period most of the mammal-like reptiles were extinct. Only a few small groups were left. Of these the cynodonts were the most important. During the early Triassic period they were the dominant carnivores. *Cynognathus* was a reptile with a dog-like head and a thick, lizard-like tail.

The cynodonts gave rise to the last of the mammal-like reptiles, the tiny tritylodonts, such as *Oligokyphus* (see page 90). And it is probable that they also gave rise to the first true mammals. But these shrew-like animals had to wait until the fall of the dinosaurs, over 150 million years later, before they could dominate the land as their ancestors had done.

Below: The Karoo region of southern Africa in the late Permian period contained many mammal-like reptiles. Here, the gorgonopsian *Lycaenops* **has attacked and killed a dicynodont. Two other mammal-like reptiles watch in the hope of getting a meal. They are related to** *Lycaenops*, **but they belong to the therocephalians—a more advanced group of theriodonts. In the background three pareiasaurs are grazing. These cotylosaurs probably had little to fear from the carnivores. Their coarse, bone-studded hides must have made them difficult to attack. The insect-eating reptile in the foreground (right) is called** *Galechirus*.

THE AGE OF REPTILES

The Mesozoic World

At the end of the Permian period, 225 million years ago, many animals and plants became extinct. These extinctions occurred both on land and in the seas. They mark the end of the Palaeozoic ('ancient life') era and the beginning of the Mesozoic ('middle life') era. This era lasted for 160 million years. Geologists divide it into three periods—Triassic, Jurassic and Cretaceous (see the Geological Time Scale on pages 22 and 23).

Because many animals had disappeared, the living areas they had occupied were now empty. However, useful living areas never remain empty for long. The survivors of the Permian extinctions began to evolve rapidly and many new types of animal appeared to recolonize the world.

In the seas there were new groups of echinoderms, bivalves and gastropods. Ammonites and belemnites were abundant, particularly in the Jurassic and Cretaceous periods.

On land there were amphibians and a few small mammals. But the Mesozoic land really belonged to the reptiles, particularly the dinosaurs. In fact, the Mesozoic era is often called the Age of Reptiles. This is not only because reptiles dominated the land. They also dominated the sea and the air. Ichthyosaurs and plesiosaurs ruled the seas; and pterosaurs, or flying reptiles, were the first backboned animals to acquire the power of flight.

The plant life of the land was dominated by gymnosperms for most of the era. Conifers, cycads, bennettitaleans and ginkgos flourished all over the world. But during the Cretaceous period the flowering plants began to take over. By the end of the era this group of plants was more abundant and widespread than any

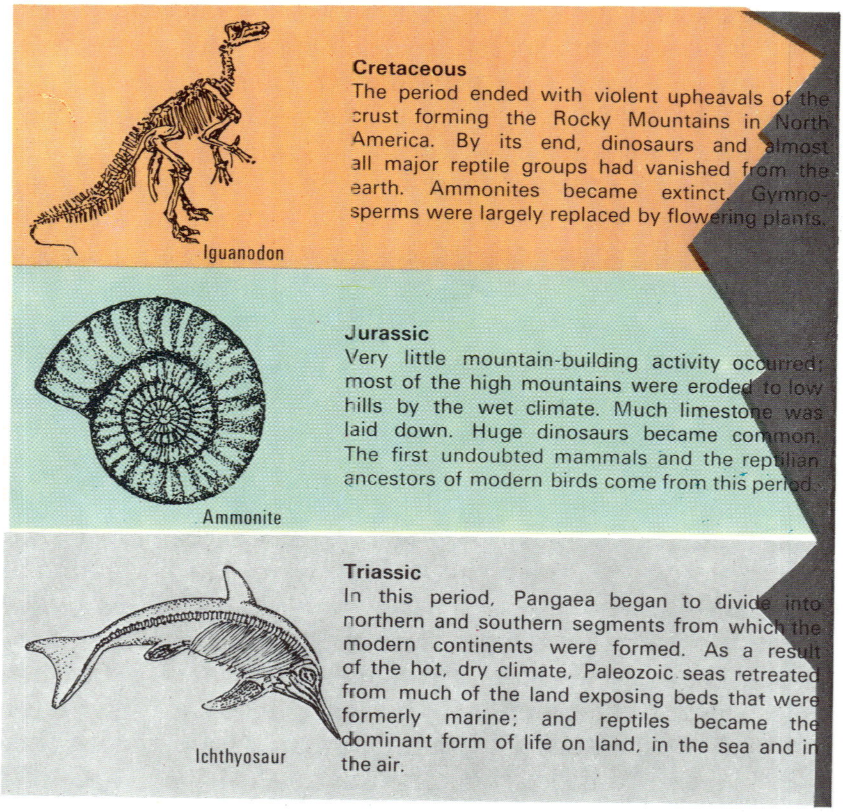

Below: A model of the Triassic reptile *Ornithosuchus*. Some scientists regard it as a primitive dinosaur, but it probably belonged to a group known as thecodonts. This was the group from which the dinosaurs evolved. Notice that *Ornithosuchus* ran on its hind legs, a characteristic commonly found among the dinosaurs. *Ornithosuchus* was a fairly large carnivore. It grew to about 3.5 metres long. However, it was dwarfed by the later flesh-eating dinosaurs.

Right: A view across some craggy mountain tops in the Andes of South America. These mountains began to rise in the late Cretaceous period. As South America began to drift westwards away from South Africa, the edge of the continent began to push against one of the oceanic plates. The continental plate was pushed downwards and the edge of the continent began to fold and buckle. Volcanic activity also helped in the formation of these mountains.

other. The gymnosperms became less important and many kinds disappeared.

At the start of the era the supercontinent of Pangaea existed. As a result, the animals and plants of the Triassic period spread into all parts of the land. But by the end of the Triassic period Pangaea had begun to break up. Gondwanaland in the south began to drift away from Laurasia in the north (see page 12). During the Cretaceous period both Gondwanaland and Laurasia began to break up.

As the continents spread apart, the dry Triassic climate gave way to a rainy, sub-tropical climate during the Jurassic period. The rains wore away the existing mountains, and low-lying, swampy plains were formed. During the Cretaceous period the seas engulfed large areas of land. Thick beds of chalk formed from the empty shells of tiny sea animals. During all this time the Mesozoic animals thrived. The climate was fairly constant and mild and there were no noticeable differences between the seasons.

However, as the Cretaceous period came to an end, the world began to change more dramatically. A period of mountain-building began. The climate cooled, particularly near the poles, and there was a greater difference between summer and winter temperatures. It seems that such changes may have been too great for animals that were used to mild conditions. By the end of the Mesozoic era many of them, including the dinosaurs on land and the ammonites in the seas, were extinct.

Above: A fossil leaf of a Cretaceous plane tree preserved as a thin film of carbon in the rock. The flowering plants were already widespread in the Cretaceous period. Several species of plane tree existed then, but only one has survived into the present.

Rise of the Reptiles

Once established on the land, the reptiles began to evolve rapidly. By the end of the Triassic period all the major groups had appeared.

The extraordinary, long-necked reptile *Tanystropheus* is something of a puzzle. It belonged to an early Triassic group known as proterosaurs, a group related to the plesiosaurs. However, scientists are not certain whether *Tanystropheus* lived in water or on land. Perhaps it lived in shallow water and fed on fish and squid, reaching out for its prey with its long neck.

The most spectacular reptiles of the Mesozoic era were, of course, the dinosaurs. But it is important to remember that many other kinds of reptiles lived at the same time. Some of them were eventually more successful than the dinosaurs in that they survived after the dinosaurs had died out.

The mammal-like reptiles of the Permian period eventually gave rise to the mammals. But most of the mammal-like reptiles did not survive the Permian extinctions. Therefore, when they died out, other descendants of the cotylosaurs (stem reptiles) were able to take over. At the beginning of the Triassic period, 225 million years ago, a tremendous radiation of reptiles took place.

The dominant land reptiles of the Mesozoic era were the archosaurs, or ruling reptiles, (see page 60). This group included the dinosaurs, the crocodiles, the flying reptiles and the ancestors of the birds. The archosaurs all evolved from a group known as thecodonts. These reptiles first appeared in the late Permian period and existed throughout the Triassic period.

Thecodonts mostly resembled lizards or crocodiles. There were several types. Some were sprawling animals with upper limbs that stuck out sideways. In others the limbs were turned in under their bodies. Thus their bodies were raised farther off the ground and they could run more easily.

Several kinds of thecodonts had long hind limbs and short forelimbs. Some, such as *Euparkeria*, were bipedal—they walked on their hind limbs only. This characteristic was typical of many of their descendants—the dinosaurs.

Meanwhile, other reptiles were returning to the sea. Such reptiles included the mesosaurs, ichthyosaurs, placodonts and nothosaurs (see page 58). However, of all the reptile sea-invaders only one group remains today, the turtles. The earliest known turtles come from late Triassic rocks. No one knows the origin of turtles, but presumably they must have evolved from a type of cotylosaur. Land tortoises did not appear until the Cenozoic era.

Most living reptiles belong to a group called Squamata, which contains the lizards and snakes. The ancestors of these reptiles were probably members of a small primitive group known as eosuchians. Fossils of this group are found in

***Kuehneosaurus* was a Triassic lizard. Like the modern flying lizard *Draco,* its ribs were extended sideways to support a membrane. Such reptiles do not actually fly, of course; they glide from tree to tree, using their membranes like parachutes.**

Key

ANAPSIDS

1. **Cotylosaurs** *(Hylonomus)*
2. **Turtles and tortoises**
3. **Mesosaurs** *(Mesosaurus)*

SYNAPSIDS (mammal-like reptiles)

4. **Pelycosaurs** *(Dimetrodon)*
5. **Therapsids** *(Cynognathus)*

EURYAPSIDS

6. **Ichthyosaurs** *(Ichthyosaurus)*
7. **Placodonts** *(Placodus)*
8. **Nothosaurs** *(Nothosaurus)*
9. **Plesiosaurs** *(Plesiosaurus)*

LEPIDOSAURS

10. **Eosuchians**
11. **Rhynchocephalians (Tuatara,** *Sphenodon)*
12. **Lizards and snakes (Monitor,** *Varanus)*

ARCHOSAURS

13. **Thecodonts** *(Euparkeria)*
14. **Crocodiles** *(Deinosuchus)*
15. **Ornithischians** *(Stegosaurus)*
16. **Saurischians** *(Tyrannosaurus)*
17. **Pterosaurs** *(Pteranodon)*

BIRDS

18. *Archaeopteryx*

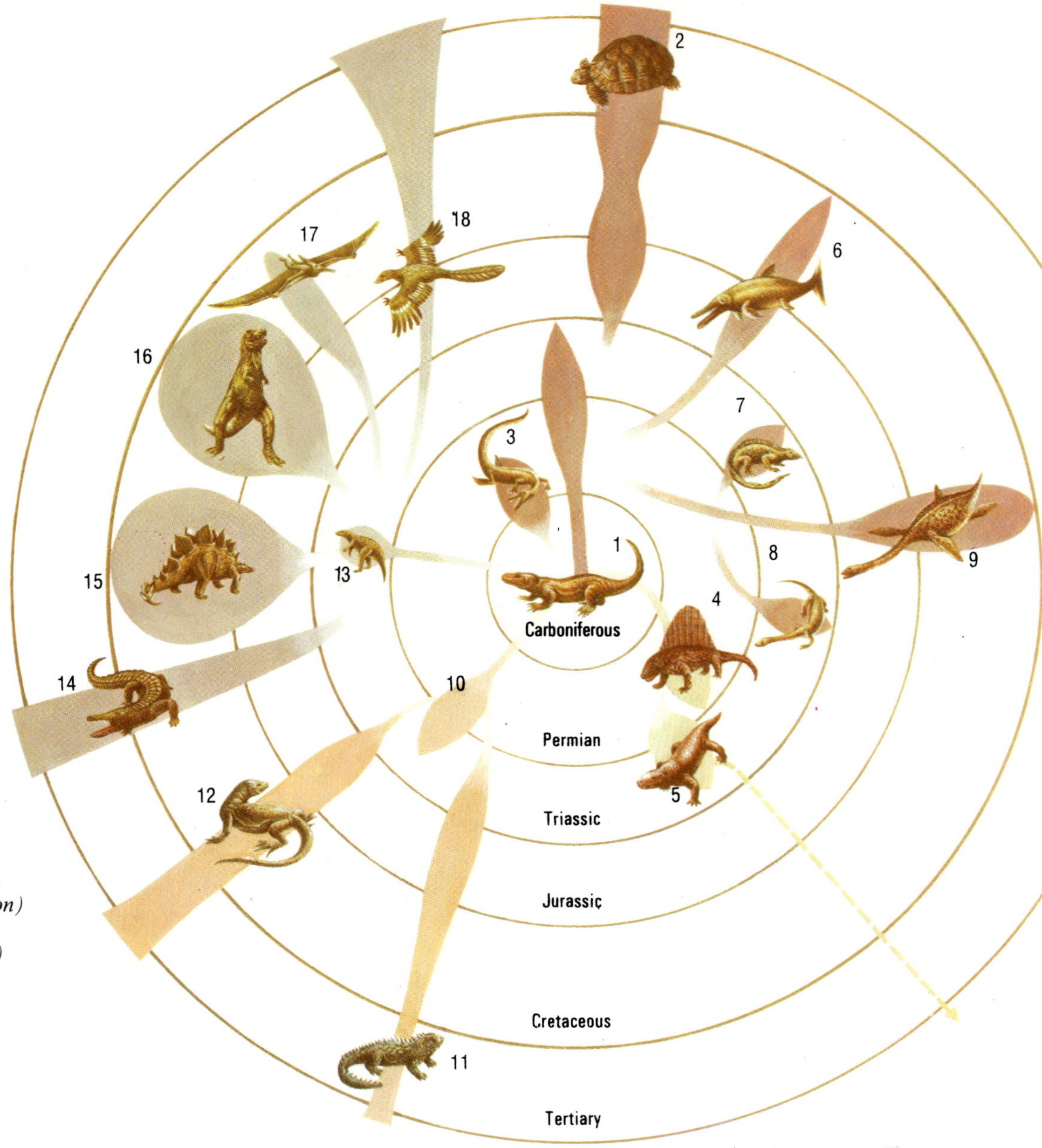

Above: A chart showing the evolution and relative abundance of the main reptile groups.

Below: *Scaphonyx,* **a rhynchosaur from South America. It had nutcracker jaws and was probably a plant-eater. Rhynchosaurs were Triassic rhynchocephalians.**

Permian and Triassic rocks. Eosuchians also appear to be related to thecodonts (their skulls show similarities). Perhaps both groups evolved from a common ancestor.

True lizards first appeared in the Triassic period. They were insect-eating types, similar in appearance to the lizards of today. Some were already highly specialized; for example, the flying lizard *Kuehneosaurus.* By the Cretaceous period most of the modern groups of lizards had appeared. In addition there were some groups, such as the mosasaurs, that had returned to the water.

Snakes also appeared in the Cretaceous period. They probably evolved from lizards that lived in burrows and ceased to use their limbs.

One other group also evolved from the eosuchians. The rhynchosaurs were a Triassic group of reptiles. They were heavily built animals, about one metre long. They evolved rapidly but they died out by the end of the Triassic period. The only living relative of the rhynchosaurs is the lizard-like tuatara (*Sphenodon*).

Back to the Sea

The Mesozoic seas teemed with fish and invertebrates. Many kinds of reptile returned to the water to take advantage of the abundant food supply.

The ichthyosaurs and plesiosaurs are well known. And these two groups were the most successful of all the sea reptiles. But they were not the first. Right from the start of reptile evolution, there were those that turned to a life in water.

Mesosaurus was an early Permian sea reptile. It was a strange creature, with a lizard-like body, a long eel-like tail and a crocodile-like head. Its webbed feet were broad and paddle-like for swimming. It measured about 40 centimetres in length and fed on other fish.

During the Triassic period there were several kinds of sea reptile. Placodonts were large, newt-like creatures. Their bodies were armoured with bony lumps and they had flat teeth for crushing shellfish. By the end of the Triassic period placodonts were extinct. Shellfish-eating rays had taken their place.

The nothosaurs also appeared in the Triassic period. This group probably gave rise to the later plesiosaurs. Nothosaurs were amphibious creatures with long necks and webbed feet. In some parts of the world they were very common.

By the beginning of the Jurassic period the true plesiosaurs and the ichthyosaurs had appeared. Plesiosaurs evolved into two main types. Long-necked plesiosaurs, such as *Plesiosaurus*, had small heads and

Above: A fossil *Ichthyosaurus* with its outline preserved in the rock.

Below: *Peloneustes* (left) was a late Jurassic pliosaur. It was about 3 metres long. Designed for powerful swimming, such short-necked plesiosaurs could make deep dives in search of their cephalopod prey. The dolphin-like *Ichthyosaurus*, (right) however, was designed for high speed sprinting.

needle-like teeth for catching fish. The limbs of a long-necked plesiosaur were paddled and the whole body was adapted for twisting and turning as the reptile chased its prey. The later plesiosaurs had very long necks indeed. *Elasmosaurus*, a Cretaceous type, had 70 neck bones and was about 10 metres long. It spent most of its life in water, because on land *Elasmosaurus* was unable to support its neck.

The short-necked plesiosaurs, or pliosaurs fed mainly on squid and other cephalopods. They swam powerfully and caught their prey in strong jaws armed with large teeth. The largest plesiosaurs were about 12 metres long. Both long- and short-necked plesiosaurs survived until the end of the Cretaceous period.

Ichthyosaurs were superbly adapted for life in the sea. By the middle of the Jurassic period they had evolved a perfect streamlined shape. Their fish-like tails propelled them through the water at high speed. Triassic ichthyosaurs had sharp teeth and fed on fish. But by the Cretaceous period some ichthyosaurs were almost toothless and fed entirely on cephalopods. They began to die out early in the Cretaceous period. Possibly they could not compete with the plesiosaurs.

Other sea reptiles included sea crocodiles, in the Jurassic period, and sea lizards. Mosasaurs were giant Cretaceous lizards. They reached lengths of up to 10 metres and swam by using their long, flattened tails. The shape and size of their teeth would seem to indicate that they probably fed on fish.

Finally, of course, there were the turtles. Triassic types had largely been land-dwellers, but by the mid-Jurassic period sea turtles had appeared. The largest was the Cretaceous *Archelon*. It was 4 metres long.

Above: Nothosaurs were common along the shores of the Tethys Sea, which lay between Gondwanaland and Laurasia (see page 12). They caught fish with their sharp teeth. Some kinds were up to 6 metres long.

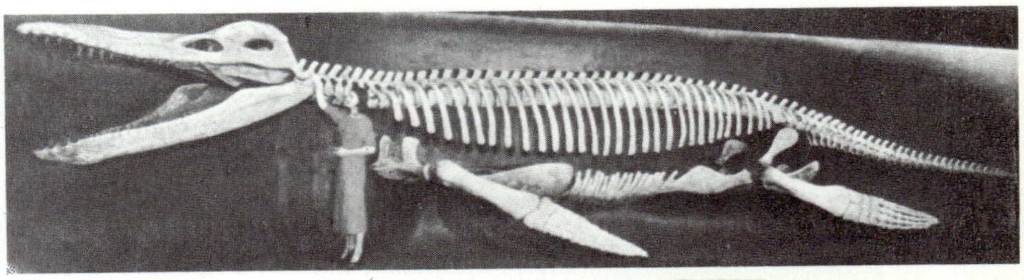

Below: ***Kronosaurus*** **was a large pliosaur. Its skull alone was nearly 3 metres long.**

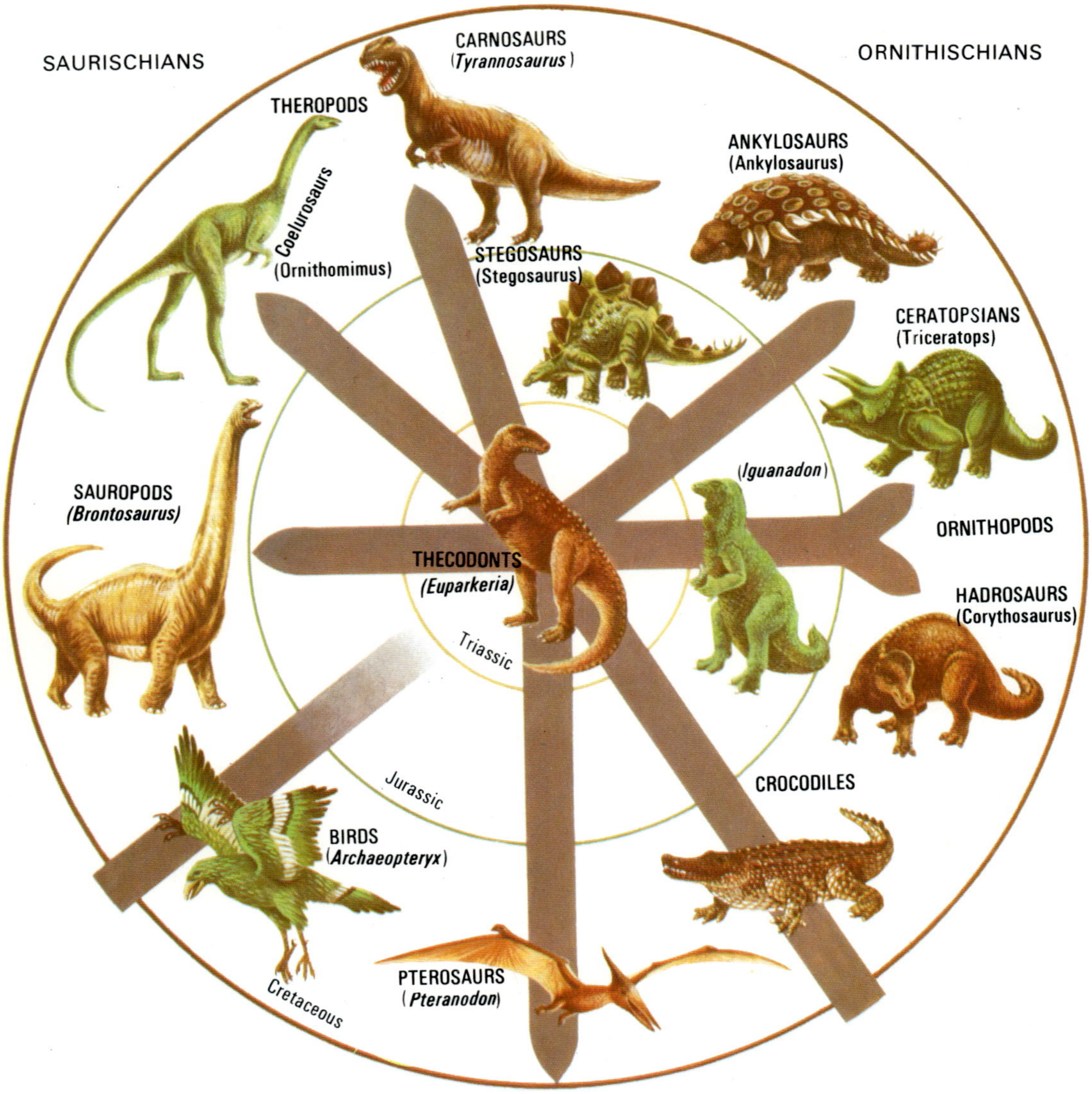

Left: The archosaurs or ruling reptiles. The thecodonts gave rise to the crocodiles, the pterosaurs and two groups of dinosaurs—the saurischians and ornithischians. Saurischian dinosaurs included the giant sauropods (see page 62) and the flesh-eating theropods such as *Tyrannosaurus* (see page 70) and *Ornithomimus* (see page 75). Ornithischian dinosaurs included the ornithopods, such as *Camptosaurus* (see page 66), *Iguanodon* (see page 77) and the duck-billed dinosaurs, or hadrosaurs (see page 72). This group also included the plated dinosaurs, such as *Stegosaurus* (see page 64), the horned dinosaurs, such as *Triceratops* (see page 68) and the armoured dinosaurs, such as *Ankylosaurus* (see page 69) The ancestors of the birds (see page 84) are also believed to have been among the ruling reptiles. However, the origin of birds is not known.

The Ruling Reptiles

For 150 million years the world was dominated by reptiles. Dinosaurs ruled the land and pterosaurs ruled the skies.

The name 'dinosaur' means 'terrible lizard'. And some of the dinosaurs were truly terrible. The huge, flesh-eating monsters, such as *Tyrannosaurus*, must have been a terrifying sight. Even the more peaceful plant-eaters often had formidable horns, spikes and armour with which to defend themselves. And the sheer lumbering size of the giant sauropods, such as *Brontosaurus*, made them almost invincible.

Below: *Rutiodon* was a late Triassic phytosaur. It was about 3 metres long. Unlike crocodiles, the nostrils of these animals were placed near the eyes (in true crocodiles the nostrils are at the end of the snout). Like other thecodonts, phytosaurs had front limbs that were stronger than the hind limbs. Phytosaurs lived in the northern hemisphere during the Triassic period.

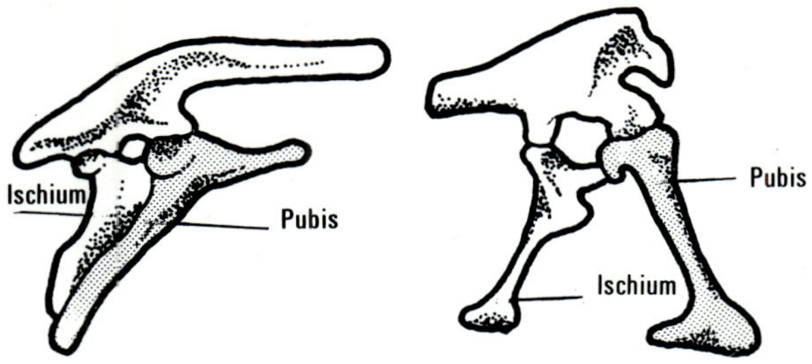

Above: The two main groups of dinosaurs are distinguished by the arrangement of their hip-bones, or pelvic girdles. Each side of the pelvic girdle is made up of three bones—the ilium, ischium and pubis. In the ornithischian girdle (left) the ischium and pubis are parallel. In the saurischian girdle (right) the pubis points downwards and forwards.

The ancestors of the dinosaurs were thecodonts. From these reptiles evolved three important types. The first type were four-footed, sluggish creatures that took to living in swamps and rivers. Two lines evolved—the phytosaurs and the crocodiles. The phytosaurs were crocodile-like creatures that soon became extinct. But the true crocodiles were a highly successful line that has survived to the present.

The second type of thecodont took to life in the trees. Soon they evolved parachute membranes between their legs. These were the pterosaurs that dominated the early Mesozoic skies (see page 82).

The dinosaurs themselves evolved from thecodonts that took to running on their hind legs. Some modern lizards can do this and it is a very fast way of moving. Bipedalism, as it is called, is a strong characteristic of the dinosaurs. Even though many of them went back to walking on four feet, they often had long hind legs and short front legs like their thecodont ancestors.

Scientists divide dinosaurs into two main groups. Those with lizard-like hip-bones are called saurischians. Those with bird-like hip-bones are called ornithischians. These two groups also had different kinds of teeth. Most saurischians had teeth all the way round their jaws. But most ornithischians had no front teeth. Instead they had a horny beak. All ornithischians were therefore plant-eaters, but many saurischians were flesh-eaters.

Modern reptiles are cold-blooded animals. But there is some evidence that the dinosaurs may have been warm-blooded, like the birds and mammals.

Below: The early saurischian plant-eaters, such as *Plateosaurus*, could grow to lengths of 8 metres. But despite their size they were easy prey for carnivores like the thecodont *Ornithosuchus*. Later herbivores were even larger, but so too were the carnivores.

Giants Among Giants

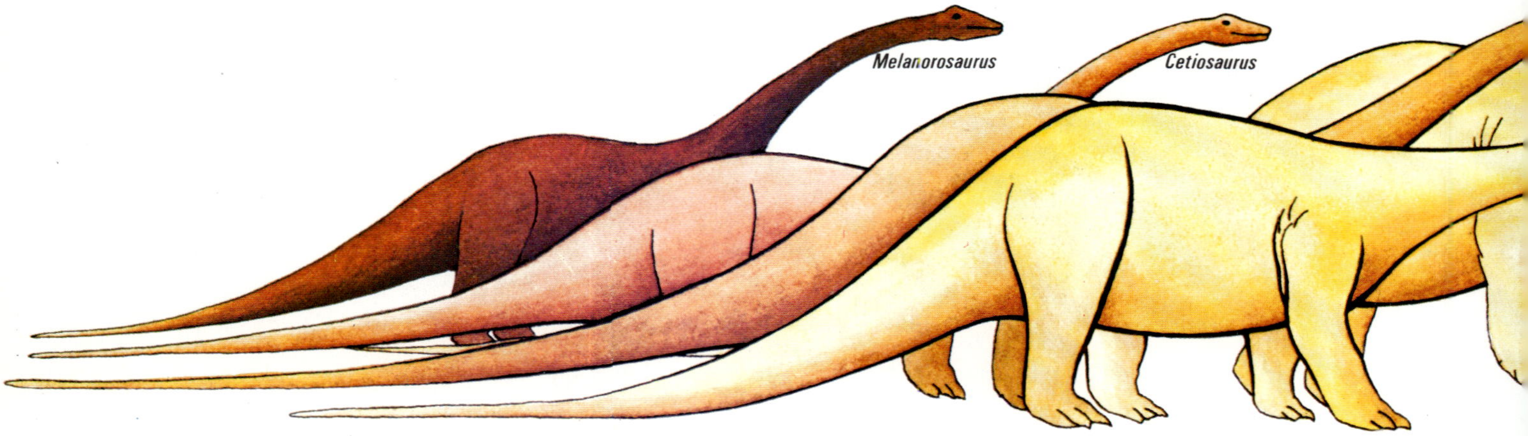

The huge sauropods were the largest animals that ever lived. But despite their size they were peaceful, plant-eaters.

It is easy to see why the sauropods are among the most popular and well-known dinosaurs. If biggest is best, then the sauropods win by a long head. In fact, these reptiles were so enormous that it is hard to comprehend their size. Even if you go to museums to see their skeletons, it is difficult to imagine what it would have been like to stand near a living, breathing, moving sauropod, towering over 6 metres above you, staring at you with its tiny head.

Scientists used to believe that sauropods spent all their lives in deep water, using their long necks to hold their heads above water. In this way they could have kept out of the way of predators. However, it is likely that the pressure of water on their bodies would have prevented them from breathing. And their elephant-like feet would probably have got struck in the mud. Scientists now believe that sauropods were true land animals. Their long necks enabled them to reach leaves high up in the trees. However, they could and did wade through rivers and lakes.

Nor would sauropods have been totally defenceless on land. Their size alone would have discouraged many predators. And when provoked, a sauropod could probably deliver a massive, rib-crushing blow with its powerful hind legs and solid, whip-like tail.

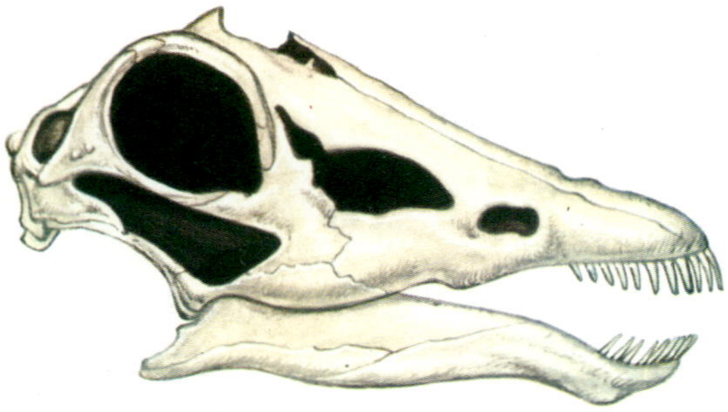

Left: The skull of *Diplodocus.* This sauropod browsed among the trees, using its peg-like teeth to pull off the leaves. For its size *Diplodocus* had a very small brain—only 10 centimetres long. However, it may also have had a 'secondary brain' or 'relay station'—a swelling in the spinal cord near the base of the tail.

Left: A sauropod compared in size with three modern buses.

Left: Some of the giant sauropods that lived in the Jurassic and Cretaceous periods.

Sauropods are often popularly known as brontosaurs. But *Brontosaurus* was only one of many. Among the early sauropods was *Cetiosaurus*. It belonged to a family of sauropods that had relatively short necks. This family also included the most massive of all the sauropods, *Brachiosaurus*. Some individuals are estimated to have weighed between 80 and 100 tonnes! Such animals would have had to eat over 400 kilogrammes of plant material each day to keep them alive.

The most advanced sauropods included *Brontosaurus*, *Diplodocus* and *Barosaurus*. *Diplodocus* was the longest of them all—it measured up to 25 metres from head to tail.

Sauropods were very common during the Jurassic period. However, during the Cretaceous period they became rarer. Possibly they could not compete with the duck-billed dinosaurs.

Cetiosaurus was an early Triassic sauropod. It was about 18 metres long and its name, which means 'whale lizard', was given to it to create an impression of its size. Its strong legs supported the immense weight of its body. When such dinosaurs walked across mudflats or the bottoms of lakes, they often left footprints that later became fossilized. Such footprints show that sauropods usually walked very slowly. But it is possible that they could move quite quickly when necessary. Sauropods had three claws on each foot. These may have been used for digging up roots from the ground.

The Plated Herbivores

The smaller herbivores needed to protect themselves against predators. Some developed plates and spines. But how much protection did such weapons give their owners? And was this their real function?

Stegosaurus **was a large, plant-eating reptile—larger than two modern cars (above). So it must have needed a lot of plant material to keep it going. However, it had simple teeth and a very small head (below). Therefore it can only have taken small mouthfuls of plant material. Some scientists think that it must also have eaten carrion (the flesh of dead animals) to get sufficient nourishment.**

The plated dinosaurs, or stegosaurs, appeared in the Jurassic period and survived into the start of the Cretaceous period. The group is named after *Stegosaurus*, the largest and best known of all the plated herbivores. Only a few other types are known. Their fossil remains come from very different parts of the world.

The earliest known stegosaur is *Scelidosaurus* from

Right: The first fossil bones of *Stegosaurus* were discovered in 1877. From these it was possible to reconstruct a skeleton. Such reconstructions show that *Stegosaurus* had hoof-like feet and the typical ornithischian hip-bone arrangement. *Stegosaurus* had a very small brain, but it also had a 'secondary brain'—a large swelling in the spinal nerve cord near the hips. This may have helped to control the rear end of the animal.

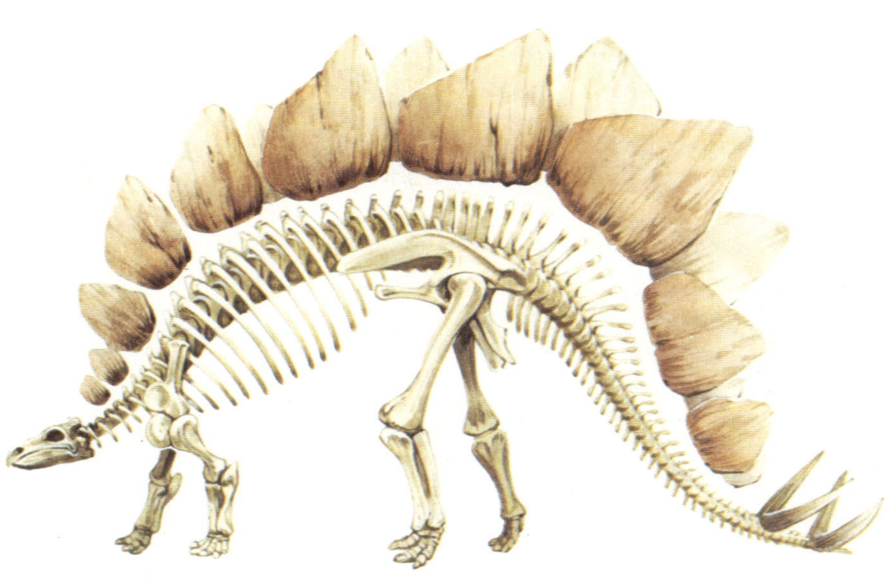

Below: Scientists had great difficulty positioning the plates on the skeleton. In 1899 it was suggested that the plates lay flat against the animal's body and that pairs of spines stuck out between them (top). Today, however, it is generally believed that the plates ran down the back, sticking out vertically. Another recent suggestion is that the plates stuck out sideways (bottom). This might have given the animal more protection, but the plates could not then have been used for efficient temperature control.

southern England. This reptile was about 4 metres long. It had several rows of small plates along its back. Like other stegosaurs, it walked on all four feet and its hind legs were much longer than its front legs.

The mid-Jurassic stegosaur *Chialingosaurus*, from China, was a slender animal with small, plate-like spines. Late Jurassic stegosaurs included *Dacentrurus* (Europe), which was armed with spines but no plates. *Kentrosaurus* (Africa) was about 5 metres long. At the front end of its body it had two rows of small plates along its neck and back. The rear end and tail were armed with eight pairs of long heavy spines, which looked extremely menacing, if not very effective.

Stegosaurus itself was a late Jurassic reptile that lived in North America. It reached lengths of up to 9 metres. Along its back were two rows of large plates and its tail was armed with two pairs of large spikes. The largest plates, each about one metre wide and weighing a considerable amount, were in the hip region.

So what were these plates and spines for? It is often supposed that they were armour for protection against predators. However, such protection could not have been very effective. It is unlikely that the small plates and spines of early stegosaurs would have discouraged determined predators allowing them to survive and the species to develop. Even *Stegosaurus* was extremely vulnerable on its flanks and belly. And its tail was probably not very useful as a weapon.

But, it is possible that the early stegosaurs do represent the first stages in the evolution of armour plating. They could be the ancestors of the much more successful Cretaceous group—the ankylosaurs, or armoured dinosaurs (see pages 68–69).

Stegosaurus itself, however, may have used its plates for another purpose. Inside each plate there were a number of channels. These opened into the animal's body and were probably filled with blood. Thus the plates could have been used for controlling the animal's body temperature—like the 'sails' of some of the mammal-like reptiles (see page 52).

On the other hand dinosaurs may have been warm-blooded animals; that is, they may have generated heat inside their bodies. *Stegosaurus*, therefore, may have used its plates for cooling its blood by exposing them to the wind. The two rows of diamond-shaped plates were staggered. Experiments have shown that this arrangement would have made an efficient cooling system.

Life in the Jurassic Period

Between 190 and 135 million years ago, dinosaurs were well established on the land. Plant-eaters browsed in the thick vegetation that flourished in the warm, wet climate. Flesh-eaters preyed on the plant-eaters.

Life was easy for the Jurassic animals. There were no extremes of temperature and there was plenty of food. Many species flourished during this period.

In the seas the ammonites spread rapidly. Some swam near the surface; others crawled along the bottom. Squid-like belemnites were also abundant. Crabs and lobsters appeared. Fishes were mostly primitive holosteans. Teleosts (the main group of modern fishes) began to appear at the end of the period.

The main enemies of fish were the sea reptiles, particularly ichthyosaurs and plesiosaurs. But there were also large sea crocodiles.

On the land, of course, the reptiles ruled supreme. Dinosaurs reached enormous sizes. The reason for this is uncertain. It may just have been competition between carnivores and herbivores; as one type grew larger, so did the other.

Furthermore, dinosaurs had no hair or feathers to protect them from the cold. A large object cools down more slowly than a small one. So large dinosaurs would not have been affected by small, everyday changes in temperature.

Of course, the opposite is also true. If a large dinosaur got cold, the Sun's heat would have taken a long time to warm it up again. This suggests that dinosaurs may have been warm-blooded. Another piece of evidence for this is the fact that many flesh-eating dinosaurs were built for fast running (see page 70). This characteristic is not found in the larger cold-blooded animals of today, such as the monitor lizard. Even the massive sauropods may have been able to move faster than the slow plod that is often suggested. Their legs were held vertically under their bodies, like those of elephants. Even so, their top speed was probably only about 16 kilometres per hour.

Other Jurassic reptiles included bird-footed dinosaurs, or ornithopods, such as *Camptosaurus*. Stegosaurs, which had evolved from Triassic ornithopods, appear to have been particularly vulnerable to predators (see page 64) and were extinct by the early Cretaceous period. However, despite its apparent handicaps, *Stegosaurus* survived for several million years.

In this Jurassic scene *Allosaurus,* a large carnosaur, is chasing the small coelurosaur *Ornitholestes.* In the background two *Brachiosaurus* (centre) browse the tops of cycads. *Camptosaurus* (left) can only reach the lower leaves. And the two *Stegosaurus* (right), with their short necks, can only graze the small, low-growing plants on the ground. High in the air, a pterosaur glides down from the conifers in search of its prey.

Horned and Armoured Herbivores

During the Cretaceous period some of the great four-footed dinosaurs developed massive armour. The ceratopsians ('horn-bearers') had enormous horned head-shields. The Ankylosaurs were covered with armour plating, like giant reptilian tanks.

Throughout the history of the dinosaurs there was constant competition between the carnivores and the herbivores. As the flesh-eaters grew larger, so also did some of the plant-eaters, such as the sauropods. But others developed efficient and specialized forms of armour to protect themselves. These included some of the strangest but most successful dinosaurs.

The ceratopsians, or horned dinosaurs, evolved from bipedal ornithopods, although the earliest ceratopsians walked on all four legs. One of these early types was *Protoceratops*. This small dinosaur had no horn, but the back of its skull was extended to form a shield. Later types, such as *Monoclonius* had single, long, rhinoceros-like horns on their noses. *Styracosaurus* also had a long nose horn, but the back of its shield had a number of horn-like projections. *Triceratops*, one of the last ceratopsians, had a short nose horn and two larger horns above and behind its eyes.

Some ceratopsians had even larger shields. The skull and shield of *Torosaurus* was 2.6 metres long. *Pentaceratops* also had a large shield and it was crowned with five horns.

The shield of a ceratopsian probably had two main uses. First, it protected the animal's neck from attack. Second, it acted as a solid base for the neck muscles. These had to be very strong in order to lift the massive horned skull. The horns themselves may have been used for protection against predators or even for attack.

One can imagine *Triceratops* making a rhino-

As the horned dinosaurs evolved they increased in size. From left to right: *Protoceratops*, **2 metres,** *Monoclonius*, **5 metres,** *Styracosaurus*, **6 metres,** *Triceratops*, **8 metres.**

Below: A model showing young *Protoceratops* hatching from their eggs, reconstructed from fossil skeletons and nests of eggs found in Mongolia. The young were only 30 centimetres long when they hatched.

Above: In the late Cretaceous period the last of the dinosaurs included *Triceratops* (left) and *Ankylosaurus* (right). Some ankylosaurs, such as *Scolosaurus* (inset right) had spikes on their clubbed tails.

ceros-like charge. However, it is more likely that the horns were used in combat between rivals. Two males would have locked heads and engaged in a sort of pushing match.

Ceratopsians probably fed on very tough plants. Their parrot-like jaws were armed with long teeth that slid up and down against each other like shears. Such teeth were suited for slicing and chopping.

The armoured dinosaurs, or ankylosaurs, appeared in the early Cretaceous period. They may have been descendants of the stegosaurs. At first they were lightly armoured. But by the late Cretaceous period there were tank-like creatures that must have been almost impossible to attack. They had squat bodies and short legs. And their backs were covered with many bony plates and spikes. If an ankylosaur dropped onto its belly, its armour would have protected it from the most savage assault.

Many ankylosaurs also had heavy clubs on the ends of their tails. And sometimes there were spikes as well. These clubs must have made formidable weapons. A single, well-aimed blow could have broken the leg of any would-be attacker.

Left: Three carnosaurs. *Megalosaurus* **and** *Allosaurus* **could both grasp their prey with their 'hands'. But the tiny, two-clawed forelimbs of** *Tyrannosaurus* **were almost useless.**

Below: This fossil carnosaur tooth is shown here at its actual size of 17 centimetres. It was serrated like a saw-blade along its edges and must have been an effective tool for cutting up flesh.

Terrible Teeth

The name dinosaur, or 'terrible lizard' truly applies to the carnivorous dinosaurs. Some of these flesh-eating reptiles were huge and ferocious.

The flesh-eating theropod dinosaurs are divided into two main groups—the coelurosaurs and the carnosaurs. The coelurosaurs were small, lightly-built reptiles. They ran on their hind legs and many of them could grasp objects with their 'hands'. Triassic and Jurassic coelurosaurs were flesh-eaters. They included such types as *Coelophysis, Compsognathus* and *Ornitholestes* (see page 66). Some of the later coelurosaurs, such as *Ornithomimus* (see page 75) were toothless. They probably raided the nests of other dinosaurs and fed on the eggs, sucking out the yolk with their beaks.

The carnosaurs were all fierce predators. The first types appeared in the late Triassic and early Jurassic periods. Most of them were fairly small. But by the middle of the Jurassic period more massive carnosaurs had appeared. These were the megalosaurids, such as *Megalosaurus* itself and *Protocerato-saurus,* which had a horn on its snout. Late Jurassic megalo-saurids were larger still. *Ceratosaurus* (another horned type) was about 6 metres long and *Allosaurus* (also known as *Antro-demus*) appears to have reached 12 metres in length, the length of three elephants.

The dominant predators of the Cretaceous period were the tyrannosaurids. These giants had tiny forelimbs and relied on their massive, sharp-toothed jaws for catching their prey. *Albertosaurus* was about 10 metres long. *Tyrannosaurus* itself is by far the largest carnivorous animal that the world has ever seen.

It was 14 metres long and stood 5 metres tall. Its teeth were over 15 centimetres long!

The legs of a large carnosaur were wide apart and it probably walked with a waddling, duck-like gait. The weight of its forward-leaning body was balanced by the heavy, almost rigid tail. It is unlikely, therefore, that carnosaurs could run very fast. So their prey probably consisted mainly of wounded or sick animals. And they probably scavenged for carrion.

Coelurosaurs, however, could run very fast. It has been calculated that *Ornithomimus* could have reached speeds of up to 80 kilometres per hour. But no sluggish, cold-blooded reptiles could have reached anything like such speeds. This is further evidence to suggest that dinosaurs were warm-blooded animals.

Above: *Tyrannosaurus* **stood taller than a giraffe and its head was as large as a new-born calf. It weighed about 100 tonnes.**

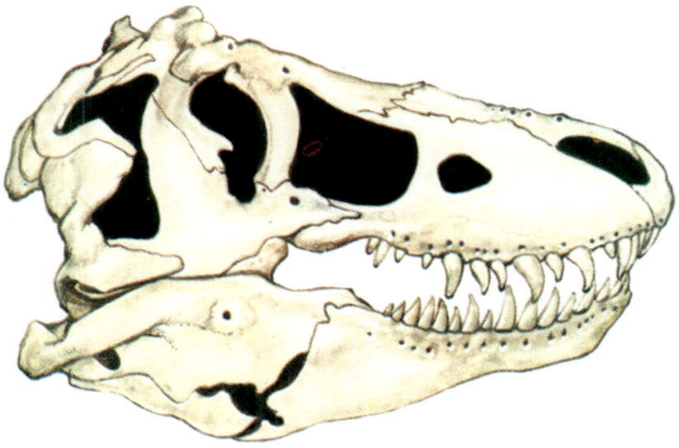

Above: The skull of *Tyrannosaurus* **with its array of sharp, curved teeth.**

Below: A scene in North America in the Cretaceous period. The vulnerable *Corythosaurus* **(see page 72) struggles in vain in the vice-like jaws of** *Tyrannosaurus.* **The heavily-armoured ankylosaur in the background has nothing to fear.**

Duck-billed Dinosaurs

The duck-bills were one of the most successful groups of Cretaceous dinosaurs. But we know very little about them. What did they feed on? And what was the purpose of their strange crests?

Above: *Anatosaurus* **may have fed on twigs and leaves, using its array of crushing teeth (up to 60 closely-packed rows in each jaw) to grind them up.** *Anatosaurus* **was an early, uncrested hadrosaur. It may have spent some of the time on all fours, but when it stood up it was as tall as a giraffe (top).**

Right: A herd of *Parasaurolophus* **keep a wary eye on an approaching** *Tyrannosaurus* **as they feed.**

The hadrosaurs, or duck-billed dinosaurs were a late Cretaceous group. They evolved from ornithopods and were the last members of this line. But they were a very successful group. They appear to have taken over from the sauropods in North America and eastern Asia. In these places hadrosaurs became very common.

The early hadrosaurs were uncrested types, such as *Anatosaurus*. Later types, such as *Saurolophus* had small, backward-pointing crests on the backs of their heads. But the most advanced hadrosaurs had large crests. *Corythosaurus* had a rounded, helmet-like crest (see page 71). *Lambeosaurus* (see page 74) had a hatchet-shaped crest. And *Parasaurolophus* had a long, curved crest projecting backwards from its head.

Scientists have found mummified specimens of hadrosaurs, complete with skin as well as bones. So we have a fairly clear idea of what these animals looked like. All those mentioned here grew to about 10 metres in length. But how they lived and why they developed crests remains something of a mystery.

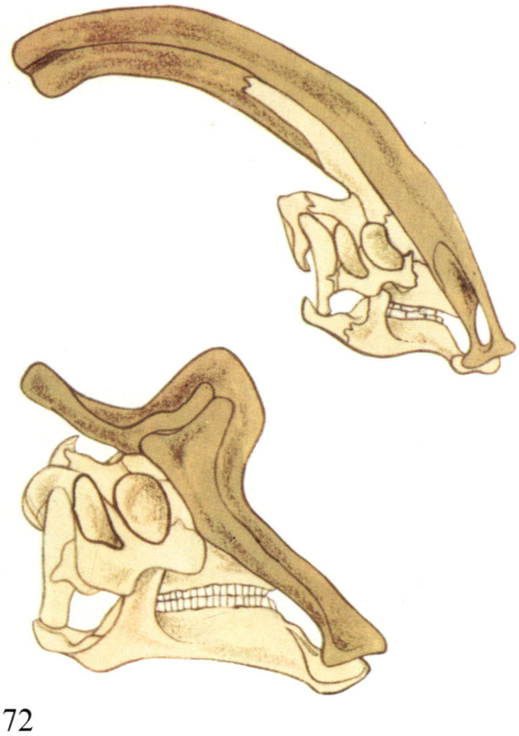

Below: The crested skulls of *Parasaurolophus* **(top) and** *Lambeosaurus* **(bottom). Such crests may have distinguished males from females. They could also have acted as resonating chambers, producing very distinctive mating calls.**

With their long, three-toed hind limbs, hadrosaurs were obviously bipedal animals. But the structure of their 'hands' suggests that they regularly walked on all fours—perhaps when eating. Their long, flattened tails suggest that they were good swimmers. Thus scientists have come to the conclusion that hadrosaurs lived in marshes.

The duck-like beaks of hadrosaurs would seem to support this idea. They suggest that hadrosaurs lived on water plants. However, inside the mouth of a hadrosaur there were up to 1,000 tightly-packed crushing teeth. These formed two 'grindstones' that were much more suitable for pulverizing hard food than for chewing soft water plants. In addition, scientists have found one fossil hadrosaur with the contents of its stomach preserved. The animal had eaten twigs and conifer needles as well as other plant material. So it would seem, it must have browsed in the forest.

Finally, there is the mystery of the crests. What were they for? They contain passages that link up with the nasal (nose) tubes in the skull. An old idea was that such crests were used as snorkels to help hadrosaurs breathe underwater. However, this is unlikely. They may have enhanced the animals' sense of smell. Or it may be that only males had crests, acting as a distinguishing feature between the sexes. Or the crests may have acted as resonating chambers, increasing the volume of the animals' bellows. We have yet to find out for certain.

Life in the Cretaceous Period

During the Cretaceous period, 135–65 million years ago, the dinosaurs reached the peak of their evolution. But there were also many other kinds of animal present.

For most of the Cretaceous period the climate was warm and mild. As a result many species flourished and a large number of highly specialized forms appeared.

In the seas there were many invertebrates, including reef-forming corals, brachiopods, sea urchins and bivalves. Ammonites were abundant, but belemnites began to decline early in the period. Teleost fishes took over from the more primitive holosteans. Sea reptiles included ichthyosaurs, mosasaurs and plesiosaurs. Of these, however, only the plesiosaurs lasted for the whole of the Cretaceous period.

On land the dinosaurs still ruled. Horned, armoured and duck-billed dinosaurs were all highly specialized plant-eaters. Other herbivores included ornithopods, such as *Iguanodon* and the strange bone-headed dinosaurs, or pachycephalosaurs. Specialized predators included the giant carnosaurs and small, agile coelurosaurs.

Meanwhile, other reptile groups had been making progress. There were tailless, toothless pterosaurs in the skies (see page 82), but by now they were not alone. They had been joined by a number of toothed birds. And there were flightless birds on the ground (see page 86).

A scene in the late Cretaceous period. During this time many dinosaurs were present, including the hadrosaur *Lambeosaurus* (centre, foreground) and the coelurosaur *Ornithomimus* (right, background). Other reptiles included pterosaurs, lizards, crocodiles and turtles. Some of the small mammals hunted insects. Flowering plants were beginning to dominate the vegetation.

Right: *Ornithomimus* was as long as a modern car. Scientists have calculated that its long legs could have allowed it to run at 80 kilometres per hour. However, studies of its footprints seem to show that it rarely travelled faster than 20 kilometres per hour.

WARM-BLOODED DINOSAURS?

Warm-blooded animals, such as mammals and birds, produce the heat they need inside their bodies. Cold-blooded animals, such as reptiles, gain their heat from the outside environment. Dinosaurs were reptiles, but there is evidence indicating that they were warm-blooded.

1. Size and speed

The largest modern lizards are the monitors. The Komodo dragon reaches lengths of over $2\frac{1}{2}$ metres. It can move quite quickly as long as it can get sufficient heat from the Sun. Some dinosaurs, however, were considerably larger. If they were cold-blooded, they must have been sluggish creatures. They could not have gained enough heat from the Sun for rapid movement. However, even the largest dinosaurs were built for quite fast movement. This would have been possible only if they were warm-blooded.

Many smaller dinosaurs were fast runners. *Deinonychus* was a fast-running, flesh-eating coelurosaur. It was about 3 metres long. It ran on its hind legs and its 'hands' were armed with fearsome claws. It appears to have had keen sight and an acute sense of smell. This late Cretaceous predator was probably able to hunt agile prey at night. To have the energy for this it must have been warm-blooded.

2. Predators and prey

Warm-blooded animals, such as the tiger, need a considerable amount of food to keep them going. Cold-blooded carnivores, however, eat much less; a crocodile eats about $\frac{1}{8}$th of the amount that a tiger eats. This is shown in the balance of nature. For a given weight of prey there are far fewer tigers than crocodiles. The same sorts of predator-prey ratios can be seen in the fossil record. *Dimetrodon* was a carnivorous, cold-blooded mammal-like reptile. Seven *Dimetrodon* fossils are found for every ten fossils of its prey animals. However, among the dinosaurs the numbers are very different. Only one fossil carnivore is found for every nine fossil prey animals. This seems to indicate that flesh-eating dinosaurs, like tigers, needed large numbers of prey to survive.

3. Bones

Studies of the microscopic structure of dinosaur bones appear to show that they were much more like the bones of mammals than the bones of lizards.

4. Hearts

We have no idea of what a dinosaur heart was like. However, the hearts of crocodiles, the only living archosaurs have four chambers, like the hearts of mammals. Other reptiles have three-chambered hearts.

Lizards were common in the Cretaceous period and there were many kinds of crocodiles. These included the early forms of modern crocodiles. *Deinosuchus*, which grew to 16 metres long, was a late Cretaceous member of this group. It had many characteristics familiar to the modern crocodile-watcher.

Finally, several kinds of early mammals were also present. Most of these were small, shrew-like creatures. The great expansion of the mammal line was yet to come.

Throughout the Mesozoic era the dinosaurs had thrived in the warm climate. Meanwhile, the break-up of Pangaea had been progressing rapidly. By the end of the Cretaceous period the continents seem to have moved far enough apart to cause dramatic changes in the climate. Winters became more severe and ice caps formed at the poles. The weather became much more changeable. At the same time the Mesozoic mountains had been worn down and the seas were retreating from the land.

These changes affected the lives of many animals. In fact, it seems that a number of animals were so badly affected that they became extinct. On land the dinosaurs disappeared, together with the pterosaurs and the toothed birds. In the seas many kinds of invertebrates died out, including some bivalves, some gastropods, some echinoderms and all the ammonites. Plesiosaurs and mosasaurs also disappeared. These extinctions mark the end of the Cretaceous period in the fossil-bearing rocks.

Pachycephalosaurs, or bone-heads, existed in a few parts of the world during the late Cretaceous period. The skull of a pachycephalosaur (above) was dome-shaped. The dome was formed from a solid mass of bone, 25 centimetres thick. On the front of the face there were a number of short knobs and spikes. The purpose of this heavy skull is not really known. However, it may have been used as a kind of battering ram in conflicts with either predators or rival pachycephalosaurs (below).

Iguanodon was a large, early Cretaceous ornithopod. It grew to about 8 metres in length and stood as tall as an elephant (above, left). It fed on plants, grinding them up with several rows of teeth. As these wore down, new ones erupted from below to replace them. Its name literally means 'iguana tooth'. Its main enemies were the large carnosaurs that existed at that time (left). The thumb of *Iguanodon* was a sharp spike and this may have been used as a defensive weapon.

Many modern plant-eating animals move about in large herds. Members of a herd stand a much better chance of avoiding being caught and eaten by predators. It seems reasonable to suppose that plant-eating dinosaurs may also have lived in herds. One piece of evidence for this came from the discovery of a group of 31 fossil *Iguanodon* skeletons near a Belgian coal mine. They all appear to have died together, perhaps as the result of falling into a ravine in their rush to escape a predator. The skeletons are now displayed at the Royal Institute of Natural Sciences in Brussels (above).

The End of the Dinosaurs

The last dinosaurs disappeared at the end of the Cretaceous period. What happened?

The sudden extinction of the dinosaurs has been a mystery to scientists for many years. A number of theories have been suggested; small mammals ate their eggs; a nearby supernova (exploding star) bombarded them with lethal cosmic rays; they were poisoned by chemicals in flowering plants; they were killed by a virus or bacterial disease; and many others. However, none of these ideas stands up to close examination.

There are two important things to remember. First, the word 'sudden', in geological terms, does not mean days, years or even hundreds of years. In fact it took 10 million years to wipe out the dinosaurs. Second, the extinction of dinosaur species was nothing new. Many dinosaurs had become extinct long before. The difference was that this time, as old species died out no new species evolved to take their places. Most people now believe that the mass

If dinosaurs like you don't hurry up and evolve, you're going to die out.

Watched by one of the last sauropods (right), a wounded carnosaur (centre) dies of cold. Even the ornithopods (left), a group that had been successful since the middle of the Triassic period, did not survive the Cretaceous extinctions. The comment in the cartoon (above) is true, but hardly fair. The conditions that existed in the late Cretaceous period probably made it impossible for dinosaurs to evolve new species.

extinctions of the Cretaceous period were due to a combination of changing climate and geography. The land was becoming colder. And here size was an important factor. The true land animals that survived (mammals, birds, snakes and lizards) all weighed less than 10 kilogrammes. Mammals and birds could tolerate cold because of their warm coverings. Small reptiles could hibernate or burrow in the ground. But large dinosaurs could not avoid the cold and so they began to die out.

Even so, we might expect to find that new species of dinosaurs evolved and adapted to the new conditions. But no new species did evolve. The reason for this may have been the geography of the land. New species evolve only in small, isolated areas. But by the late Cretaceous period the land was fairly flat and there were no barriers to stop large animals from roaming where they liked. Therefore, there were no small, isolated communities and new dinosaur species could not evolve.

The retreat of the shallow seas left marshlands. These were excellent places for crocodiles and turtles and so these groups survived. In the seas themselves, the living space was reduced, so many groups died out. However, this by itself would not account for the extinction of all the plesiosaurs and ammonites. There must have been at least some suitable areas left. Perhaps a small drop in the sea temperature resulted in the loss of huge numbers of the tiny animals and plants known as plankton. This would have reduced the numbers of animals that fed on plankton. And the predators that fed on the plankton-feeders would have suffered from a severe shortage of food.

The Dinosaur Hunters

Above: The campsite of one of the joint Polish-Mongolian expeditions to Mongolia. Here, between 1963 and 1971, scientists found the remains of many late Cretaceous animals, including dinosaurs and mammals. In particular, they found the remains of many *Protoceratops*—not only adults but also young individuals and nests of fossilized eggs.

During the 1800s the giant fossil bones of dinosaurs caught people's imagination. Then the race was on. Who would be the first to find new dinosaurs?

The first dinosaur bones were discovered during the 1700s. But it was a long time before such fossils were identified and named. People simply could not believe that such creatures had existed. One of the first dinosaurs to be named was *Megalosaurus*, a name which simply means 'large lizard'. Then in 1822 the wife of the eminent British geologist Gideon Mantell discovered a fossil tooth in Tilgate Forest in Sussex, England. Later, some huge bones were found in nearby rocks. Gideon Mantell described this newly-discovered reptile and named it *Iguanodon*.

By 1841 another large reptile, the primitive armoured dinosaur *Hylaeosaurus*, had also been discovered. Sir Richard Owen, a British palaeontologist, examined the bones of these creatures very carefully. He decided that they could not belong to any known group. So he named the new group the Dinosauria. Many years later it was discovered that there were actually two groups of animals—the Saurischia and the Ornithischia. So the name Dinosauria was dropped from

Above: Mary Anning (1799-1847) made a profession of collecting fossils and selling them to scientists. She lived in Lyme Regis in Dorset, England and made some spectacular finds in the local rocks. She discovered the first complete ichthyosaur and plesiosaur skeletons and the first British pterosaur.

Othniel Marsh (1831-1899) (far left) and Edward Cope (1840-1897) (left) were bitter rivals in the early days of dinosaur hunting. They sent out teams to hunt for fossils in the rocks of Wyoming and Colorado. Each man tried to keep his fossil sites secret from the other.

Right: Excavating the fossil bones of a sauropod at Altan Ula in Mongolia.

Left: In 1909 Werner Janensch of the Berlin Museum of Natural History led an expedition to the Tendaguru region of East Africa. There the scientists discovered the remains of many dinosaurs. Among the finds were the huge bones of *Brachiosaurus.* Here, one of the bones is displayed by the team of diggers.

Below: The hind limb bones of a *Diplodocus* exposed in the rocks of the Morrison formation of North America. This expedition was financed by the American millionaire Andrew Carnegie. He donated replicas of this gigantic sauropod to several museums. The Morrison formation consists of Jurassic rocks in the Western USA. It stretches down from Montana in the north, through Idaho and Wyoming, Utah and Colorado, to New Mexico in the south.

scientific classifications. However, the term 'dinosaur' has remained in popular use.

Now that the true importance of such fossils was realized, more and more bones were discovered. Scientists raced to find new fossils. They were often jealous of their finds and sometimes fierce rivalry existed between dinosaur hunters. During the late 1800s many tons of bones were excavated from Jurassic and Cretaceous rocks in North America. In one place in Wyoming scientists discovered that a local shepherd had built a cabin entirely out of dinosaur bones. During the early 1900s expeditions went to many parts of the world to find dinosaurs. Fossils were found in Africa, South America, Europe and Central Asia. Dinosaur fossils are still being excavated. And occasionally new species are discovered.

Below: ***Dimorphodon*** **was a primitive Jurassic pterosaur. It had several reptile-like features, including its large skull, many biting teeth and long tail. Its wings were two leathery membranes and its wingspan was about 1.5 metres.**

Above: ***Pteranodon*** **was a late Cretaceous pterodactyl. It had no tail and kept itself stable in the air by making conscious movements of its body, head and limbs. To coordinate such movements it had a relatively large brain. It had a wingspan of over 8 metres and its huge crest probably acted as a rudder or stabilizer. Scientists have calculated that** ***Pteranodon*** **could glide very slowly and it probably soared over the oceans, like a modern albatross. It probably caught fish in its toothless beak and carried its prey in a throat sac.**

CONQUEST OF THE SKIES

Flying Reptiles

The pterosaurs, or 'flying lizards' probably evolved from thecodonts that took to living in trees. One of the ancestors of the pterosaurs may have been a small Triassic archosaur called *Podopteryx*. This reptile lived in trees and glided from one tree to another, using parachute membranes stretched between the limbs on each side of its body.

The first pterosaurs appeared in the Triassic and Jurassic periods. *Eudimorphodon* and *Dimorphodon* were primitive, tailed pterosaurs with large heads. *Rhamphorhynchus* was more lightly built. Its tail had a leaf-shaped structure on the end which was jointed in such a way that it probably acted as a stabilizer.

The later pterosaurs, known as pterodactyls, had no tails. Some, like *Pterodactylus*, were small, sparrow-sized creatures. Others were giants; *Pteranodon* had a wingspan of over 8 metres and *Quetzalcoatlus* had a wingspan of 10 metres.

Pterosaurs had many of the adaptations needed for flight. Their wings were membranes that stretched all the way down the body to the hind legs. Movements of the wings were controlled by the front limbs and the leading edge of each wing was supported by the greatly lengthened bones of the fourth finger. Pterosaurs were very light creatures. They had very thin bones and, as in birds, there were air spaces inside the bones to lighten the weight.

To fly well requires great strength and stamina. A pterosaur had strong shoulders and its breast-

Rhamphorhynchus **(left) was a late Jurassic pterosaur. Its skull was much lighter than the skull of** ***Dimorphodon*** **and it had fewer teeth. The teeth all pointed forwards and scientists believe that they were used for spearing fish (below). However,** ***Rhamphorhynchus*** **could not have dived into the water or even landed on the surface. Instead, it may have skimmed along the surface, spearing fish with darting movements of its head. Its wingspan was about 1.8 metres. It probably used its rudder-like tail to keep it stable in the air.**

Below: ***Dimorphodon*** **compared in size to** ***Archaeopteryx,*** **the first known bird (see page 84), and a modern pigeon.**

bone had a keel to which the wing muscles were attached. However, the keels of pterosaurs were not as well developed as those of birds. As a result pterosaurs could only flap their wings rather feebly. But they were expert gliders and could probably glide for miles.

On the ground, however, pterosaurs were clumsy, awkward creatures. They could only hobble about on their clawed feet. Their wings dragged along the ground and could easily be torn. And a torn wing was probably fatal.

Once on the ground, it is difficult to see how pterosaurs launched themselves into the air. Some kinds of pterosaurs probably rested on the edges of cliffs, from where they could take off easily. Small types may have clung onto the sides of cliffs or hung, bat-like, from their hind-legs. However, *Quetzalcoatlus* was a vulture-like creature that lived around inland plains and fed on carrion. Unless it swooped down and gathered up its food without landing, it must have had some method of getting off the ground.

Gliding flight requires very little energy. But the constant flow of air over the body of a pterosaur must have caused it to lose heat rapidly. At least some pterosaurs may have kept themselves warm with a covering of hair. The pterosaur *Sordes pilosus* ('hairy devil') was discovered in Russia in 1971. Surrounding the fossil bones were what appeared to be the remains of a furry coat. At the same time, pterosaurs may have overcome the problem of heat loss by generating their own heat; that is, they may have been warm-blooded. Certainly, if dinosaurs were warm-blooded, there is no reason why pterosaurs could not have been warm-blooded as well.

Pterosaurs became extinct at the end of the Cretaceous period. The cause of their extinction is not known. However, the same conditions of climate and geography that appear to have caused the extinction of the dinosaurs and other animals probably also caused the extinction of the pterosaurs. In addition pterosaurs had competition from the birds, which were the true conquerors of the skies.

From Reptiles to Birds

Above: A reconstruction of *Archaeopteryx*.

Right: One of the fossils of *Archaeopteryx*, showing the bones with impressions of feathers around them.

Below: The skeletons of *Archaeopteryx* and a modern bird. Notice the large, keeled breast-bone of the modern bird. For a long time scientists believed that *Archaeopteryx* had no breast-bone at all (jumbles of fossil bones are often difficult to interpret). However, it is now known that there was a small, poorly developed breast-bone (not shown in this reconstruction).

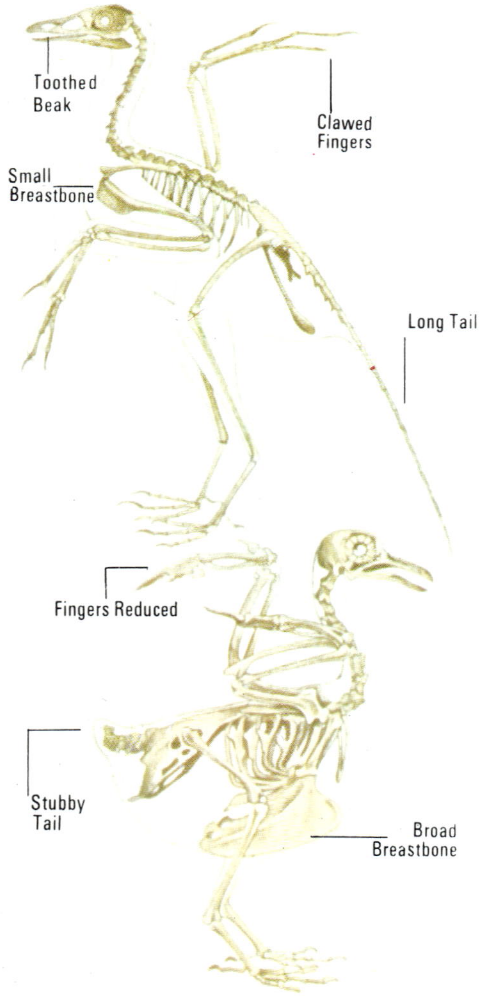

Since the Cretaceous period, birds, with their complete mastery of flight, have been the true rulers of the air.

The basic characteristics of a bird are that it is a vertebrate with two wings and two feet. The earliest bird so far discovered is the late Jurassic animal known as *Archaeopteryx* ('ancient feather'). Five fossil skeletons and one fossil feather are known. Three of the skeletons have definite impressions of feathers around them.

The skeletons of *Archaeopteryx* are remarkably like those of small coelurosaurs, such as *Coelophysis*. So scientists believe that the ancestors of *Archaeopteryx* may have been early dinosaurs. On the other hand, the true ancestors of Archaeopteryx may have been among the Triassic thecodonts.

Whatever its ancestry, *Archaeopteryx* had a number of bird-like and reptile-like characteristics. It had wings and its whole body was covered in feathers. However, its beak contained many small, sharp teeth. It had claws on its wings. Its tail had a long row of bones down the middle—like the tail of a lizard. Its bones did not contain air spaces.

Feathers were not originally developed for the purpose of flight. This was a secondary advantage that came later. Feathers evolved, presumably from the scales of reptiles, for insulation. But why did they evolve? Feathers would have been a distinct disadvantage to cold-blooded reptiles. With such insulation they could not have gained heat from the Sun. However, for warm-blooded animals feathers would have been very useful for keeping heat in. Therefore, scientists now believe that the dinosaur or thecodont ancestors of *Archaeopteryx* that originally evolved feathers must have been warm-blooded.

Archaeopteryx could not fly very well. It did not have a keel on its breast-bone, so there was nowhere for strong wing muscles to be attached. Therefore, it was probably a gliding animal. But scientists disagree about the kind of life it led. It may have lived in trees, using its claws to help it scramble from branch to branch. Using its wings it could have glided from one tree to another. However, some scientists think that the feathers would have been damaged by scrambling about in trees. *Archaeopteryx* may have lived on the ground. Its wings would have been useful in taking off from high ground to escape from predators of which there were many at this time. It is likely that its wings were not powerful enough to lift the bird off the ground from a standing start. However with a run and a skip it is possible that *Archaeopteryx* would have evaded capture.

Archaeopteryx is, unfortunately, very much on its own in the fossil record. Its ancestry is pure guesswork and no other Jurassic birds are known. And the fossil history of most of its Cretaceous descendants is rather poor.

Early Cretaceous birds still had several reptile-like feathers. They had teeth and some had reptile-like jaws. There were two main groups.

The first group were all flightless birds. They had lost the use of their wings. The best-known type is *Hesperornis*. This was a large bird that grew to about one metre long. Some

The cumbersome membrane wing of a pterosaur (right) was supported by the long arm and fourth finger. The light, feathered wing of a bird (below) is operated by a short powerful arm. The wing of a bird is superior in other ways as well. It can be folded up when not in use and feathers are much less easily damaged than a membrane. A bat wing (below right) is a membrane supported by both limbs and by four long fingers. It can be folded up when the animal is resting. Bats have strong shoulders and keeled breast-bones for the attachment of flight muscles.

Below: *Hesperornis* **was a toothed sea bird that dived for fish in the early Cretaceous seas. It could not fly. The tern-like bird,** *Ichthyornis* **also hunted fish, but it was an excellent flier. It is not known if** *Ichthyornis* **had teeth or not.**

Above: The fossil skeleton of an Eocene bat. The membrane wing has been reconstructed on top of the fossil bones.

individuals appear to have reached 1.8 metres in length. *Hesperornis* had a streamlined, cigar-shaped body and its feet were placed well back on its body. The feet were probably difficult to use on land, but they would have propelled the bird swiftly through water. *Hesperornis* probably spent nearly all its time in water, diving for fish.

Modern penguins are similarly designed. However, penguins 'fly' through the water using their wings, which are modified into efficient flippers. The tiny wings of *Hesperornis* were almost useless.

The second group of Cretaceous birds were excellent fliers. The best known type is *Ichthyornis*. This was a tern-like bird that stood about 20 centimetres tall.

During the late Cretaceous period a number of different kinds of flying birds appeared. And by the Eocene epoch there were primitive types of flamingos, geese, herons, game birds, pelicans and vultures.

The evolution of birds continued steadily throughout the Tertiary and Quaternary periods. Some species were very large. The largest flying bird that ever existed was the Miocene sea bird *Osteodontornis*, which had a wingspan of about 5 metres. And in the Pleistocene epoch there were giant swans, storks and vultures.

Among the most spectacular prehistoric birds were some that gave up flying and returned to ground-living. *Diatryma*, an Eocene bird, and *Phororhacos*, which lived in the Miocene epoch, both stood 2 metres tall. Some of the largest types only died out in the Pleistocene epoch. *Aepyornis*, a Madagascan elephant bird, reached 3 metres in height. *Dinornis*, the largest of the New Zealand moas, reached 3.5 metres. Moas were probably hunted to extinction by early man.

Above: *Diatryma* was a giant flightless bird that lived in North America and Europe in the Eocene epoch. Its eating habits are not known. It could have used its parrot-like beak for cutting up flesh or plant material.

Right: *Phororhacos* was a giant running bird that lived in South America during the Miocene epoch. It had a ferocious hawk-like beak and probably preyed on goat-sized mammals.

THE AGE OF MAMMALS

The Cenozoic World

The changes in climate and geography that occurred at the end of the Mesozoic era eliminated the dinosaurs and many other animals. But among the survivors of these changes were the mammals. With the dinosaurs gone, these warm-blooded, fur-covered animals were able to spread and evolve rapidly. Many groups appeared and adapted to different ways of life in different living areas. For 65 million years the Cenozoic, or 'new life', era has been (and still is) the age of mammals.

We know a great deal about life in the Cenozoic era. Cenozoic rocks are younger and therefore closer to the surface than other rocks. In addition, fewer changes have occurred in these rocks since they were formed. Geologists divide the era into two periods—the Tertiary (third) and Quaternary (fourth) periods (the Palaeozoic and Mesozoic eras used to be known as the Primary and Secondary periods).

Many changes in climate, geography and forms of life occurred during these times. So geologists have divided these two periods into seven epochs.

By the start of the Cenozoic era the break-up of Pangaea was complete. But during the Palaeocene epoch the low sea levels left a land bridge between North America and Eurasia. Other continents may also have been linked at this time. By the Eocene epoch, the seas had once again expanded. Continents were cut off from each other. Such isolation tends to encourage the evolution of new species. Unique kinds of mammals evolved on the separated continents, particularly in South America and Australia.

The Eocene climate was generally warm. Tropical plants grew as far north as Britain. During this time many new kinds of mammal appeared. Some were the ancestors of modern mammals; others were experimental types that soon died out. Many modern groups of mammals started to evolve in the Oligocene epoch. It was the age of the giant hooved mammals that browsed in the forests.

Below: Every kind of tree has its own distinctive type of pollen grain. And some trees prefer warm conditions, where others prefer a cold climate. Fossil pollen grains can be found by examining sediments under a microscope. In this way scientists can learn what kinds of trees were growing in a particular place and draw conclusions about the climate that existed at the time.

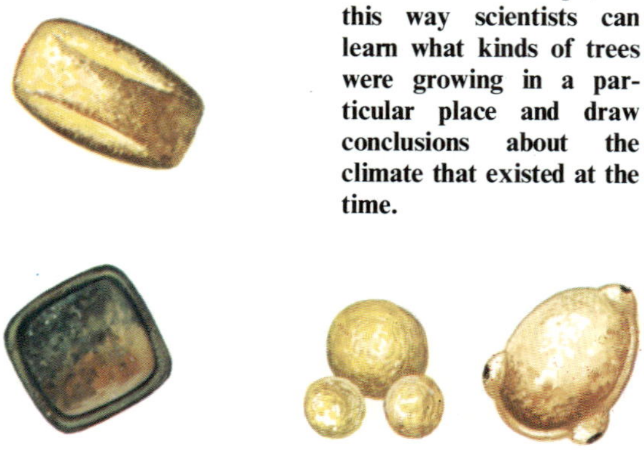

Left: The Alps are young mountains. Their jagged peaks have not yet been worn away. They began to form during the Oligocene epoch.

Below: The left-handed whelk (right), a warm-water species, was common in Britain during the early Pliocene epoch. But by the end of the epoch it had been replaced by the common whelk (left), a cold-water species. This shows that the climate must have cooled towards the end of the Pliocene epoch.

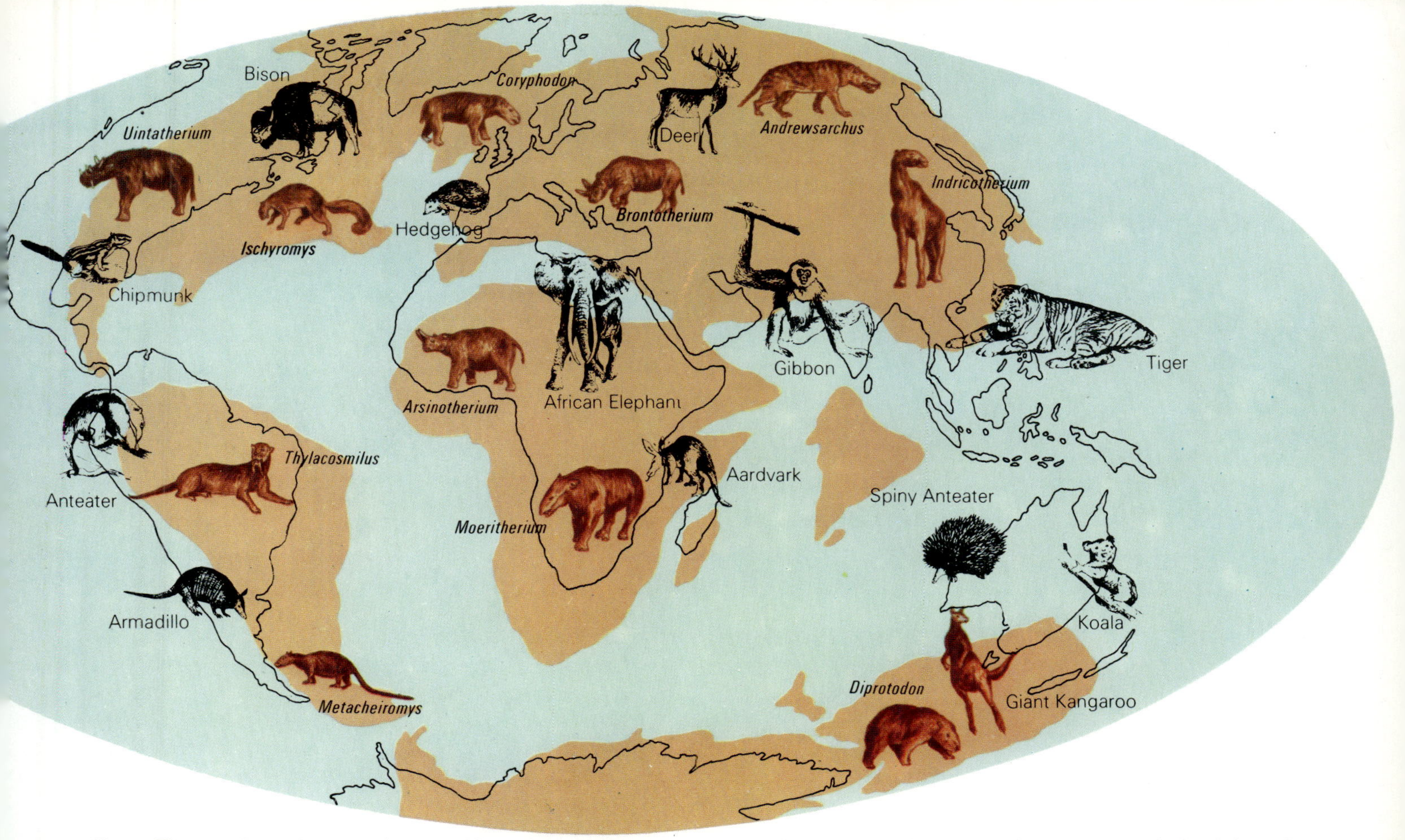

Above: The map shows the approximate positions of the continents at the start of the Cenozoic era. Their present positions are shown by the black outlines. Also shown are some of the animals that lived during the Cenozoic era (the animals that still survive are drawn in black). Marsupials evolved during the Cretaceous period, possibly in South America. From there they spread into North America, Europe and Australia (via Antarctica). Australia then became isolated from the rest of the world. Placental mammals evolved in North America and spread throughout the world (except Australia). South America then became isolated and developed its own unique kinds of animals. Some marsupials survived in South America, but in North America and Europe they were driven out by the placentals.

The Miocene epoch was a time of many upheavals in the Earth's crust. India, which had been slowly moving northwards, collided with Asia, pushing up the Himalayas. The movement of other plates caused the raising of mountain ranges formed in previous times. The Rockies, Andes, Carpathians and Alps all reached new heights. At the same time grasslands began to appear among the forests and browsing and grazing mammals were present.

The Pliocene epoch was the last epoch of the Tertiary period. The climate cooled and ice caps formed once more at the poles. During this time vast areas of grassland spread across the land. This resulted in a tremendous increase in the number of grazing animals. The continents were by now in their present positions. And in Africa the first men were beginning to evolve.

The Quaternary period is divided into two epochs. Soon after the start of the Pleistocene epoch the great Ice Age began. During this time the polar ice sheets advanced and retreated several times. In the north large areas of land were covered in ice. Woolly mammals survived in the areas of tundra; others migrated south to warmer areas. Meanwhile man was evolving rapidly. By the end of the Pleistocene epoch 10,000 years ago, modern man was living in Europe. The period of time that covers the history of man's civilization is known as the Recent, or Holocene epoch.

Period	Epoch
QUATERNARY	**Recent (Holocene)** Modern Man emerged. Civilization developed.
	Pleistocene Vast regions of the northern hemisphere covered by ice sheets which gouged out the Great Lakes. Man appeared.
TERTIARY	**Pliocene** Climate like today's. The Panamanian isthmus reappeared, re-establishing a land link between North and South America.
	Miocene Himalayas were created when India collided with Asia. Grazing mammals.
	Oligocene Alps began to form. Climate remained warm and temperate. Large browsing mammals.
	Eocene Advance of the Seas. First whales. Tropical plants crept as far north as southern Britain. Volcanic activity.
	Palaeocene Placental mammals spread.

Left: *Diademodon* **was a cynodont mammal-like reptile that lived in the early Triassic period. Cynodonts had many mammalian characteristics. For example, they had various kinds of teeth and they were probably warm-blooded. However, they could not twist their spines. Therefore they could not curl up to keep warm.**

Right: *Oligokyphus* **was a mammal-like reptile belonging to the group called tritylodonts. This was the last group of mammal-like reptiles; they survived into the Jurassic period and only died out when the multituberculate mammals appeared. They were not the ancestors of mammals, but some of them had nearly all the characteristics of mammals.** *Oligokyphus* **was covered in fine hairs. It could also bend its spine and could therefore curl up on its side. It may even have suckled its young.**

Rise of the Mammals

The first mammals appeared in the Mesozoic era. And by the time the dinosaurs died out placental mammals were ready to take their place as the dominant animals.

The history of the mammals began in the Permian period with the mammal-like reptiles (see page 52). During the Triassic period the last of these reptiles became more and more mammal-like. Many of them were probably warm-blooded and some even had hair.

True mammals appear to have evolved during the middle of the Triassic period, probably from cynodont mammal-like reptiles. Fossils of the earliest known mammals come from various parts of the world. They include *Morganucodon* (Britain), *Megazastrodon* (southern Africa) and *Sinoconodon* (China). All these types lived during

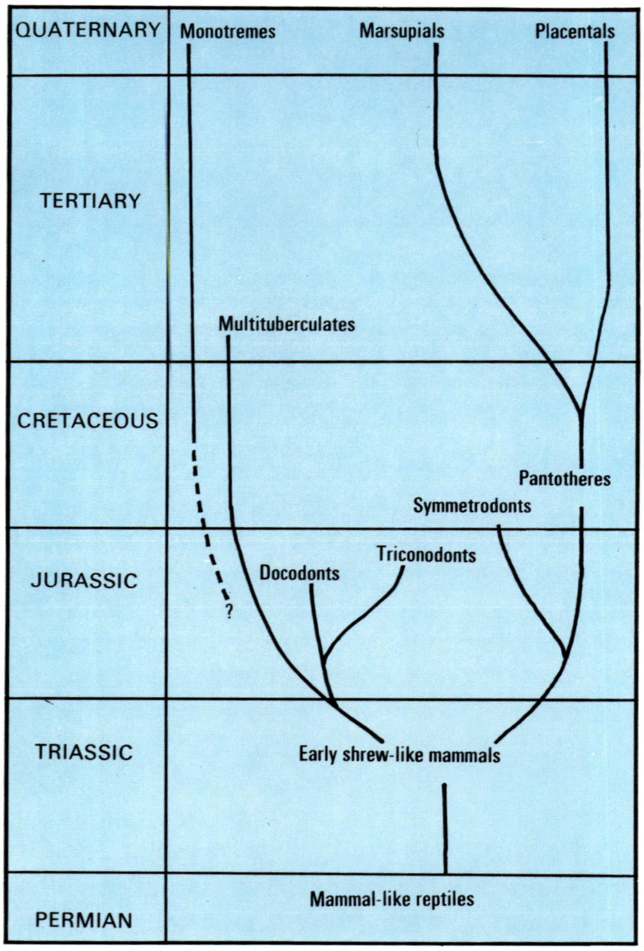

Above: A chart showing the probable course of the evolution of early mammals. During the Mesozoic era several 'experimental' groups appeared. But by the beginning of the Tertiary period most of them had died out, leaving the placentals as the dominant group.

Left: The early mammals of the Triassic period, such as *Morganucodon,* **were no bigger than the eggs of large dinosaurs. But when the dinosaurs were gone, the descendants of these mammals inherited the world.**

the late Triassic period. They were small, shrew-like creatures that probably ate insects, worms and other invertebrates. They may also have raided the nests of dinosaurs to steal eggs.

Except for one group, the multituberculates, all the Mesozoic mammals were mouse-sized animals. All these small types used to be classified together in a single group called the pantotheres. However, scientists now believe that there were several kinds of early mammals. Often, the only evidence we have of their existence consists of a few fossil bones and teeth. Hence most of the groups have been given names that describe the shapes of their teeth.

The late Triassic mammals gave rise to two main groups. The first group included the docodonts, triconodonts and multituberculates. The second group included the symmetrodonts and the pantotheres.

Docodonts existed in Europe and North America from the middle to the end of the Jurassic period. They had dumb-bell shaped cheek teeth. Triconodonts lived alongside the docodonts. Their cheek teeth had three points, or cusps, set in a row.

The multituberculates were a much more successful group. They appeared at the end of the Jurassic period and survived throughout North America, Europe and Asia until the Eocene epoch. They were rodent-like animals, with cutting incisor teeth at the front and complicated, many-cusped chewing teeth at the back. Some grew as large as foxes. They ate plant material and only became extinct when the true rodents appeared.

REPTILES V MAMMALS

Reptiles lay eggs. And most reptiles abandon their young before they hatch. All mammals (except monotremes) give birth to active young. They suckle their young and look after them for some time after they are born.

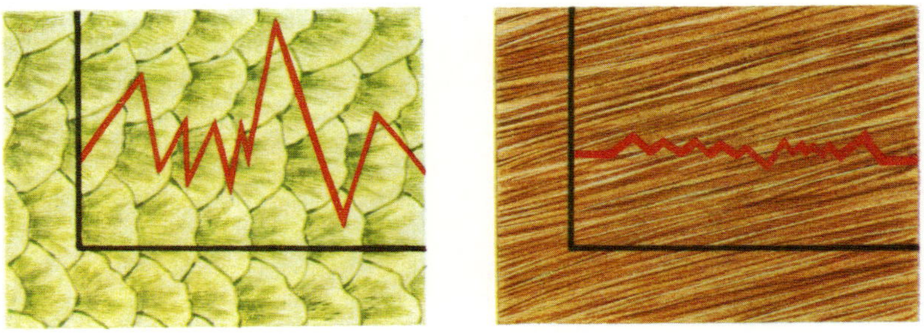

Reptiles control their body temperature by using the external environment—they heat up in the sun and cool down in the shade. Therefore the body temperature of a reptile fluctuates greatly. Mammals produce their own body heat and keep it in with a layer of fur. Therefore they maintain an almost constant body temperature.

The nasal (nose) passages of a reptile open into the front of the mouth. Therefore it cannot breathe while it eats. In a mammal, however, the nasal passages open into the back of the mouth. So a mammal can chew and breathe at the same time. Notice also that the cerebral hemispheres (grey areas) of a mammal's brain are much larger than those of a reptile. As a result mammals are better at co-ordinating the functions of their bodies.

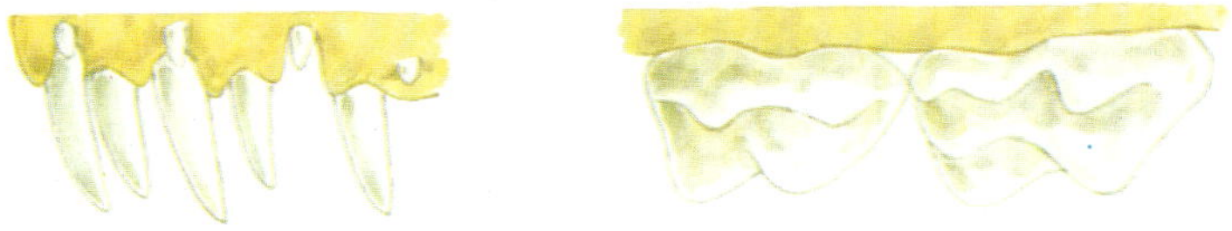

Reptiles have pointed teeth for biting and tearing. Mammals have a variety of types of teeth, including many-cusped (many-pointed) chewing teeth.

Taeniolabis **was a Cretaceous multituberculate. These rodent like mammals lived on the ground and ate nuts, fruit and other plant materials. Multituberculates appeared in the Jurassic period and survived for 100 million years—longer than any other mammal group so far. They died out in the Eocene epoch, probably as a result of competition with the true rodents that appeared at that time.**

Above: A reconstruction of the late Triassic mammal *Megazastrodon.* Fossils of this animal have been found in the Karoo region of southern Africa, along with dinosaurs and mammal-like reptiles.

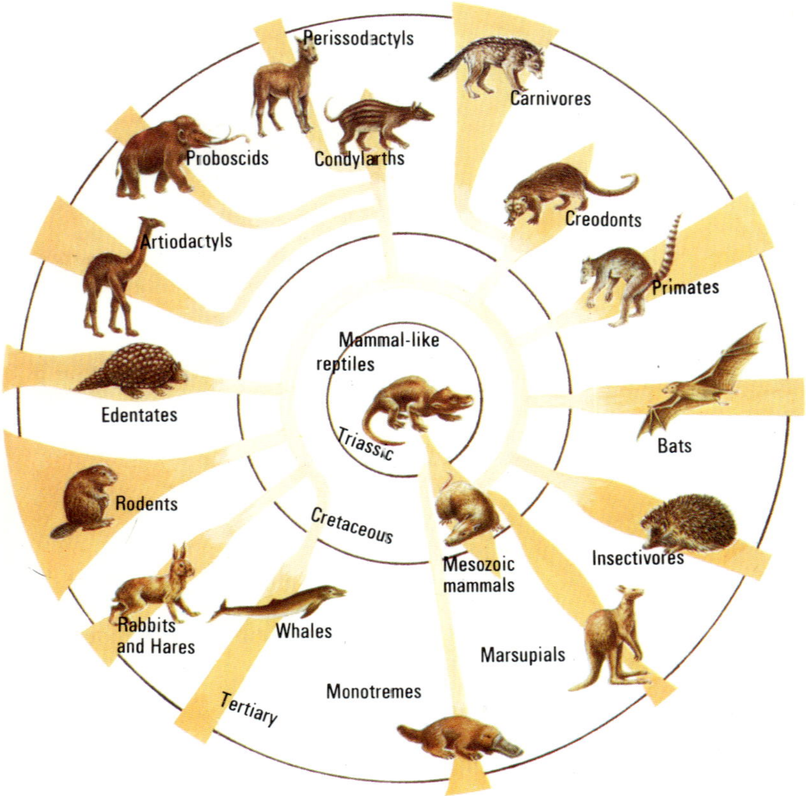

Left: A chart showing the evolution and relative numbers of the three main mammal groups. Their probable relationships are also shown. Each group is represented here by one species, as listed below. Those marked with a star are living species.

Mammal-like reptiles: *Chiniquodon*
Mesozoic mammals: *Morganucodon*
Monotremes: *Ornithorhynchus** **(duck-billed platypus)**
Marsupials: *Sthenurus* **(giant kangaroo)**
Insectivores: *Erinaceus** **(hedgehog)**
Bats: *Palaeochiropteryx*
Primates: *Notharctus*
Creodonts: *Oxyaena*
Carnivores: *Hyaena**
Condylarths: *Phenacodus*
Perissodactyls: *Hyracotherium*
Proboscids: *Parelephas*
Artiodactyls: *Alticamelus*
Edentates: *Glyptodon*
Rodents: *Castoroides*
Rabbits and Hares: *Eurymylus*
Whales: *Basilosaurus*

Opposite page: The three modern kinds of mammal. The duck-billed platypus (top) is a monotreme and lays eggs. The koala bear (bottom left) is a marsupial; the young are reared in a pouch. Mice (bottom right) are placental mammals.

Symmetrodonts were a small group of mammals that lived in the late Jurassic and early Cretaceous periods. They had symmetrical, triangular cheek teeth with three cusps.

The pantotheres were the most important of all the Mesozoic mammals. They gave rise to the marsupials and the placentals. They also had triangular cheek teeth, but these were not symmetrical and they were more complicated than the teeth of symmetrodonts. Pantotheres appear to have flourished during the late Jurassic period. But by the middle of the Cretaceous period they had been replaced by their marsupial and placental descendants.

Modern mammals belong to three main groups—the monotremes, the marsupials and the placentals. Monotremes are a small but interesting group. Like reptiles, they lay eggs and various parts of their bodies have reptile-like features. But they are warm-blooded, they are covered in fur and they suckle their young—three important characteristics of mammals. The only living monotremes are the duck-billed platypus and five species of spiny anteaters. Only a few fossil types are known and the origin of monotremes is uncertain. However, their skulls show certain features found in multituberculates, docodonts and triconodonts. Monotremes may, therefore, be related to these groups. They probably arose in the Jurassic period.

Marsupials and placentals both give birth to active young. A young placental is nurtured for some time inside its mother's body. It receives its nourishment via a structure called the placenta. Marsupials, on the other hand, have only very simple placentas. A young marsupial spends very little time inside its mother's body. And when it is born it is very undeveloped. However, it crawls to its mother's pouch, where it suckles and continues to grow.

Marsupials first appeared in the middle of the Cretaceous period. They probably arose in South America and spread into Antarctica, Australia, North America and Europe. They survived and flourished in Australia because this continent soon became separated from the others. On other continents, however, they faced competition from the placentals that evolved in North America. The marsupials of the northern continents never became widespread and finally died out during the Miocene epoch. But marsupials did survive in South America. There were two reasons for this. First, South America was separated from North America from the late Cretaceous period until the Pliocene epoch. Second, the South American placentals were all herbivores; there were no carnivores to compete with the marsupial meat-eaters.

It is not easy to explain why the North American and European marsupials did not survive competition from placentals. Zoologists usually say that placentals are 'more advanced'. Marsupials are supposed to have a primitive and less efficient method of reproduction. However, this is not really true. The ancestors of marsupials may have been a half-way stage in the evolution of placentals. But later marsupials (including modern types) were highly specialized animals. They adapted very well to many different ways of life. And their method of reproduction works very well indeed.

Placentals have better brains than marsupials. Therefore they may be quicker and better at exploiting living areas. But not all marsupials are unsuccessful. The opossums of South America survive quite happily alongside placentals. And one species, the Virginia opossum, has actually spread northwards into the USA and Canada.

But, for whatever reason, the placentals did dominate the north. By the end of the Cretaceous period there were insect-eating animals. They and their descendants would soon take over the living areas of the dinosaurs.

Early Experiments

During the Palaeocene and Eocene epochs many groups of mammals appeared. Some were successful; others soon died out.

Hyaenodon **was an Oligocene creodont. It resembled a modern hyaena and hunted small hooved mammals.**

At the start of the Tertiary period mammals evolved rapidly. Many new groups took over the living areas once occupied by the dinosaurs. By the middle of the Eocene epoch 27 different orders of placental mammals had evolved. However, not all of these were successful. Some were already extinct by the end of the Eocene epoch. Others continued until the Oligocene, Miocene, Pliocene or Pleistocene epochs. By the middle of the Pleistocene epoch only the 18 orders of modern placental mammals remained.

Unfortunately, there are very few Palaeocene deposits left in the world today. The epoch only lasted 11 million years, so only thin deposits were laid down. Many of those deposits have already been worn away. However we do know that at least nine orders of mammals appeared during this epoch.

The basic mammalian stock consisted of insect-eating animals, and insectivores are still common today. But this group gave rise to all the herbivorous and carnivorous mammals.

Palaeocene herbivores included the condylarths, tillodonts, notoungulates, taeniodonts and amblypods. Of these the condylarths were the most numerous. They were also very important, as they gave rise to all the later hooved mammals. There were many types of condylarth. Examples include the sheep-sized *Phenacodus*, the terrier-sized *Meniscotherium*, and the bear-like *Andrewsarchus*. Condylarths died out in the Miocene epoch.

Tillodonts were like large rodents. They probably evolved from early condylarths, but disappeared during the Eocene epoch. They probably could not compete with the true rodents, which first appeared at the end of the Palaeocene epoch. Notoungulates also evolved from the condylarths. They flourished in South America until the Pleistocene epoch (see page 100). Taeniodonts were large, dog-like animals that evolved directly from the early insectivores. They had strong claws and probably dug in the ground for roots.

Amblypods were less successful. They arose in the Palaeocene epoch, but by the end of the Eocene epoch they had disappeared. There were two main types. Pantodonts, such as *Barylambda* and *Coryphodon*, were powerful, hippo-like creatures. Dinocerates included the strange rhino-like *Uintatherium*.

The main Palaeocene carnivores were the creodonts. This group included a variety of animals. Some, such as the bear-sized *Patrofelis*, were slender and cat-like.

Left: *Phenacodus* **was a condylarth that lived during the Eocene and early Oligocene epochs. It was about 1.7 metres long and its feet had five hoof-like toes.**

Left: *Coryphodon* was a common pantodont amblypod during the late Palaeocene and early Eocene epochs. At 2.5 metres long it was one of the largest animals of its time. It probably spent most of its life in water.

Right: *Uintatherium* was a massive dinocerate amblypod that lived in North America during the Eocene epoch. It was about 3 metres long. On its head it had three pairs of horns.

Others, such as *Hyaenodon*, were wolf-like animals. Creodonts were the dominant predators until the Oligocene epoch. Then the true carnivores, which had evolved from early creodonts, took over. True carnivores had larger brains than creodonts, so they were probably better hunters. Creodonts finally died out in the Miocene epoch.

The primates also arose in the Palaeocene epoch. They evolved from tree-dwelling insectivores and soon became widespread. *Plesiadapis* (see page 111) became particularly common in the northern continents. The apes appeared in the Miocene epoch and man evolved in the Pliocene epoch.

By the middle of the Eocene epoch all the remaining groups of mammals had appeared. There were whales and sea-cows in the seas. The rodents spread and replaced the multituberculates. And bats evolved from tree-dwelling insectivores. In Africa the ancestors of the elephants were evolving.

All these mammal groups continued to flourish throughout the Cenozoic era. But during the Oligocene, Miocene and Pliocene epochs the most widespread land-animals were the hooved mammals.

Above: *Moeritherium* was the ancestor of the elephant. It lived in Africa during the late Eocene and early Oligocene epochs and was about the size of a modern tapir.

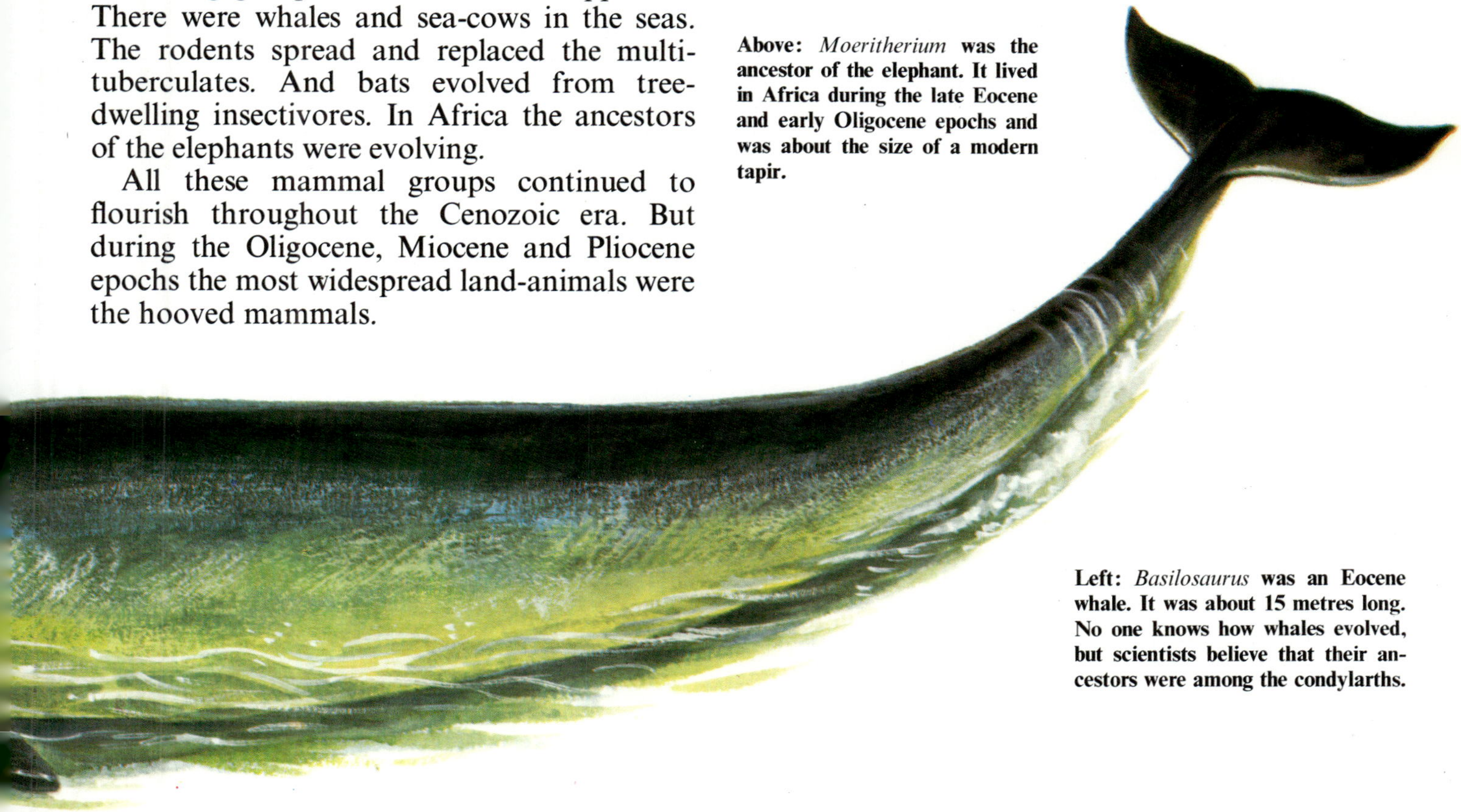

Left: *Basilosaurus* was an Eocene whale. It was about 15 metres long. No one knows how whales evolved, but scientists believe that their ancestors were among the condylarths.

The oldest known tapir lived in the Oligocene epoch. Tapirs were never common, but their fossil remains have been found in many parts of the world. Tapirs are regarded as the most primitive of the living perissodactyls.

The first horses appeared in the Eocene epoch. They were small animals with four-toed forefeet. They browsed in the forests. However, by the Pliocene epoch their descendants had become fast-running, one-toed, grazing horses.

Several other groups of perissodactyls arose at the same time as the early horses. Palaeotheres were small, horse-like animals. They became extinct by the middle of the Oligocene epoch. Brontotheres survived until the end of the Oligocene epoch. Some of them reached enormous sizes. *Brontotherium* stood 2.5 metres tall

The skeleton of *Megacerops*. Like other brontotheres it had a V-shaped pair of strong, blunt horns on its nose.

Below: Three North American hooved mammals. *Moropus* (top) was a Miocene chalicothere. Its strong claws were probably used for digging up roots. *Archaeotherium* (bottom left) was an Oligocene entelodont. It had large, bony knobs on its cheeks. *Synthetoceras* (bottom right) was a Pliocene relative of modern deer and cattle.

Hooved Mammals

During the Tertiary period many kinds of hooved mammals browsed in the woods or grazed on the plains.

Most hooved mammals, or ungulates, belong to two large orders (groups) of mammals. There are the perissodactyls, which have an odd number of toes on each foot, and the artiodactyls, which have an even number of toes on each foot.

During the early part of the Cenozoic era the perissodactyls were a very successful group. However, today only three groups remain—the rhinoceroses, tapirs and horses.

Some of the early rhinoceroses were small, fast-running horse-like creatures. Others were hippo-like, amphibious animals. Both of these types were hornless. They were extinct by the end of the Oligocene epoch. Some of the later rhinoceroses were also hornless and among these were the giant indricotheres (see page 98). Others were the more familiar horned type.

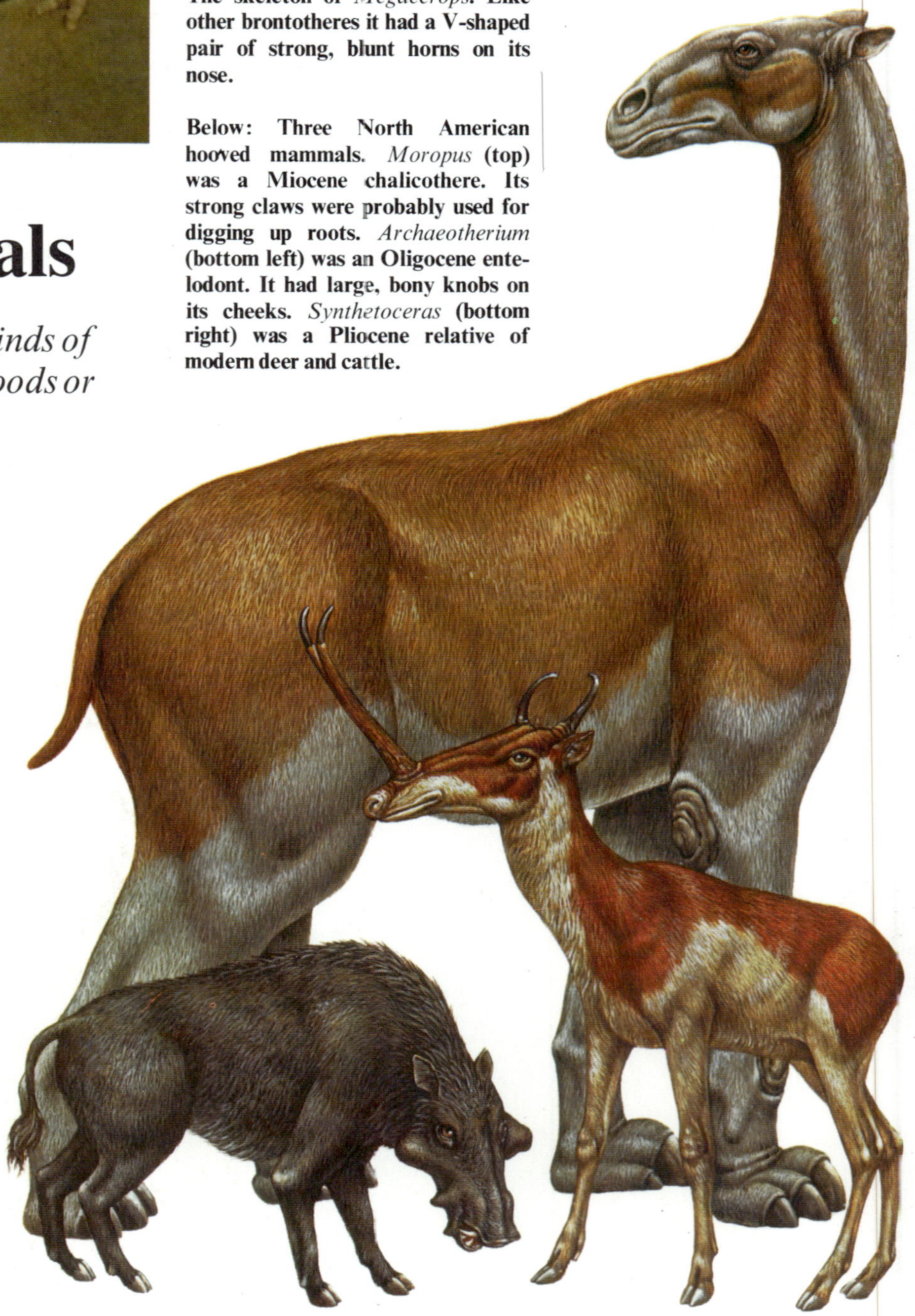

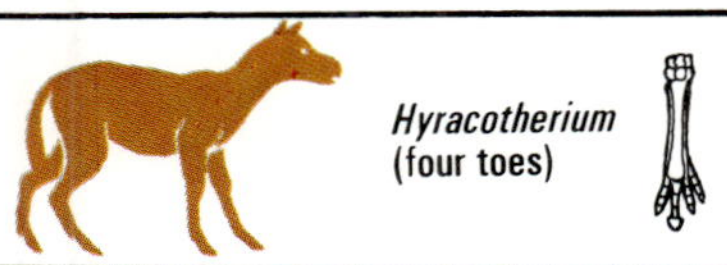

EOCENE

The age of small, four-toed, browsing horses. ***Hyracotherium*** **was followed by** ***Orohippus*** **and then** ***Epihippus*****, which had a slightly larger central toe.**

OLOGOCENE

The age of three-toed browsing horses. But the teeth of ***Mesohippus*** **and** ***Miohippus*** **were better suited for grinding up plant material. And** ***Miohippus*** **was a fairly good runner.**

MIOCENE

The descendants of ***Miohippus*** **formed two groups. Some, such as** ***Hypohippus*** **and** ***Megahippus*****, remained three-toed browsers. Others, however, walked on large central toes. And their teeth were suitable for grinding tough grass.** ***Parahippus*** **and** ***Merychippus*** **roamed the grassy plains that spread across North America during this epoch.**

PLIOCENE

Some of the descendants of ***Merychippus*** **were three-toed grazing horses, such as** ***Nannipus*** **and** ***Hipparion*****. But** ***Pliohippus*** **was the first one-toed horse.**

PLEISTOCENE

Several kinds of one-toed horse arose from ***Pliohippus*****, including** ***Hippidion*** **and** ***Onohippidion*****. But all modern horses, zebras and asses belong to the genus** ***Equus*****.**

The evolution of modern horses can be traced back to the Eocene epoch. The direct ancestors of ***Equus*** **(the modern horse) were in order,** ***Hyracotherium, Orohippus, Epihippus, Mesohippus, Miohippus, Parahippus, Merychippus*** **and** ***Pliohippus*****. During the course of this evolution horses increased in size. At the same time they began to run on fewer toes. And their teeth became suitable for grazing grass rather than browsing the leaves of trees.**

at the shoulder. Chalicotheres were the longest-lived group. They were horse-like creatures, but they had claws on their feet. Some, such as *Moropus*, were the size of large cart-horses. The last chalicotheres died out during the Pleistocene epoch.

As the perissodactyls began to decline, the other group of hooved mammals, the artiodactyls, began to spread. Modern artiodactyls include the pigs, hippopotamuses, camels, giraffes, deer and cattle. During the Oligocene epoch there were several additional kinds. Some were pig-like creatures. Entelodonts, such as *Archaeotherium* were the size of cattle. True pigs also appeared during the Oligocene epoch and hippopotamuses appeared during the Miocene epoch.

Camels first evolved during the Oligocene epoch. *Poebrotherium* was a sheep-sized animal with short legs. Later camels included the gazelle-like *Stenomylus* and the long-necked *Alticamelus*.

Deer-like animals first appeared in the Eocene epoch. But true deer are known only from the Miocene epoch onwards. Giraffes also began to appear during the Miocene epoch, together with the ancestors of antelopes, cattle and other bovids. During the Pliocene epoch the bovids began to spread to almost every part of the world.

Below: ***Hyracotherium*** **(also known as** ***Eohippus*****, or 'dawn horse') was only about 40 centimetres high at the shoulder. Its descendants, such as the Miocene three-toed browsing horse** ***Hypohippus*****, were much larger.** ***Hyracotherium*** **is often regarded as a palaeothere. It probably gave rise to other palaeotheres, such as** ***Pachynolophus*** **and** ***Palaeotherium*****. But this group soon became extinct, probably as a result of competition from true horses such as** ***Epihippus*****.**

Giants of the Land

Even though they never equalled the size of the sauropod dinosaurs, some land mammals were huge.

Like other groups of backboned animals, the mammals include a number of giant types. Some still exist today. The blue whale is the largest animal that has ever lived. And the African elephant is the largest living land animal.

Prehistoric giants include the largest land mammal of all time. This was the hornless rhinoceros *Indricotherium* (also known as *Baluchitherium*), which stood $5\frac{1}{2}$ metres high at the shoulder. In contrast the total height of a modern giraffe is only 5 metres and the largest modern elephants are less than 4 metres high at the shoulder.

Above: *Deinotherium* **was a hoe-tusker that existed in Africa from the late Miocene epoch to the early Pleistocene epoch. It stood about 3 metres at the shoulder. Its short tusks were probably used for digging.**

Below: *Indricotherium* **(top) was the largest land mammal that has ever existed. It lived in southern Asia during the Oligocene epoch.** *Platybelodon* **(bottom) was a shovel tusker. It lived in Asia during the Miocene epoch. Presumably it shovelled up food like a mechanical excavator.**

Other giants included the brontotheres (see page 96), the South American ground sloths (see page 100) and some Australian marsupials (see page 102). *Arsinoitherium* was a huge two-horned mammal that lived in Egypt during the Oligocene epoch. It reached a length of 3.3 metres.

The evolution of elephants and their relatives began in the Eocene epoch. Types such as *Moeritherium* (see page 95) were like small hippopotamuses. All the elephants, mammoths and mastodons belong to the mammal group known as proboscids. This name refers to the long trunk or proboscis (nose). As the elephants evolved they increased in size, their trunks grew longer and they developed tusks.

The earliest known mastodons are *Palaeomastodon* and *Phonia*, which lived in Africa during the Oligocene epoch. They stood about 2 metres at the shoulder and had short trunks and tusks. By the Miocene epoch there were three separate groups, all of which continued into the Pleistocene epoch. The deinotheres, or hoe-tuskers had short, downward-pointing tusks. The short-jawed mastodons had long trunks and long tusks. They resembled modern elephants. The American mastodon, *Mammut americanus*, stood about 3 metres high at the shoulder. The third group were the long-jawed mastodons. There were several kinds. An early type was *Gomphotherium*, a pig-like animal with four short tusks. It stood about 3 metres at the shoulder. Later types included the strange shovel-tuskers, such as *Platybelodon*.

Long jawed mastodons gave rise to the mammoths and true elephants. The first known elephant is *Primelephas*, which lived in Africa during the Pliocene epoch. Later elephants spread into Europe and Asia. Mammoths also evolved in Africa. The best known types are those that lived in the tundra regions during the Ice Ages. They had long woolly coats and they probably used their curved tusks to clear snow away from the grass. Mammoths became extinct during the Pleistocene epoch.

Above: The skeleton of *Arsinoitherium*. This rhino-sized hooved mammal may have been related to the elephants. But its relationships are uncertain and it is usually placed in a group by itself.

Below: Watched by the sabre-toothed cat *Smilodon*, an American mastodon struggles in vain in a pool of sticky tar. When the sabre-tooth tries to attack the dying mastodon, it too will be trapped. The remains of such tar pits have been found at Rancho La Brea, near Los Angeles in North America. Many Pleistocene mammals and birds died there and were preserved in the tar.

Mammals of South America

Right: *Pyrotherium* **was the size of a small elephant. It may have been descended from the same ancestor as the North American amblypods.**

Isolated from the rest of the world for about 60 million years, South America produced unique kinds of mammals.

During the late Cretaceous period South America, Antarctica and Australia separated from the remaining continents. By this time the marsupials were well-established in South America. They faced little competition from the few plant-eating placentals that had made their way south from North America.

The Cretaceous marsupials were insect-eating animals. But a variety of types soon evolved, including rodent-like plant-eaters. There were no placental carnivores, so marsupials also took over this role. *Borhyaena* was a fierce, hyaena-like predator; *Lycopsis* was like a dog; and *Thylacosmilus* had exactly the same appearance as the placental sabre-toothed cats.

Early South American placental herbivores included some condylarths. These animals gave rise to four unique groups of hooved mammals—notoungulates, litopterns, astropotheres and pyrotheres.

Notoungulates were a varied group. Some were small, such as the Miocene, rabbit-like *Pachyrukhos*. Others were larger, root-eating animals, such as the Oligocene *Thomashuxleya*, which was about 1.5 metres long. And some were giants. The Pliocene notoungulate *Toxodon* was about 3 metres long and was very common.

There were two main kinds of litopterns. Some were camel-like in appearance. The later forms, such as *Macrauchenia*, were large animals. Their nasal (nose) openings were placed high on their skulls. They may, therefore, have had

Macrauchenia was a camel-like litoptern

Megatherium was a giant sloth

Diadiaphorus was a horse-like litoptern

Glyptodon was a giant armadillo

short trunks. However, some scientists think that the camel-like litopterns were amphibious animals that spent a lot of time in water. High nasal openings would have allowed them to breathe while almost completely submerged.

Other litopterns were horse-like animals. *Diadiaphorus* was a small, three-toed animal. *Thoatherium* had a single hoof, very like that of a modern horse. The horse-like litopterns were very common during the Miocene epoch.

Astropotheres did not resemble any of the North American mammals. *Astropotherium* was a strange, hippo-like animal about $2\frac{3}{4}$ metres long. It may or may not have had a trunk. Astropotheres died out during the Miocene epoch.

Pyrotheres appear to have been the South American equivalent of elephants. *Pyrotherium* had high nasal openings and scientists assume that it had a trunk. Pyrotheres were extinct by the end of the Oligocene epoch.

The edentates form another unique group of South American mammals. *Metacheiromys* was an early type. Its descendants developed armour-plating over their backs. By the Pleistocene epoch there were giant, tank-like glyptodonts. Some types, such as *Doedicurus*, had bony, spiked clubs at the end of their tails. The glyptodonts were related to modern armadillos.

Other modern edentates include the sloths. And during the Pliocene and Pleistocene epochs there were giant ground sloths. *Megatherium* was about 6 metres long.

At the start of the Pliocene epoch South America became linked to North America again via the Panama Isthmus. Placental mammals, such as dogs, bears, camels, horses and mastodons, invaded South America. Many of the South American mammals could not compete. By the end of the Pleistocene epoch all the notoungulates, litopterns and marsupial carnivores were extinct.

However, not all the South American mammals were unsuccessful. Marsupials, tree sloths and armadillos still survive. Some marsupials even invaded North America. Glyptodonts and ground sloths also moved north. But they too finally became extinct at the end of the Pleistocene epoch. They were probably hunted to extinction by man.

Below: Some of the animals that inhabited South America during the Tertiary period.

Mammals of Australia

Cut off from the rest of the world for over 50 million years, Australia has developed its own very special collection of marsupials.

The origins of the Australian marsupials are not known for certain. But scientists believe that marsupials migrated from South America into Antarctica and Australia sometime during the Eocene and Palaeocene epochs. Antarctica then moved south and became covered in ice. Australia (together with its surrounding islands) was left on its own—a vast continental island. As there was no competition from placental mammals, the marsupials flourished.

The early fossil record of Australian marsupials is very poor. The oldest fossil so far discovered is of an Oligocene phalanger. But some Miocene fossils are known and there is an excellent fossil record of Pliocene and Pleistocene marsupials. Many of them were similar to modern types. But there were a few unusual forms and some were giants.

Modern marsupial carnivores include the cat-like dasyures and the Tasmanian devil. Another carnivore, the thylacine, is probably now extinct. Until recently it survived in parts of Tasmania. It was the Australian equivalent of the placental wolf. *Thylacoleo* may also have been a carnivore. It was a large, lion-like animal with slicing cheek teeth and short tusks. However, its skeleton was like that of a phalanger and some scientists think that its teeth were used for slicing up plant material.

Most Australian herbivores belong to the group called diprotodonts. This group includes phalangers, koalas, wombats and kangaroos. It also includes the largest marsupial that ever lived. *Diprotodon* was a giant, wombat-like animal, about 4 metres long. A number of well-preserved specimens of *Diprotodon* have been found in the salty mud of Lake Callabonna in South Australia.

During the Miocene epoch the Australian climate was mostly tropical or sub-tropical.

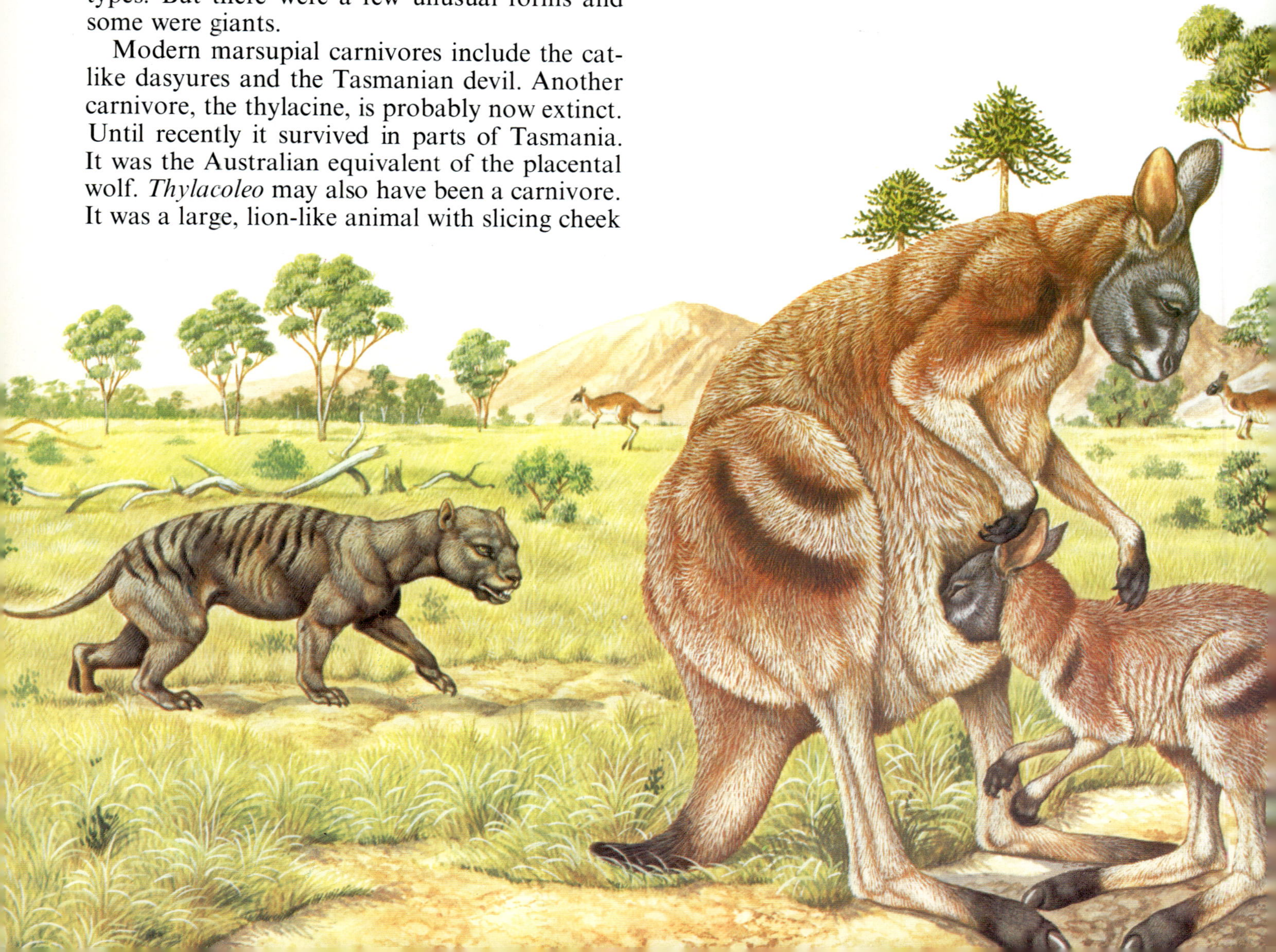

Forests covered the land and there were many lakes and swamps. During the Pliocene epoch the rainfall decreased and the forests were replaced by grassland. Kangaroos, the Australian equivalent of hooved placentals, grazed on the plains. Some of these kangaroos were giants. *Procoptodon* was over 2 metres tall and *Sthenurus* may have reached a height of 3 metres.

Unfortunately, Australian marsupials are no longer isolated. Man arrived in Australia about 25,000 years ago and introduced the dingo. This placental carnivore probably caused the extinction of the thylacine and the Tasmanian devil on the Australian mainland. More recently introduced placentals have had an even greater effect. Rabbits and deer compete with the marsupial herbivores, and foxes prey on them. Man has also taken over much of the land for growing crops and grazing domestic animals. Finally, a number of marsupials have been ruthlessly hunted in the last 200 years.

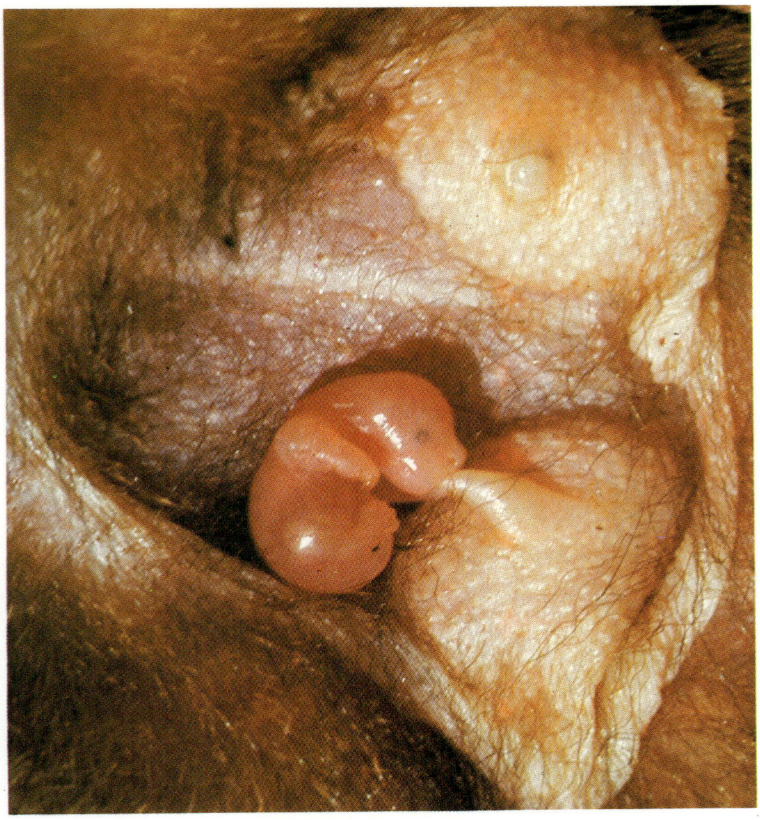

Above: A recently-born young marsupial in its mother's pouch. Notice that its forelimbs are relatively well developed. The tiny animal used these to crawl up its mother's belly. Once inside the pouch it immediately fastened on to one of the teats and began to suckle. A young marsupial gets no assistance from its mother as it crawls up to the pouch. She remains apparantly aloof and unconcerned.

Below: Australia during the Pleistocene epoch. On the left is the lion-like marsupial *Thylacoleo*. Its way of life remains a mystery. In the centre a female *Procoptodon* feeds her young. It has left the pouch and only returns occasionally to suckle. In the background a mob (herd) of these giant kangaroos bound across the plain on their long hind legs. On the right two rhinoceros-sized *Diprotodon* browse peacefully on the vegetation.

The Great Ice Ages

During the Pleistocene epoch the polar ice caps extended their grip on the world. In the north the ice advanced southwards, causing many changes in the animal and plant life.

At the end of the Pliocene epoch the world's climate became much colder. The northern grasslands once again were replaced by forests. Gradually glaciers began to form in a number of places and these thick sheets of ice advanced southwards. The forests disappeared and were replaced by tundra where it was too cold for trees to grow. In Scandinavia the ice was 3,000 metres thick and from there ice sheets extended 2,000 kilometres down into central Europe. In Britain ice sheets reached the River Thames.

When glaciers melt, they leave considerable evidence behind them. Deep U-shaped valleys, smoothed out hills and piles of boulders carried far from their parent rocks are all evidence of former glaciers. So geologists have been able to trace the course of the Pleistocene Ice Age fairly accurately by reading the rocks (see page 16).

The Ice Age actually consisted of several shorter ice ages or *glacials*. In between the glacials there were periods of warmer climate known as *interglacials*. In central Europe there were five Pleistocene glacials, known as the *Donau*, *Günz*, *Mindel*, *Riss* and *Würm* glaciations. The four North American glaciations correspond with these. The Nebrasken glaciation occurred at the same time as the Donau glaciation; the Kansan glaciation corresponds with the Günz glaciation; the Illinoian glaciation corresponds with the Mindel glaciation; and the Wisconsin glaciation covered the period of both the Riss and Würm glaciations.

Pleistocene animals responded to the changing climate in one of two ways. Some moved south to warmer regions; and many of those never returned. Others evolved and adapted to suit the new conditions. They developed thick warm coats that enabled them to survive in the tundra regions. During the glacial periods animals tended to become smaller; as a result they needed less food. Animals that evolved during the Pleistocene epoch included woolly rhinoceroses, steppe mammoths, woolly mammoths, saiga antelopes, cave bears, musk ox, reindeer, bison and polar bears. Occasionally complete bodies of mammals are found preserved in the permafrost of Siberia.

Left and below: Woolly mammoths, woolly rhinoceroses and reindeer all survived in the tundra region just south of the ice sheets.

Top right: A map of the world as seen from above the North Pole. The maximum extent of the Pleistocene ice is shown by the grey areas.

Right: During the Ice Age this valley was filled with a moving glacier that wore down the sides and bottom of the valley into a typical U-shape.

Above: The tundra today. During the Ice Age large areas of North America and Europe would have looked very much like these barren wastes around the Arctic Ocean.

Above right: Gentians prefer a cold climate. During the Ice Age they grew all over Europe. But today they are found only in the tundra and on Alpine mountain tops.

Right: High in the Swiss Alps, this glacier is a relic of the last glaciation. When the next glacial arrives, it will advance downhill to the lowlands again.

During the warmer periods, or interglacials, other kinds of animals appeared. Straight-tusked elephants, hippopotamuses, giant elk, aurochs, monkeys and deer reappeared in northern Europe. However, each interglacial appears to have been slightly colder than the previous one. By the end of the Pleistocene warmth-loving animals had either died out or moved permanently south. Mammoths and woolly rhinoceroses also died out, but not because of the cold. Man appeared during the Pleistocene epoch and probably hunted these animals to extinction for food, using their hide for clothes and their tusks for tools.

Ice ages have occurred several times in Earth's history, notably in Precambrian and Permian times. No one really knows what causes them. But they may be connected with variations in Earth's angle of axis (tilt) combined with variations in its path around the Sun. Mountain building may also be involved and the position of the continents also appears to affect climate.

The last ice sheets began to retreat about 15,000 years ago and we appear to be living in another interglacial. Northern temperatures reached a maximum about 5,000 years ago and have been getting steadily lower ever since. Some scientists believe that the ice sheets will return within a few thousand years.

WESTERN EUROPE DURING THE ICE AGES

The climate was warm enough for hippopotamuses. Food was plentiful for the ancestors of modern man and the early neanderthals.

Horses roamed the grasslands and were hunted by cave lions. Beavers lived in the birch and aspen woods.

Large mammals, such as straight-tusked elephants roamed the broad-leaved forests. *Homo erectus* hunted animals and gathered fruit.

Life in western Europe changed several times as the glacials and interglacials came and went. During the glacials nothing lived on the ice sheets, but the snowy wastes just south of the ice sheets supported a wide variety of life. During the interglacials many warmth-loving animals lived in Europe. Much the same kinds of animals inhabited North America during the Pleistocene epoch. This chart does not show the Donau glaciation, which only seems to have affected the Alpine regions of Europe.

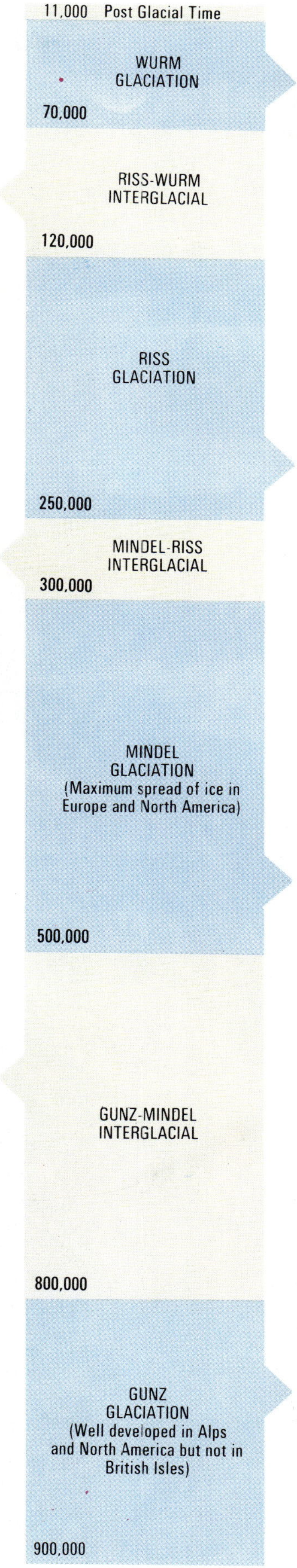

The last glaciation. Conifers and willows dominated the vegetation. Neanderthal man hunted reindeer and other animals.

Woolly mammoths were probably hunted by early man of their hides and meat. As a result they and other animals became extinct.

The coldest period of all. But animals such as musk ox and wolves survived in the tundra.

Wild boar and brown bears lived in the coniferous forests just below the tundra region.

THE SCALE OF LIFE

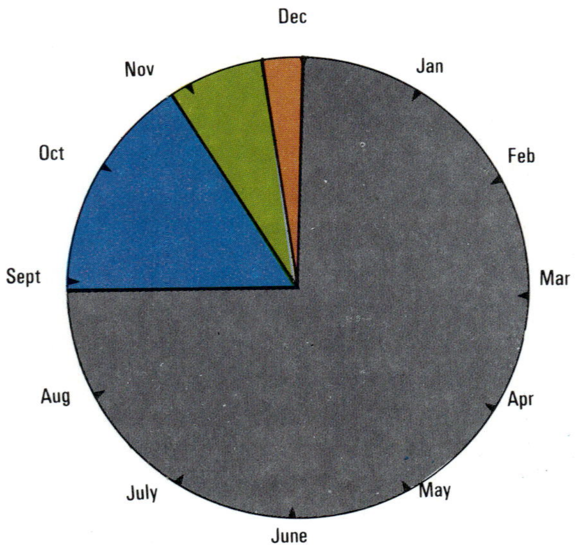

Above: The time scale of life is often difficult to comprehend. Here, the whole of the history of life on Earth has been condensed into a single year. On this scale the Cambrian period—the start of the main fossil record—did not begin until late September. The first fishes appeared during the third week of November, closely followed by the first amphibians and reptiles. Mammals began to appear at the beginning of December, but they did not begin to dominate the world until late in the month. Man appeared only late in the evening of December 31st. The last 6,000 years (the span of recorded history) occupy a mere ninety seconds. One human lifetime lasts just one second.

Compared with some of the giants that have existed in the past, man is a rather small animal. Even *Protoceratops*—tiny compared to its relatives (see page 68)—was a formidable size.

This tendancy towards gigantism is found in all the main groups of vertebrates and even among some invertebrates—*Meganeura* was the size of a large modern bird! Large size has its obvious advantage; there is less chance of being eaten. But it seems that large, specialized animals are easily brought to extinction. They need a lot of living space and large quantities of food. When conditions change they cannot adapt.

Pteranodon
Brontosaurus
Archaeopteryx
Baluchitherium
Homo sapiens
(Man)
Iguanadon
Sthenurus
Diatryma

THE ASCENT OF MAN

Above: A modern tree shrew. Tree shrews are squirrel-like animals that can run along the branches of trees using their claws. Like primates they have colour vision and rely on sight rather than smell. These characteristics evolved independently in the tree shrews. However, they and the primates may have had a common ancestor and tree shrews may resemble early primates from which man eventually evolved.

Below: A ring-tailed lemur. Lemurs are primates and are found only in Madagascar. They disappeared from other parts of the world during the Oligocene epoch due to competition from the monkeys. The arrival of man on Madagascar caused the extinction of many species. The largest of the lemurs, the calf-size *Megaladapis* appeared in the Pleistocene epoch and became extinct about 300 years ago.

Before the Monkeys

Man belongs to the mammal group known as the primates. This group evolved early in the history of the mammals, during the late Cretaceous period. The ancestors of primates were tree-living, insectivorous animals. They were probably very much like the modern tree shrews of south-east Asia.

Primates all have certain characteristics in common. They have five fingers and toes; and their hands (and often their feet) can be used for grasping objects. Instead of claws they have flattened nails that help protect the pads of the fingers and toes. They have four kinds of teeth—incisors, canines, pre-molars and molars. Their faces are often flattened and primates have forward-pointing eyes. This gives them binocular, or stereoscopic, vision, which allows better judgement of distance. Primates usually have large eyes and good vision. On the other hand, their sense of smell is less good than in other animals.

Another important characteristic of primates is that they care for their young for much longer than other mammals. This gives the young a greater chance of learning from their parents; and as a result primate young have a much greater learning ability than other mammals. At the same time the long period of parental care seems to have resulted in the formation of family groups with complicated social structures. Social behaviour is one of the most important characteristics of man.

However, despite these general characteristics, primates have never become highly specialized animals. As a result they have never been restricted to a particular way of life. Of course, evolution has taken place

and there are obvious differences between man, apes and other primates. But man is a generalized rather than a specialized animal. It is this feature that has made him so adaptable and, therefore, so successful.

Man, apes and monkeys belong to the primate group known as the anthropoids. The remaining primates all belong to the group known as prosimians—a name that literally means 'before monkeys'. Modern prosimians include lemurs, lorises, bushbabies and tarsiers.

Scientists think that *Purgatorius*, which lived in the Cretaceous period, is the earliest known primate. However, this creature was very like a condylarth and its classification as a primate is uncertain. The earliest certain primate is *Plesiadapis*, which lived in the Palaeocene epoch. This rodent-like animal had claws and a pointed snout. It may have lived on the ground or in the trees, running along the branches like a squirrel.

During the Eocene epoch various kinds of prosimians appeared. Some of them, such as *Tetonius* and *Necrolemur* were like modern tarsiers. Others, such as *Adapis* and *Notharctus*, were like lemurs. The Eocene prosimians were tree-living animals that fed on insects, leaves, fruit and birds' eggs. They had relatively large brains, forward-pointing eyes and grasping hands. Some of them were well-adapted for leaping from branch to branch. One group, the omomyids, probably gave rise to the apes and monkeys.

Above left: A reconstruction of *Plesiadapis*. Its teeth had some rodent-like features. This suggests that the plesiadapid primates and the rodents were closely related.

Above: A bushbaby. Like most prosimians, bushbabies are nocturnal animals. They survive in East Africa because they do not compete directly with monkeys for food.

Man's Ape Ancestors

Twenty million years ago apes roamed the forests of Africa. Then, about 10 million years ago, grasslands began to replace the forests and man's ancestors descended from the trees.

The first primates appeared in North America. And from there the prosimians spread throughout most of the world. However, as the continents drifted apart, their descendants evolved into two different groups. The New World monkeys are those that live in the Americas. They have broad, flat noses and their nostrils are far apart and open to the side. Many of them have grasping tails. Old World monkeys are those that live in Africa and Asia. Their nostrils are close together and open to the front. None of them have grasping tails.

These two groups of monkeys appeared in the Oligocene epoch and they may have evolved from different prosimian ancestors. The apes also appeared in the Oligocene epoch but they were (and still are) confined to the Old World. One of the main physical differences between apes and monkeys is that monkeys have tails, apes do not.

Above: A fossil skull of *Aegyptopithecus*. This animal had a very small brain and its pointed snout was more like the snout of a prosimian than an ape. However, it had large canine teeth and its lower jaw was heavy and ape-like.

Below: A reconstruction of *Oreopithecus*. This mid-Miocene ape is difficult to fit into the evolutionary story of the monkeys, apes and man. It was a tree-dwelling animal that lived in the swamp forests of southern Europe. It had a curious mixture of monkey-like, ape-like and man-like features. Its ancestors are not known and it appears to have had no descendants.

Below: An orang-utan, one of the modern great apes. With its long arms and strong, grasping hands it is well-adapted for swinging slowly through the trees. Presumably, the ancestors of the orang-utan were Miocene apes that remained tree-dwellers when other apes began to live on the ground. When an orang-utan does descend from the trees, it walks on the knuckles of its hands.

APES V MAN

Gorilla

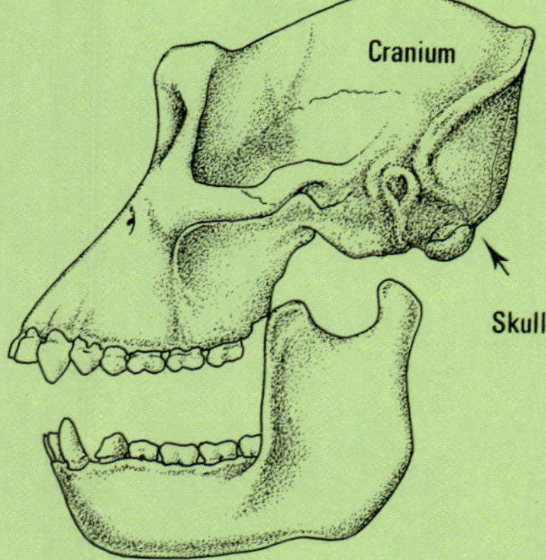

Man

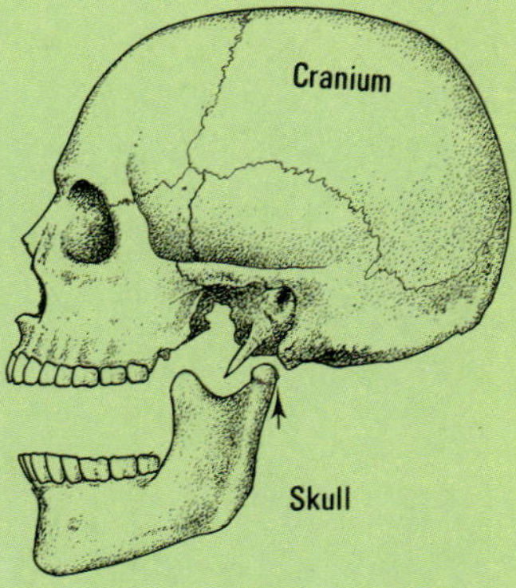

Man has a much flatter face than an ape. The cranium, or brain case, is larger—which reflects man's greater intelligence. Also, the skull is set on top of the spine, whereas an ape's skull is slung forward. As a result an ape's skull needs large muscles to hold it up. The ridges and crests on the back of the skull are for the attachment of these muscles. Apes need powerful jaws to chew their plant food. The brow ridges above the eyes act as shock absorbers as the jaws pound away. Man, on the other hand eats less tough food. The jaws are therefore more delicate and there are no brow ridges.

An ape has large teeth, including shearing incisors that project forward, and tusk-like canines. Man has smaller and more even teeth. In addition the jaw of an ape is U-shaped, whereas man's jaw is more rounded.

An ape walks on its feet and the knuckles of its hands. Man walks in an upright position. The shapes of their pelvic girdles (red) and spines are therefore very different. Man's spine is S-shaped so that the centre of gravity of the body lies directly above the feet.

Both apes and man have grasping hands. But man's thumb is longer in relation to the fingers. This allows a precision grip between the thumb and forefinger.

Apes have grasping feet. Man's feet, on the other hand, are adapted for upright walking. The big toe lies alongside the others, there is a definite heel and the foot is arched.

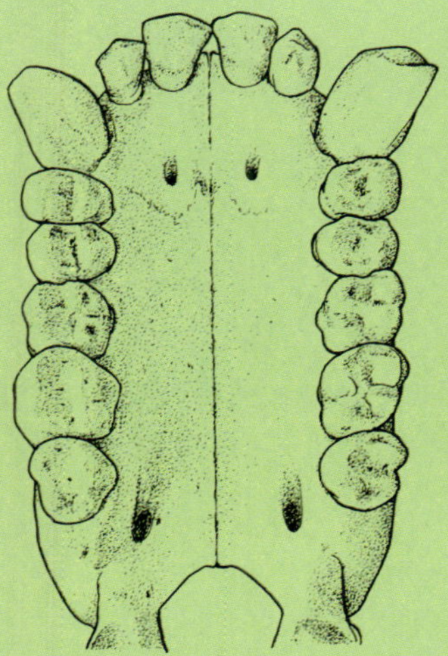

Upper Jaw

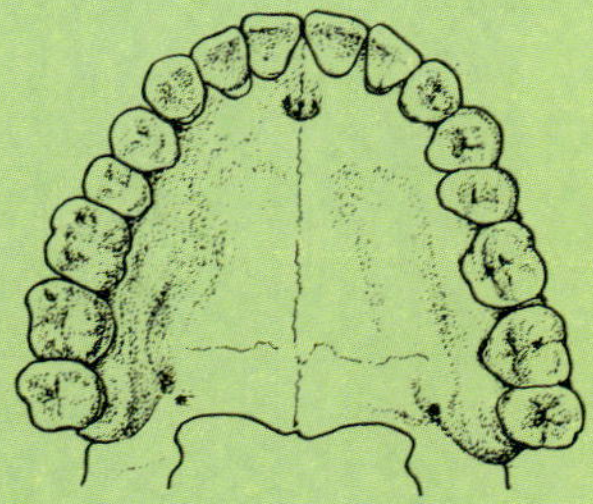

Upper Jaw

Skeleton

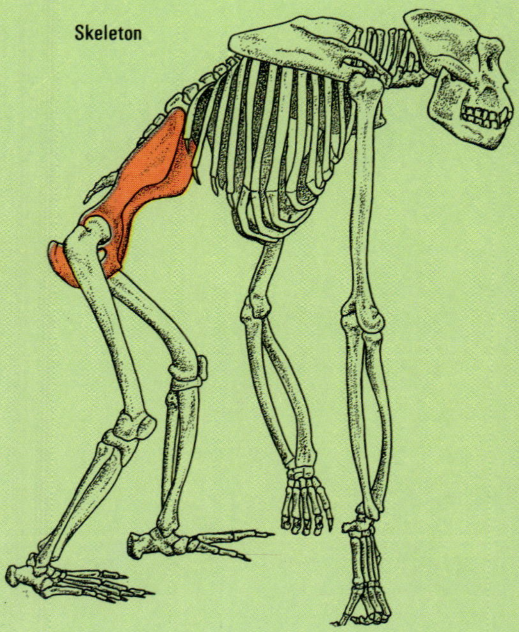

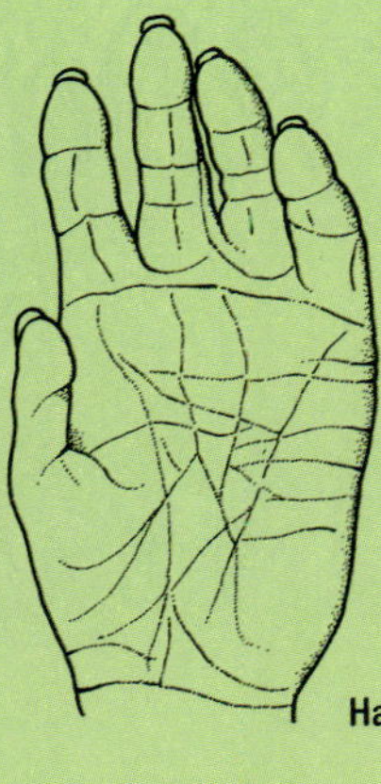

Hand

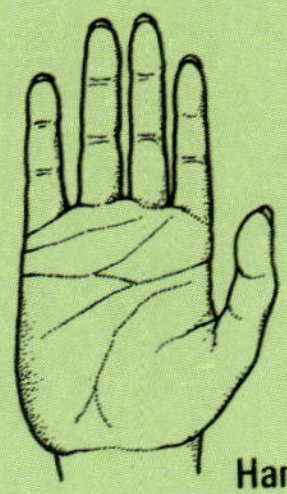

Hand

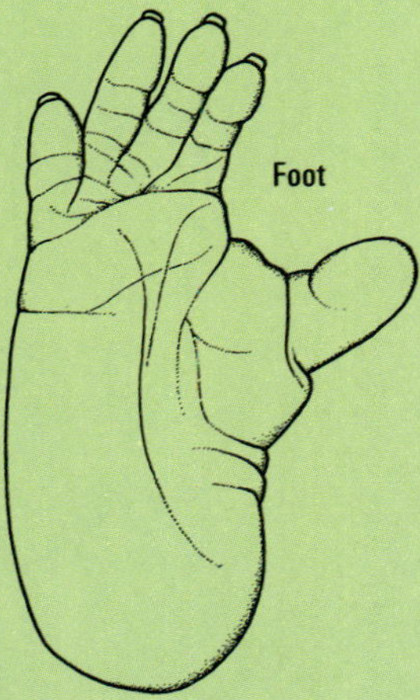

Foot

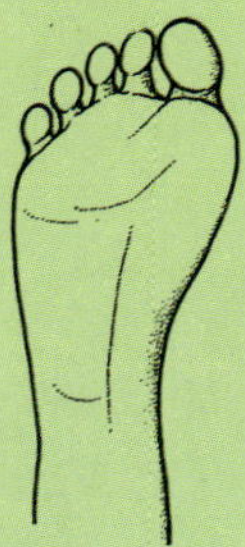

Foot

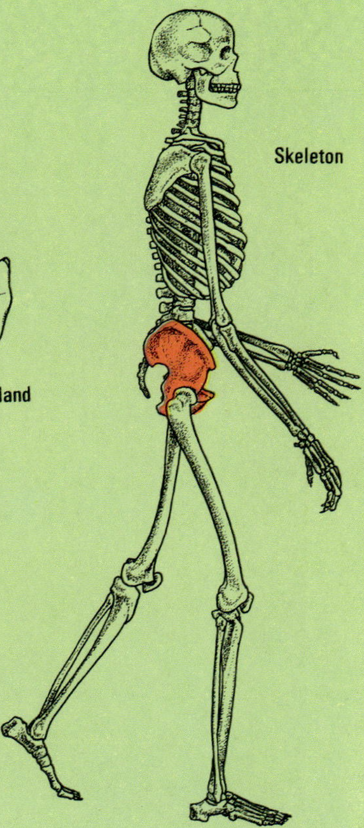

Skeleton

The earliest known anthropoids are *Oligopithecus*, *Propliopithecus* and *Aegyptopithecus*. Their fossils are known from the Oligocene deposits at Fayum in Egypt. During this epoch the Fayum region (now desert) was covered with forests and large rivers. *Oligopithecus*, the oldest of the three, had some characteristics of omomyid prosimians as well as some ape-like features. *Propliopithecus* was a more advanced form and may have been the ancestor of all the later Old World monkeys, apes and man. *Aegyptopithecus* was a small, tree-living creature with definite ape characteristics.

During the Miocene epoch apes lived throughout Africa and even spread into Europe and Asia. The Miocene apes are usually all grouped together as the dryopithecines, or 'oak apes'. Their fossils are often found by the leaves of oak trees.

Early Miocene types include *Proconsul*, *Rangwapithecus*, *Limnopithecus* and *Dendropithecus*. All of these had disappeared by the middle of the Miocene epoch. They were replaced in the late Miocene by several species all included in the genus *Dryopithecus*. *Dendropithecus* is thought to have been the ancestor of modern gibbons. The relationships of the other species are not known.

Two other Miocene species are particularly interesting, although they were certainly not man's ancestors. *Oreopithecus* was a swamp-dweller that, in addition to ape characteristics, had characteristics of both monkeys and man. However, it appears to have developed these characteristics independently and has no known descendants.

Gigantopithecus was larger than a gorilla. It was therefore probably the largest ape that has ever lived. But, again, it has no known descendants—unless, of course, the abominable snowman really does exist!

Towards the end of the Miocene epoch the climate of Africa changed. The forests began to disappear and grasslands spread across the land. Some of the apes succeeded in adapting to this new environment. They came down from the trees and began to feed on the ground.

One of these apes is known as *Ramapithecus*. Fossil skulls of this animal have been found in Kenya and in various parts of Asia and Europe. The skull of *Ramapithecus* was generally ape-like, but it had a few man-like features. As a result, *Ramapithecus* is generally thought to be man's ape ancestor. It may have fed on grass seeds. If so, it would probably have sat on the ground and picked the seeds with its hands.

Following *Ramapithecus* there is a long gap in the fossil record. Only a few fragments of fossils are known from the next five million years. But during this time the first truly man-like creatures evolved.

Right: Reconstructions of the lower jaw (top) and lower face (bottom) of *Ramapithecus.* The face was flatter than the faces of other apes and the incisor teeth and canines were smaller. It had grinding molar teeth. These could have been an adaptation for eating the hard seeds of grasses.

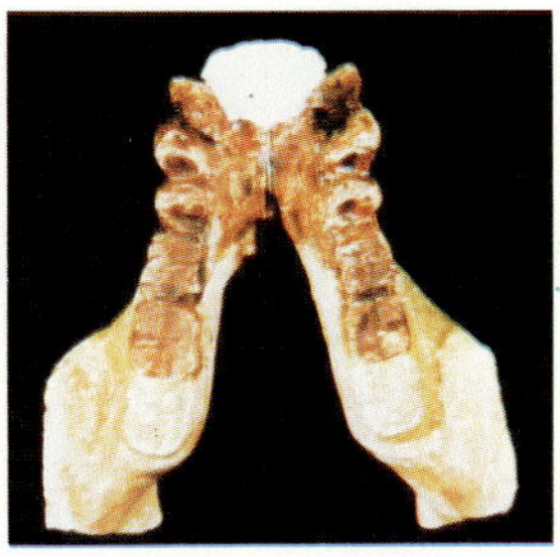

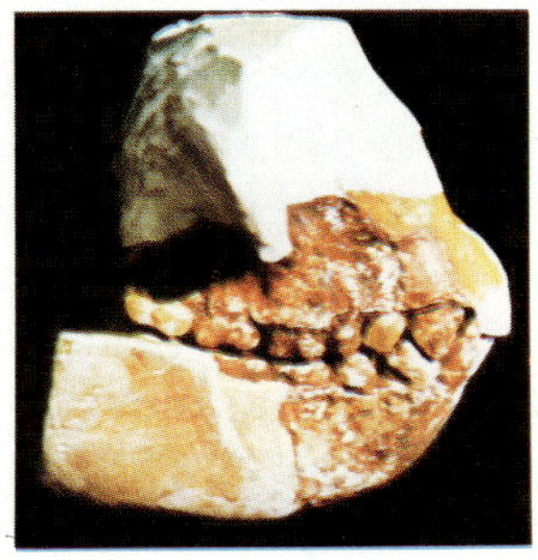

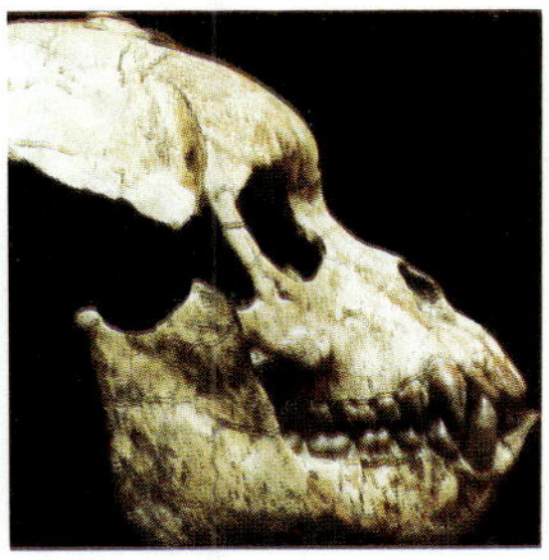

Above: A reconstruction of *Proconsul,* a chimpanzee-like early Miocene ape that lived in trees. It has been suggested that one species, *Proconsul africanus,* was the ancestor of the chimpanzee and that another, *Proconsul major* was the ancestor of the gorilla. However, there is no evidence that links *Proconsul* with any of the later apes.

Left: A fossil skull of *Proconsul.*

Below: A scene in East Africa during the early Miocene epoch. Above the lowland forests were a number of volcanoes and the fossils of dryopithecine apes are found near the remains of these volcanoes. They probably lived in the forests and on the slopes above. The volcanic activity would have caused the environment to change frequently. This may have encouraged the rapid evolution of the Miocene apes. Other animals shown here include a two horned rhinoceros, deinotheres, creodonts and two aardvarks.

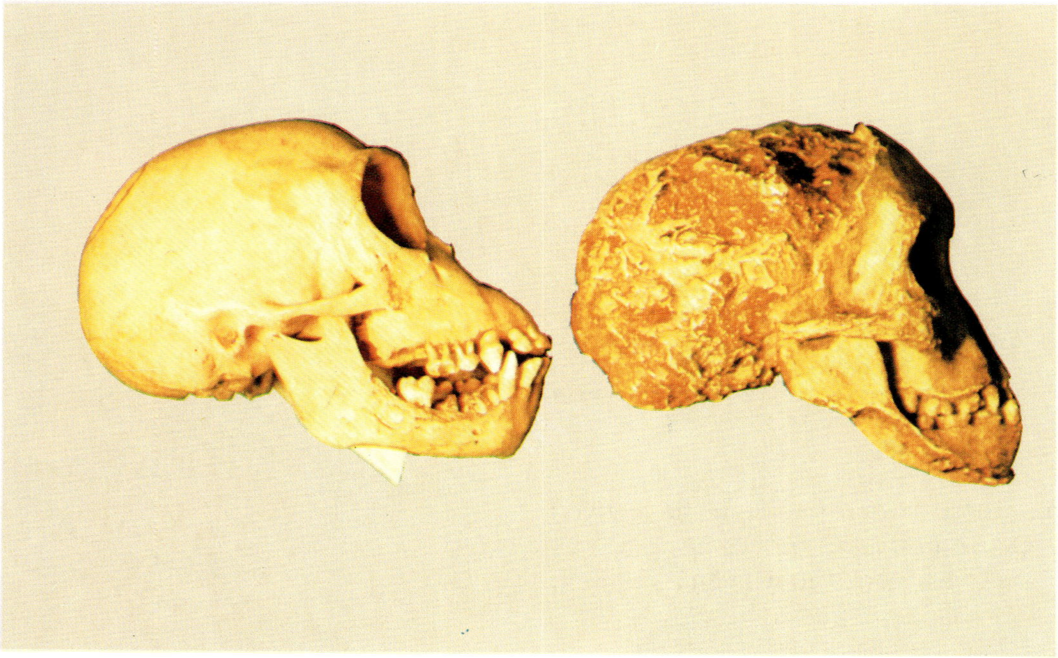

Left: The Taung *Australopithecus* skull (right) compared with the skull of a young chimpanzee (left). The Taung skull belonged to a child about six years old. Its face was flatter than a young chimpanzee's and it had smaller canine teeth.

Above: The lower jaw of the Taung child (left) compared with the lower jaw of a young chimpanzee. The Taung jaw has smaller teeth at the front and more human-like teeth at the back.

Australopithecus and Handy Man

About five million years ago the first hominids appeared in Africa. They walked on their hind legs and may have used weapons and tools.

Below: The pelvic girdle (hip girdle) of *Australopithecus* was much more like that of a human than that of a chimpanzee. This indicates that *Australopithecus* walked in an upright position.

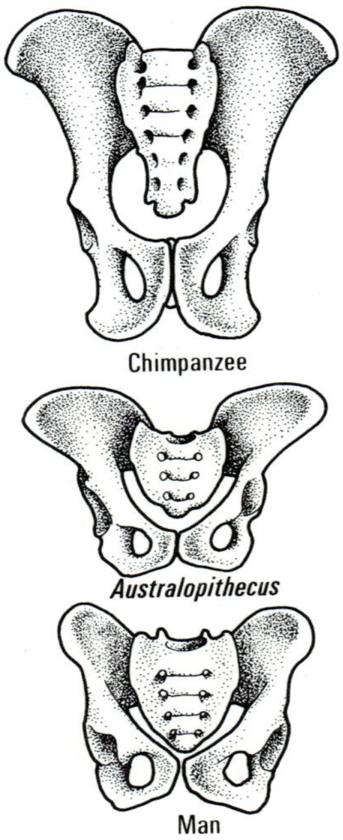

The earliest known hominids (members of the family of man) belong to the group known as australopithecines, or 'southern apes'. These hominids were totally different from *Ramapithecus*. They had developed the habit of walking on their hind legs. How this ability came about is uncertain. Various theories have been put forward. Perhaps the descendants of *Ramapithecus* began to stand up in the long grass in order to see predators. Or perhaps they stood up to defend themselves with sticks and bones. These theories are not totally satisfactory and the development of upright walking has yet to be properly explained. In any case, the early hominids could now use their hands for carrying hunting weapons and food.

The first australopithecine skull was found in 1924 at the Taung cave in South Africa. One year later Professor Raymond Dart described it to an audience of scientists and non-scientists. He called it *Australopithecus africanus* and said that it was an early hominid. However, most people did not believe this. At that time Piltdown man (see page 122), with its large human-like brain and ape-like jaw (the exact opposite of *Australopithecus*), was thought to be man's ancestor. However, when Piltdown man was later exposed as a hoax, *Australopithecus* was recognized as being an early form of man.

Australopithecus remains were later found at other cave sites in South Africa. It soon became apparent that there were two different types. *Australopithecus africanus* (or 'gracile' *Australopithecus*) was a small, lightly-built hominid with a small brain and human-like teeth. *Australopithecus robustus* (also known as *Paranthropus*) was much larger. It had powerful jaws and brow ridges like those of a

Right: Hunting fossil man in Kenya. Scientists search every inch of ground for fragments of bones and skulls. These are later painstakingly pieced together.

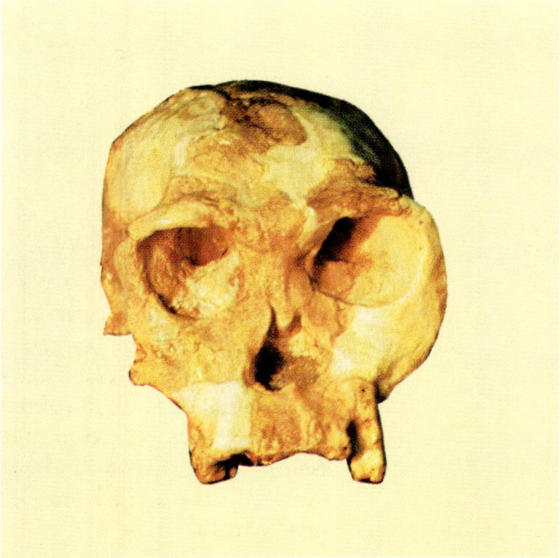

Left: The skull of 'Twiggy', one of the *Homo habilis* fossils found at Olduvai gorge.

Right: Some of the cave-dwelling australopithecines may have been the victims of leopards. A number of fossil bones have leopard tooth marks. Trees often grow outside caves and a leopard carried its prey into a tree to eat it at its leisure. This could explain why so many skull and neck bones are found. These would have been the first parts to be bitten off. They would then have fallen down in front of the cave entrance.

gorilla. It is thought that these two forms may have lived alongside each other. *Australopithecus africanus* appears to have been a scavenger and a hunter. It may even have used sticks and bones as weapons. *Australopithecus robustus,* however, seems to have lived mainly on tough plant food. At the same time it is now thought that neither of these hominids were the direct ancestors of man.

In 1959 Louis and Mary Leakey were excavating in Olduvai Gorge in Tanzania, East Africa. Here there were stone tools belonging to the Oldowan culture (see page 130). Among the pebble tools they found a massive hominid skull. They nicknamed it 'nutcracker man'. Later, it was realized that this was another robust australopithecine and it was named *Australopithecus boisei.*

To begin with the Leakeys thought that they had discovered the maker of the stone tools. The whole collection of fossils was dated at about 1.75 million years old and these were therefore the oldest known tools. But then they found the remains of another, more lightly-built hominid. This was very different from the australopithecine fossils. Its limbs and feet showed that it walked well. And it had a strong hand grip. It was much more likely that the stone tools were made by this hominid. So the Leakeys named it *Homo habilis*, or 'handy man'.

One of the clearest differences between 'handy man' and the australopithecine was brain size. *Australopithecus boisei* had a 500–550 cc brain, whilst *Homo habilis* had a brain size of 650 cc. The two Olduvai hominids are thought to have lived alongside each other until about one million years ago. *Homo habilis* may even have hunted *Australopithecus boisei*. Excavations have uncovered the remains of occupation sites and places where animals were killed and cut up.

When it was discovered, *Homo habilis* was thought to be the direct ancestor of modern man. But during the last ten years or so the situation has become very complicated. Hominid fossils have been found at Lake Rudolf (Lake Turkana) in Kenya, Laetolil in Tanzania, Swartkrans in South Africa and Omo and Hadar in Ethiopia. Many of these fossils are australopithecines. The Hadar finds include a half complete skeleton of a gracile australopithecine nicknamed 'Lucy'. But some of the finds are much more human-like. In 1972 at Lake Rudolf, Richard Leakey (the son of Louis and Mary Leakey) found pieces of skull that belonged to an apparently advanced hominid. It had a much larger brain than *Homo habilis*. Leakey included it in the genus *Homo*, but it has not yet been given a species name. It is just known by its find number, 1470. It is believed to be about two million years old.

Some of the hominid remains from Laetolil and Hadar are also included in the genus *Homo*. But these hominids

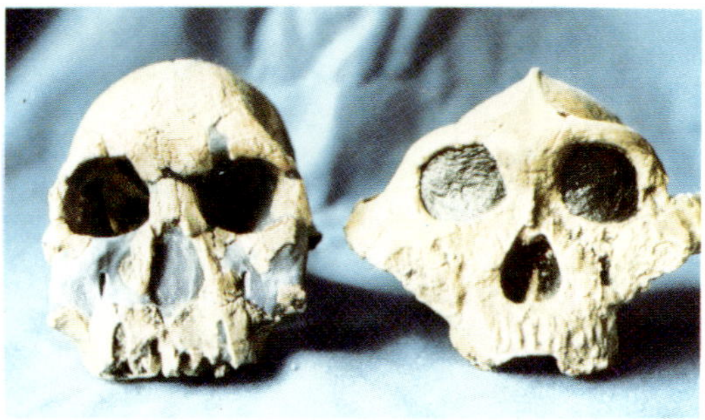

Above: The fossil skull of the Olduvai hominid 1470 (left) and an *Australopithecus robustus* skull found at the same site. Notice the large rounded skull of the 1470 hominid compared with the flat, ridged skull of *Australopithecus robustus*.

Right: The area east of Lake Rudolf today, showing one of the excavation sites where hominid fossils have been found.

Below: The area east of Lake Rudolf two million years ago. A group of *Australopithecus robustus* (left) peer over the rocks at a group of advanced 1470 hominids. These primitive men were able to use tools and build stone wind-breaks.

lived between three and four million years ago. Presumably, therefore, they must be the ancestors of the Olduvai and Lake Rudolf hominids. Scientists are now debating two main questions. Were there two, three or many hominid groups living in Africa two million years ago? And which group gave rise to the first true men? The evidence suggests that there were at least three or four groups. And of these the 1470 hominids are the most probable ancestors of modern man.

The First True Men

Between two million and one million years ago the descendants of the early hominids evolved rapidly and spread into Asia and Europe. True man had appeared.

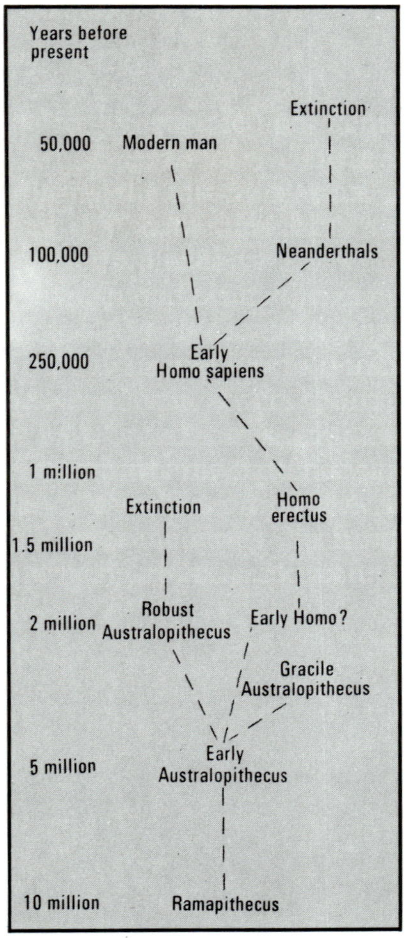

In 1871 Charles Darwin suggested that man's ancestors would be discovered in Africa. He has, of course, been proved completely correct. But at that time there were others who suggested that the orang-utan—the 'old man of the forest'—was close to man's ancestry. Therefore, man's ancestors would be found in Asia.

Among those who believed in Asia as the cradle of man was the Dutch anatomist Eugene Dubois. In 1891 he was searching for fossil remains of man at a place called Trinil on the banks of the River Solo in Java. There he discovered the top of a fossil skull. Later he found a tooth and a thigh bone. He decided that he had found the remains of early man and called his find *Pithecanthropus erectus*.

Scientists did not accept *Pithecanthropus* as being a hominid for many years. But after the discoveries of the Heidelberg jawbone in 1908 and the supposed Piltdown fossils in 1912, they began to take *Pithecanthropus* more seriously.

In 1927 Davidson Black at the Peking medical school in China examined fossil teeth that had been found in a large cave at Choukoutien ('Dragon Bone Hill'). He announced that they belonged to a new hominid, which he called *Sinanthropus pekingensis*. Later, at the same site many more fossils were discovered. They were the remains of about 40 individuals, including 14 partly complete skulls.

During the 1930s more fossils were discovered in Java. And in recent years similar fossils have been discovered in Africa, notably

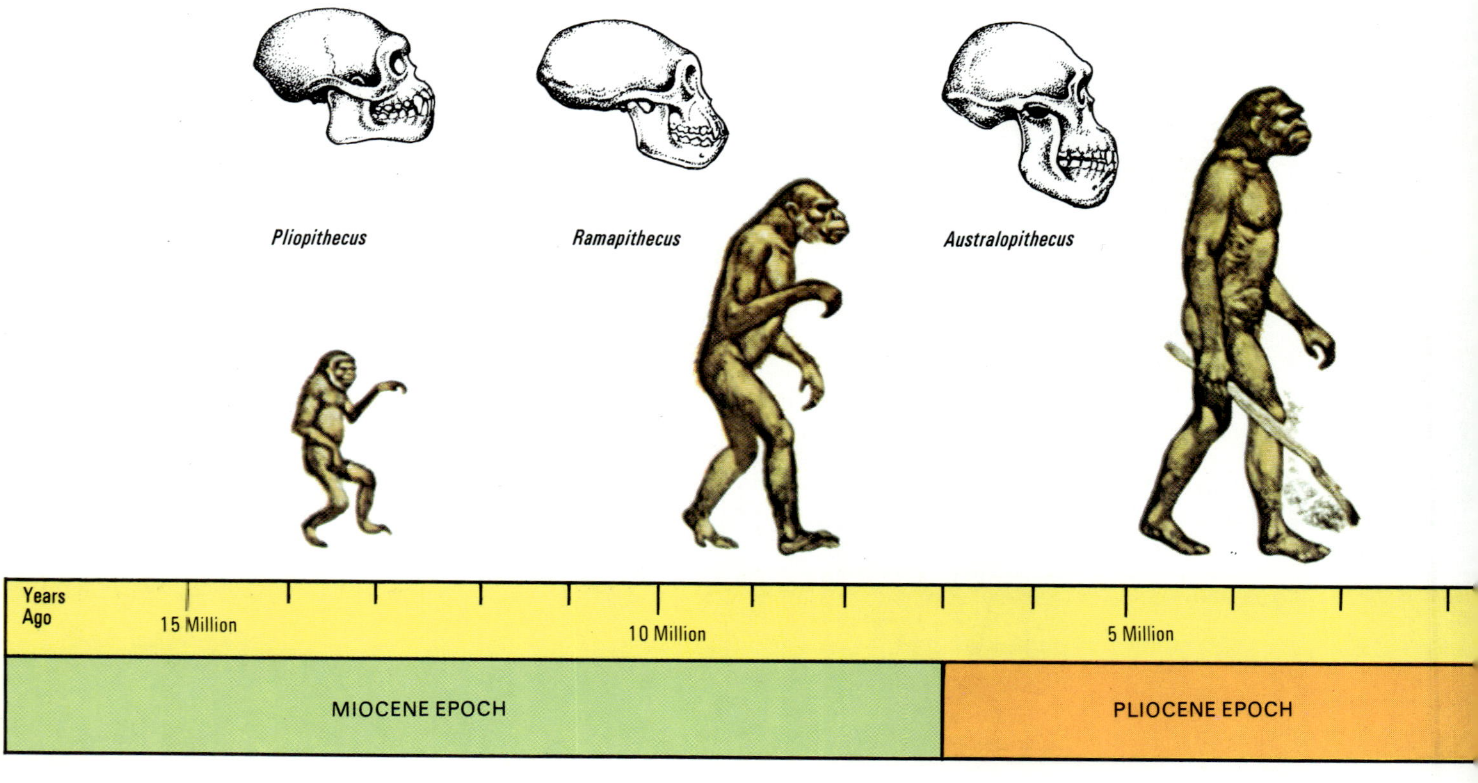

at Ternifine in Algeria and at Olduvai in Tanzania. Like Java man and Peking man these fossils were all given different names when they were found. But they are now all grouped under one name—*Homo erectus*. Some of the fossils found in Europe are also included under this name.

Homo erectus was very different from the earlier hominids. The skull was thicker and there were large brow ridges above the eyes. The brains of these early men were much larger and they walked in a more upright position. Some of them were as tall as modern man. The change is related to the transition from small-scale scavenging to large-scale hunting.

Scientists do not yet know how *Homo erectus* evolved from the early hominids. There is not enough fossil evidence. Nor do they know for certain how hunting and toolmaking developed. However, there is no doubt that *Homo erectus* was a hunter and toolmaker.

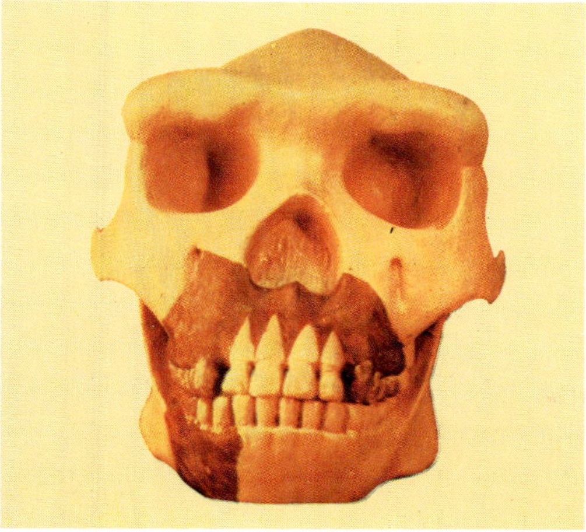

Above: A reconstruction of the skull of Java man made using pieces of skull found at Modjokerto. It shows that early *Homo erectus* had a rugged face and large brow ridges.

Left: A chart showing the probable course of man's evolution. *Homo erectus* may have evolved from a 1470 type hominid. And over five million years ago the australopithecines, *Homo habilis* and 1470 hominids probably had a common ancestor.

Right: Louis Leakey (1903-72) (left) at work with his wife Mary and two colleagues. Louis Leakey discovered the remains of fossil ape and man at several African sites. His most famous discoveries were made at Olduvai gorge. Mary Leakey is still excavating in Africa.

Below: Man's progress from the apes. *Pliopithecus* was an early form of gibbon and was not one of man's direct ancestors. *Ramapithecus* was an ape, but is generally thought of as the first of man's known ancestors. *Australopithecus* could walk upright and may have used weapons. *Homo erectus* was the ancestor of both Neanderthal man and modern man.

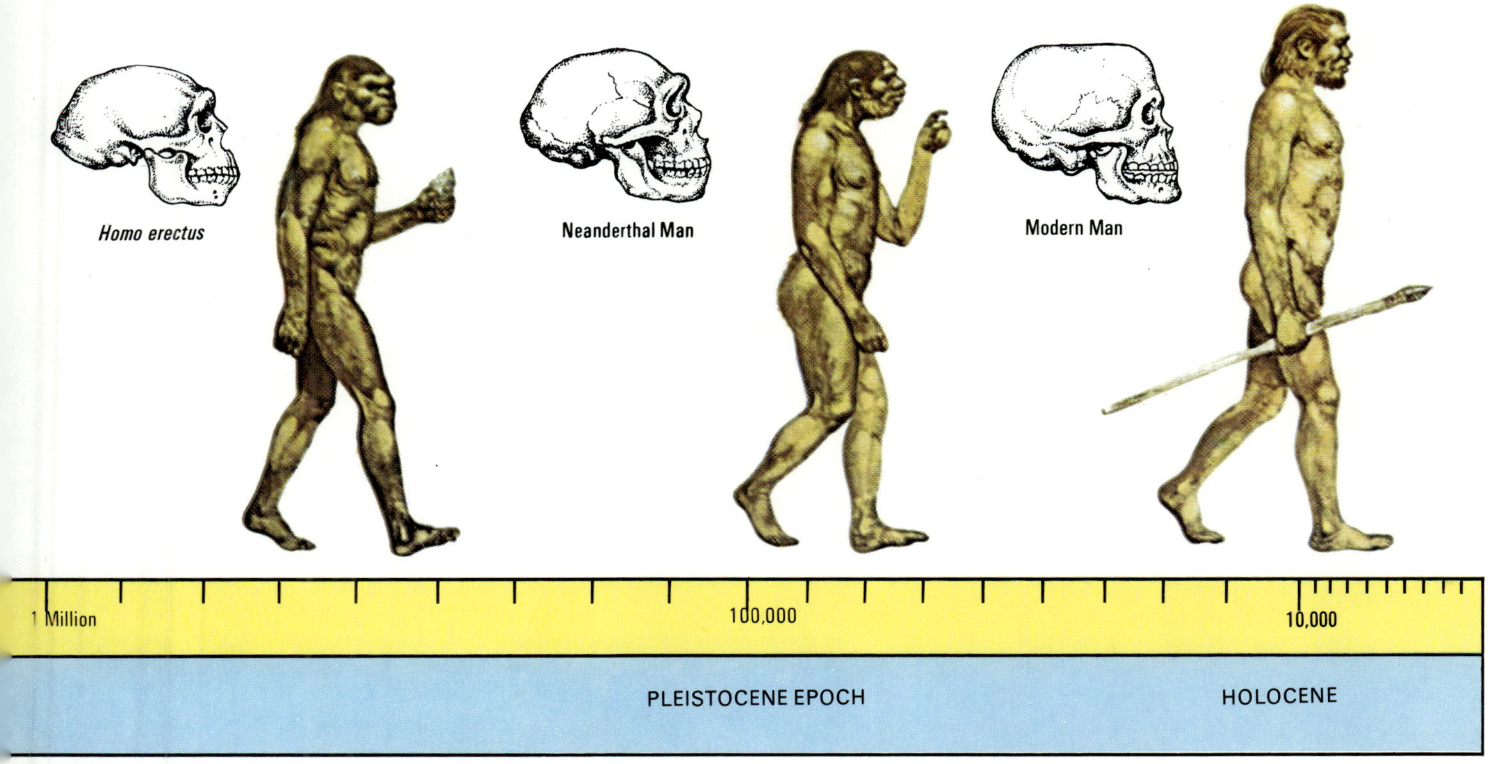

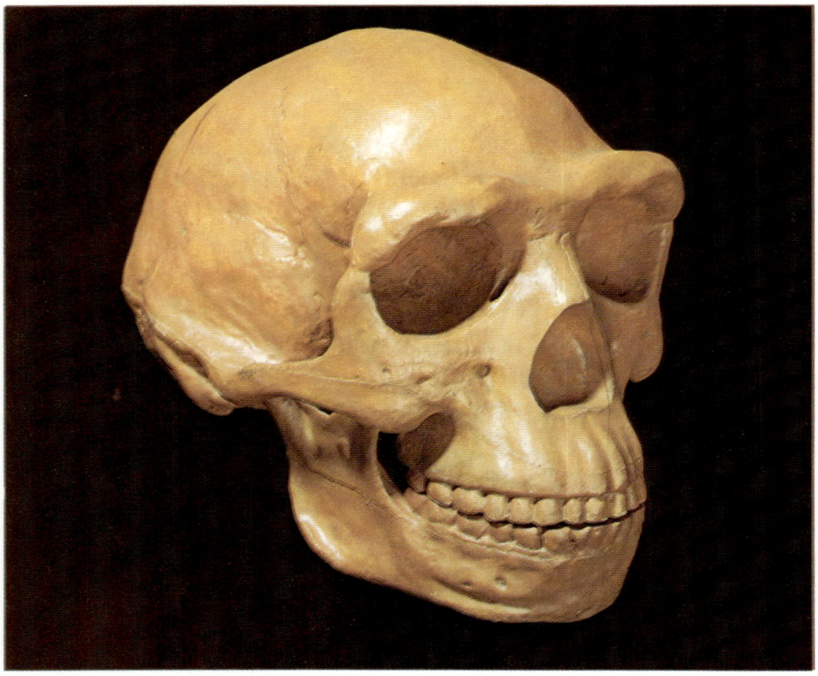

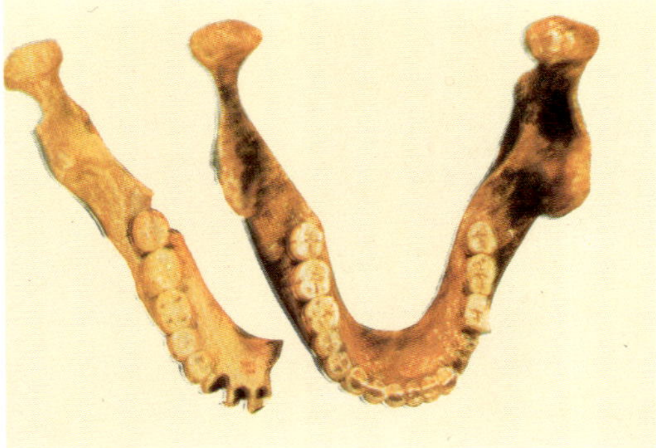

Above: A cast of the Heidelberg jaw (left) compared with a jawbone found at Arago in France. The Arago jaw is about 200,000 years old and the Heidelberg jaw is about 450,000 years old. But the Heidelberg jaw has small, modern teeth. It may have belonged to a type of man half-way between *Homo erectus* and *Homo sapiens.*

Left: A reconstruction of a Peking man skull. Peking man was more advanced than Java man. He had a less rugged face and a larger brain.

If *Homo erectus* was the descendant of the known early hominids, then it is logical to suppose that he evolved in Africa. Evidence from Olduvai points to this. The Olduvai fossils are dated at about one million years old and *Homo erectus* seems to have lived alongside the last of the robust australopithecines. However, the earliest Java fossils also date from about this time. So *Homo erectus* must have begun to migrate out of Africa at a very early stage.

Two large jaw bones found in Java, Asia pose a problem. They appear to have belonged to a gorilla-sized creature and have been given the name *Meganthropus*, or 'giant man'. Some scientists believe that this was a large form of *Homo erectus*. Others say that these jaws belonged to a form of australopithecine. If this is so, then perhaps the australopithecines and early hominids both migrated out of Africa. *Homo erectus* then evolved in Asia and migrated back to Africa. But this idea is regarded as unlikely. There is no real evidence and the oldest stone tools used by *Homo erectus* come from Africa.

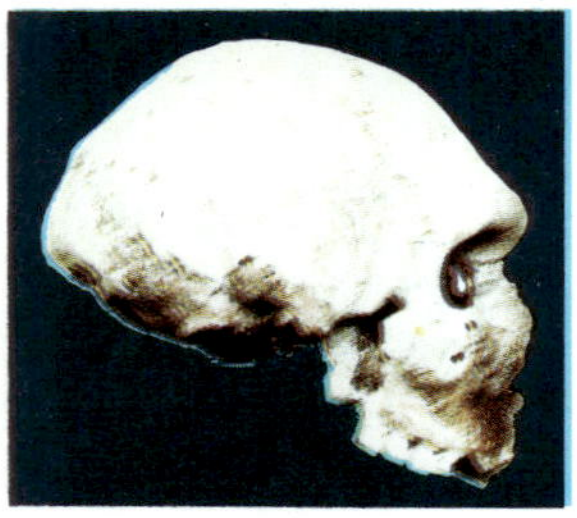

Right: A fossil skull found in a cave at Petralona in Greece. It has a large brain case, but many of its features are those of *Homo erectus.* It probably dates from about 400,000 years ago.

Wherever he came from, *Homo erectus* was certainly living near Peking in China about 500,000 years ago. The Choukoutien cave site contains evidence that these early men used chopper-core tools (see page 130). They were hunters; the bones of many animals were found in the cave. Many layers of ash were

PILTDOWN MAN—A FOSSIL FAKE

The reconstructed Piltdown skull.

In 1912 Sir Arthur Smith Woodward, an eminent British palaeontologist, was shown some pieces of skull by Charles Dawson, an amateur archaeologist. Charles Dawson told him that he had found the pieces in a gravel pit at Piltdown in Sussex. They returned to the pit and found some more fragments of skull and a jawbone. The following year a canine tooth was found, together with some stone tools and the bones of some Pleistocene animals.

Using the pieces Sir Arthur Smith Woodward reconstructed the skull. *Eoanthropus*, or 'dawn man', as it was called, hit the headlines. Everyone was delighted with the find. Here was the oldest known example of fossil man, much older than Neanderthal man.

When the first australopithecine skull (the Taung skull) was described, most scientists did not believe that it could be a relative of man. It did not fit in with the Piltdown fossil. However, as more australopithecines were found, people began to wonder about Piltdown man.

By 1953 there were better methods of dating and the Piltdown remains were subjected to the fluoride test. This showed that they were in fact only a few hundred years old. Further tests showed that the pieces had been stained to make them look old. And the jaw actually belonged to an orang-utan; the teeth had been filed down to make them look human. Piltdown man was a hoax—he never existed.

No one knows for certain who played this trick. But whoever it was fooled many eminent scientists for a number of years.

The techniques of making both chopper-core tools and hand axes moved up into Europe during the middle of the Pleistocene epoch, about 450,000 years ago. However, it is not clear who the European toolmakers were. At many tool sites there are no fossils, and where there are fossils there áre sometimes no tools. The Heidelberg jaw, for example, came from a site without tools.

It is likely, however, that advanced forms of *Homo erectus* lived in Europe. These people would have led a nomadic life. Wandering from site to site at different times of year. When animal and plant foods became scarce in one area they moved on to another.

Food was their main concern. They were almost certainly skilled hunters, and they probably hunted in groups. To catch large animals, such as mammoths, they may have used traps, such as deep pits with pointed stakes at the bottom. The tools they made would have been used for skinning animals and making wooden implements.

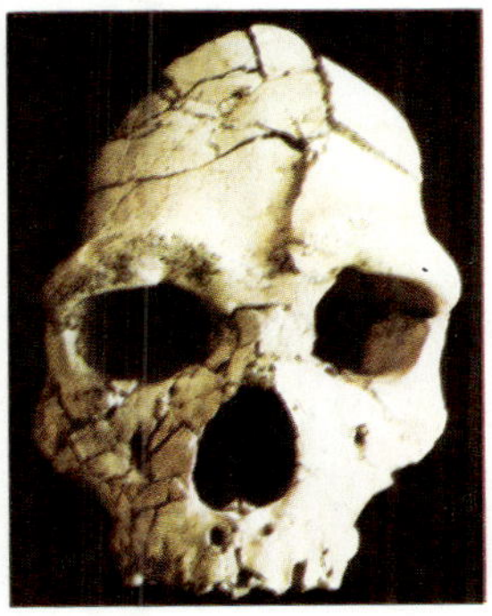

Left: A fossil skull found at Arago in France, dating from about 200,000 years ago. It may have been an early form of *Homo sapiens,* but it still has a broad face and large brow ridges.

Above: At Ambrona in Spain scientists have found evidence of how early man hunted 300,000 years ago. Signs of fire and many fossil bones indicate that grass and brushwood were set alight to drive herds of elephant into swampy ground. There they were killed and cut up for meat. The tools used for butchering have been found scattered over the site. In one place a line of bones indicates that severed limbs may have been used as stepping stones.

Below: Some of the main sites where fossil hominids have been found.

also found. This shows that Peking man knew how to kindle and tend a fire. He could keep a fire going for a very long period of time. He cooked his meat on the fire and it was probably very important for keeping warm and driving away predators.

The chopper-core tools of Peking man were more advanced than the Oldowan tools of *Homo habilis* and similar tools have been found at sites throughout Asia. *Homo erectus* also learned how to make and use hand axes. This technique of tool-making seems to have developed in Africa. Some of the oldest known hand axes have been found at Olduvai.

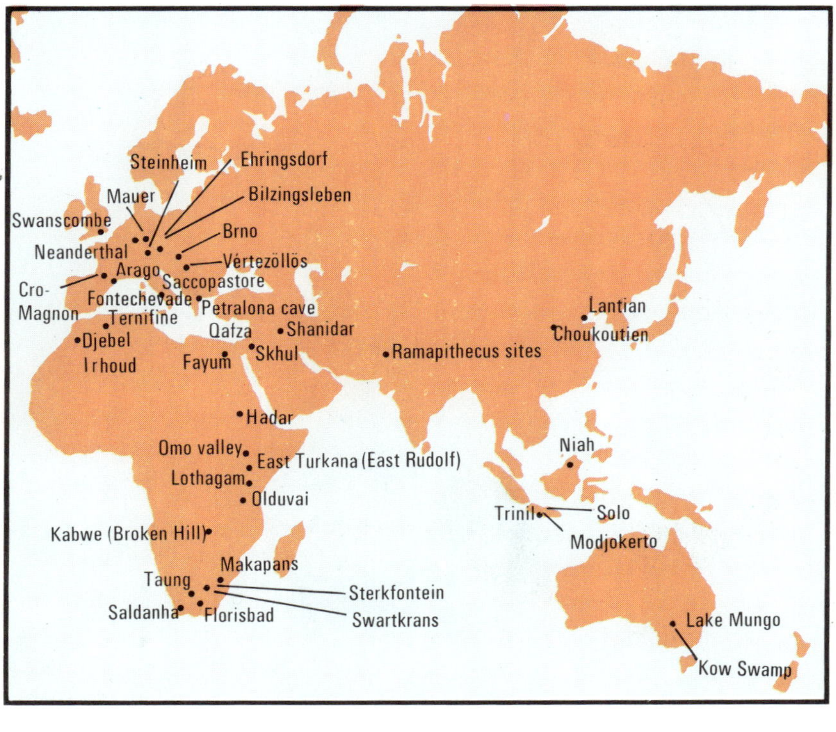

The Neanderthals

Between 100,000 and 70,000 years ago Neanderthal man, a close relative of modern man, appeared in Europe.

As the ice ages came and went in Europe, so too did *Homo erectus* and early *Homo sapiens*. These early men could not tolerate the cold. But during the last glaciation, which began about 70,000 years ago, Neanderthal man managed to survive the harsh conditions.

Neanderthal man, or *Homo sapiens neanderthalensis*, is named after the Neander valley in Germany, where Neanderthal remains were found in 1856. Since then about 60 skeletons have been found in Europe, Russia and North Africa.

The Neanderthals were shorter and more thick-set than modern man. They had broad faces, chinless jaws, low foreheads, heavy brow ridges and probably flattened noses. At the back of the skull there was a strange bun-like projection. But despite his primitive appearance, Neanderthal man was far from unintelligent. To survive in ice age Europe he had to be resourceful and adaptable.

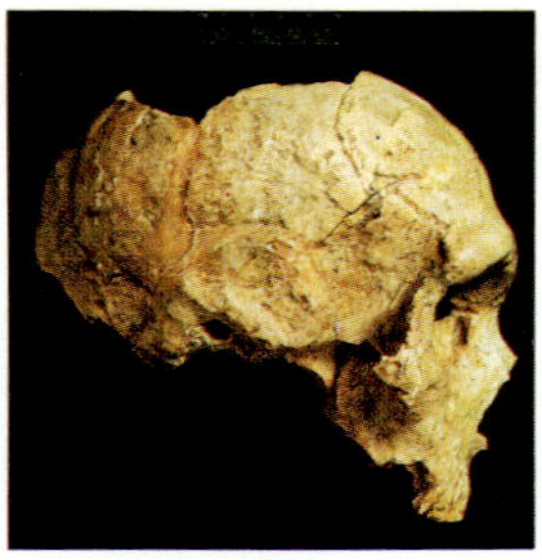

Above: A Neanderthal skull found in a quarry in Gibraltar. It was discovered in 1848, but its importance was not realized until after the Neander valley remains were found in 1856.

Below: Neanderthal man hunted with spears, stones and balls of hard clay. He used fire to provide warmth and probably cooked his food. Fire torches provided light. Neanderthals lived in caves and thus competed with cave bears for shelter. Torches and spears would have been useful for driving such animals away. Neanderthals may have had some kind of religion, such as a cave bear cult. Carefully arranged cave bear skulls and other objects have been found at some Neanderthal sites. They probably communicated with each other by signs and facial expressions. They may even have had a primitive language but it has been calculated that they could not produce the full range of human sounds.

Neanderthal man was a skilled hunter and lived off the plentiful herds of ice age mammals, such as woolly mammoths, woolly rhinoceroses, reindeer and bison. He lived in natural shelters, such as caves. He used fire and wore the skins of animals to keep warm. The flint tools he made belong to what is called the Mousterian industry (see page 130). Flakes of flint were used as scrapers and knives. Pointed flakes may have been bound to wooden handles and used as spears.

The Neanderthals also showed concern for their dead. They were buried in shallow graves. And sometimes flowers and tools were placed in a grave with the body. Perhaps Neanderthal man had some kind of religion and believed in a life after death.

The Neanderthals disappeared about 35,000 years ago. It is not known why this happened. They may have been wiped out by more advanced men who invaded from the east. Or they may have interbred with the invaders, and the new population evolved into modern man.

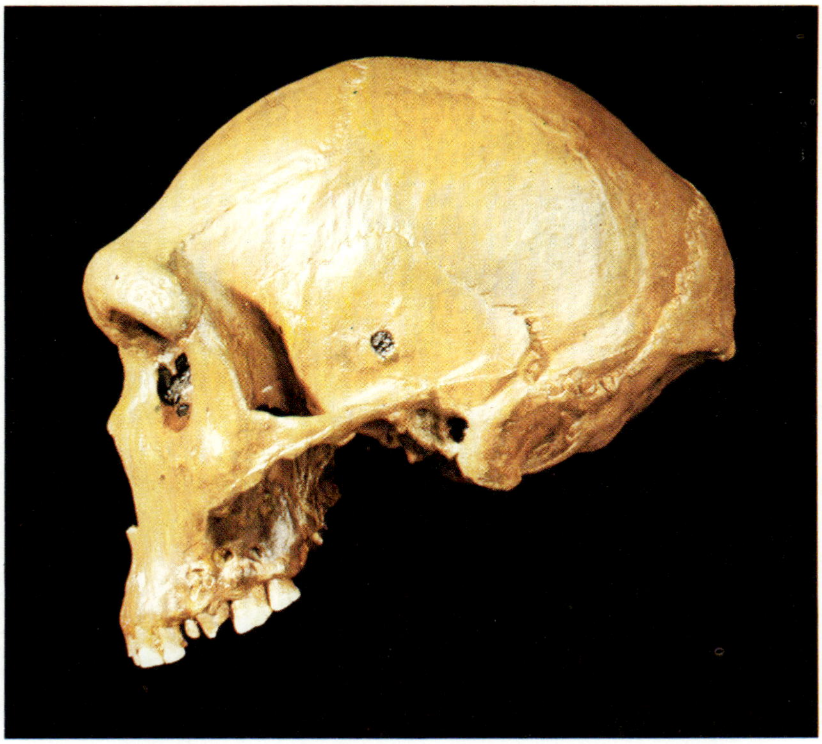

Above: A Neanderthal-like skull found at Kabwe in Zambia (formerly Broken Hill in Northern Rhodesia). Although it has many features of Neanderthal man, it also has features of modern man. Another similar skull was found at Saldhana in South Africa. These skulls are between 70,000 and 120,000 years old. It seems that there was a separate and distinct African variety of man that arose from a *Homo erectus* type and later became extinct. This variety is known as *Homo sapiens rhodesiensis*, because it was discovered in Rhodesia.

The Rise of Modern Man

About 30,000 years ago modern man was living in Europe. His fossil remains, tools and paintings show that he was very different from Homo erectus *or Neanderthal man. But modern man appeared suddenly and his origins are uncertain.*

Below: The brain case of a skull found in the Omo valley in Ethiopia. It has a mixture of *Homo erectus* and *Homo sapiens* features. Dated at about 120,000 years old, it could have belonged to the earliest known ancestor of modern man.

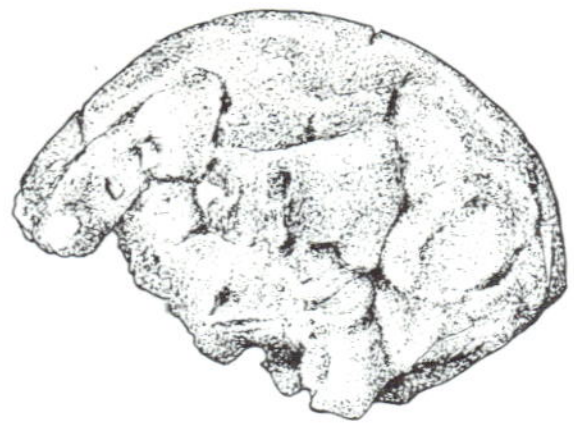

Below: One of the skulls found at Qafza in Israel. It belonged to a fairly robust form of modern man. The peoples of the Middle East and South West Asia may have been the descendants of a North African group and the ancestors of the European Cro-Magnons.

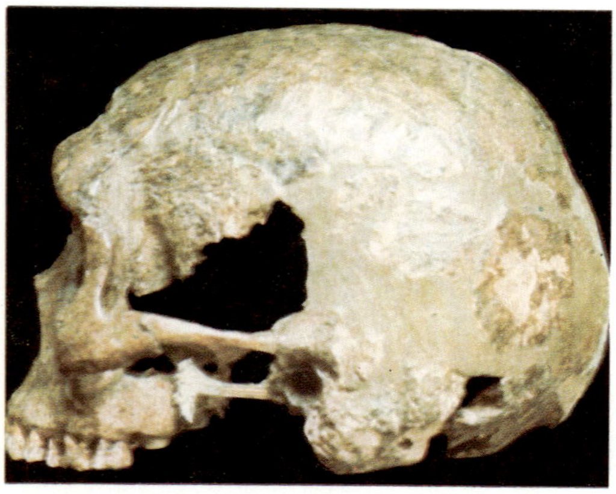

Below: The braincase of a skull found near the River Solo in Java. It is possibly 100,000 years old and resembles earlier fossil skulls of *Homo erectus*. However the brain case is much larger than that of *Homo erectus* and so it is classed as an early form of *Homo sapiens*. Possibly there was a group of people living in Java who were directly descended from the Asian forms of *Homo errctus*.

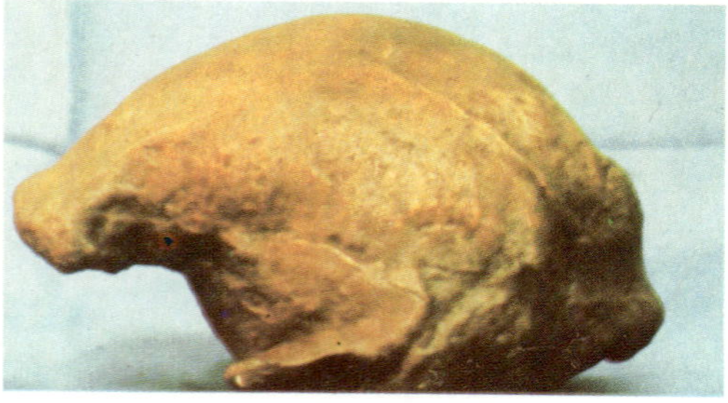

Modern man is known by the Latin name *Homo sapiens sapiens*. And the early modern men probably looked very much like ourselves. The race of modern men who lived in Europe 30,000 years ago are known as the Cro-Magnons. This name comes from an important site in France. There the skeletons of five adults were found. Other sites have shown that southern Europe was one of the main areas of human occupation for about 20,000 years.

Little is known about the origins of Cro-Magnon man. There is evidence that forms of man more advanced than *Homo erectus* were living in Europe about 250,000 years ago. Pieces of skull have been found at Swanscombe in England and Steinham in Germany. These men may have been half-way forms between *Homo erectus* and *Homo sapiens*. The 200,000 year old Arago fossils (see pages 122–3) may also belong to this group.

The first evidence of modern man comes from skulls found in Israel. These date from 35,000 to 50,000 years ago. A much older skull, perhaps 120,000 years old, has been found in Ethiopia. Possibly, therefore, the ancestors of the Cro-Magnons lived in North Africa. From there they migrated to the Middle East and Asia. Towards the end of the last ice age they moved into Europe. There they either displaced or interbred with the Neanderthals.

Whatever his origins were, Cro-Magnon man was still a hunter. He kept no animals and grew no crops. He lived in caves and made extremely good stone tools. The remains of Cro-Magnon tools have been found at a large number of sites. A series of industries or cultures (see page 130) are named after these places and they show a progression of increasingly more advanced toolmaking techniques.

At the same time man was beginning to develop an artistic ability. Hunting probably took up very little time, so the Cro-Magnon people had plenty of time to devote to other matters. About 25,000 years ago some of the European peoples were modelling small clay figures and carving miniature ivory statues. They also made jewellery from shells, teeth, bone, clay and other materials.

The Cro-Magnons lived near the openings of caves. And possibly they moved a little bit farther in during the winter. But deep inside their caves they began to make drawings on the walls. At first these were outline drawings made with a finger or stick. But even these drawings show that the artists had an excellent knowledge of animals and their anatomy. Later they began to colour the drawings using pigments from the local earth. Paint brushes were probably made using

Above: The Cro-Magnons lived in cave shelters They used animal skins for clothing and to make inner shelters in the caves. Their tools were made from stone flints and bones.

Below: Deep inside their caves the Cro-Magnons painted superb pictures of animals. This picture of a bison is in a cave at Niaux in southern France. It was painted over 15,000 years ago.

animal hair, chewed ends of sticks or pads of moss. Often an artist would engrave part of his picture on the cave wall.

No one knows why these pictures were done so deep inside the caves. Working there must have been very difficult. Crude ladders made from the branches of trees were used to reach high parts of the cave walls. Light was provided by a candle that consisted of a moss wick burning in a limestone cup of animal fat. Some of the paintings were probably done just for pleasure. Others may have been concerned with religion or magic. They may have been done to ensure success in hunting. Or they may have formed part of initiation rites when boys grew old enough to become hunters.

The Cro-Magnons were the last of the Palaeolithic (Old Stone Age) hunters. As the ice sheets began to retreat 12,000 years ago, the Mesolithic (Middle Stone Age) cultures began to develop. By this time man had spread to almost every part of the world and the various races of modern man were evolving.

Stone Age Hunters

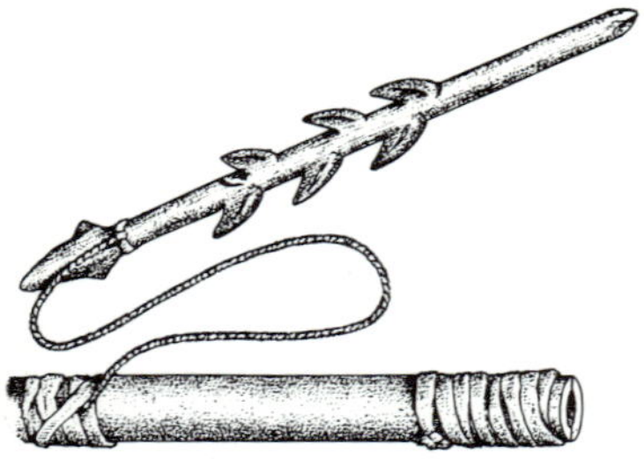

For well over two million years the way of life of man and his ancestors was based on hunting.

Above: A late Palaeolithic (Old Stone Age) harpoon used for hunting reindeer about 13,000 years ago. The barbed head was made from an antler, and was attached to the shaft by a cord. The swelling at the lower end of the head fitted into the hole at the top of the shaft. When the harpoon was thrown, the head embedded in the animal's side and the shaft became entangled in its feet.

Below: Two Mesolithic (Middle Stone Age) hunting weapons. The wooden arrow (top) was tipped with a tiny chisel-shaped piece of flint. The fish spear (bottom) was made of bone into which small flints were inserted as barbs.

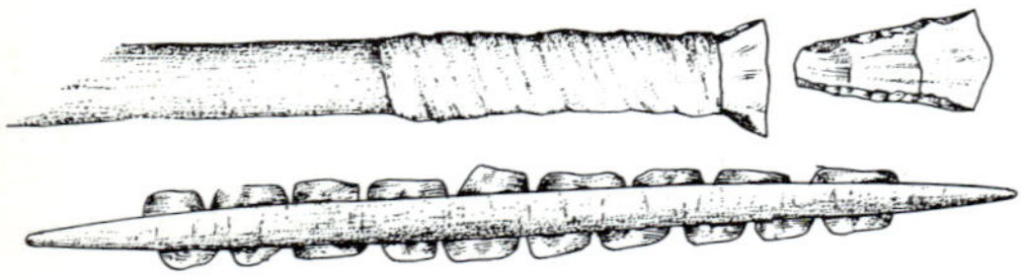

The first hominids probably used sticks and stones for defence and for hunting small animals. The australopithecines may have used fragments of broken bones as tools. But when man actually began to make stone tools and fashion hunting weapons, he began to hunt larger animals. This more than anything else governed the development of social groups and cultures.

One large animal would provide meat for many people. But to hunt a large animal early men had to learn to work together. Everyone had to know his own task and carry it out. Together they carried their kill back to the base camp. There, the women, old people and children would be waiting. They performed the easier tasks that could be done in and around the camp, such as gathering berries and cooking.

A camp site in northern Europe 23,000 years ago. These people hunted mammoths and wild horses (background). They used wooden spears tipped with flints or ivory lances fashioned from the tusks of mammoths. The tents were built over bowl-shaped hollows. Inside each tent a fire was kept going constantly. The fuel was coal (right) mined from local surface workings. These northern people also seem to have worn warm, eskimo-type clothing. Animal skins were prepared using flint scrapers (foreground right). Flint tools do not remain sharp for very long. So the old flint worker (foreground, left) was probably kept very busy.

All this required a group of people who would co-operate with each other. Division of labour was essential. And some sort of communication was necessary. Children had to be taught what to do and adults had to be able to convey information to each other. Communication probably began with signs and sounds that later developed into language.

Hunting also contributed to the spread of man. One group of people needed a fairly large area in which to hunt. When game became scarce or the local population became too large, some groups would move on to new areas. There, if they were successful, they remained and continued to spread.

Food was perhaps man's main concern. But shelter was also important, particularly in Europe during the Ice Age. Caves were often used by early man. But in some places there were no suitable caves and people began building their own shelters. To begin with these were crude 'tents' made of branches and thatched with brushwood and grass. Then skins were used as a covering. About 25,000 years ago, in cold parts of Europe and Asia, people were building thick-walled huts from mammoth bones and stones.

During the Mesolithic period hunting techniques became highly advanced. The bow came into use and arrows were tipped with barbed flints. Hooks were used for fishing. But in some places the hunting way of life was soon abandoned. About 9,000 years ago Neolithic (New Stone Age) people began to settle down in one place and farm the land.

Above: A reconstruction of a Neolithic (New Stone Age) deer antler hood, dating from about 7,500 years ago. It may have been used on ceremonial occasions. Or it may have been worn by a hunter as a disguise.

Man the Toolmaker

Prehistoric men fashioned tools from flint and other stones. Over thousands of years they gradually perfected the techniques of toolmaking.

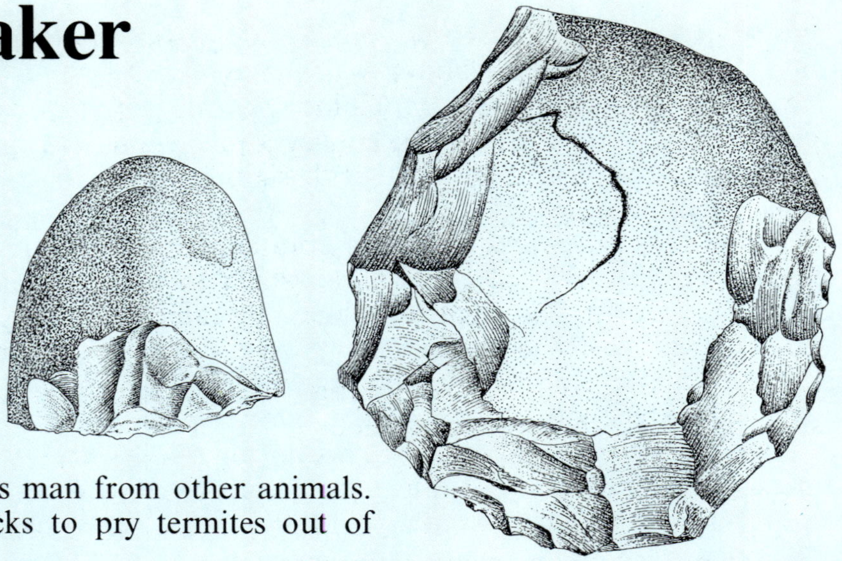

Above: An Oldowan pebble tool (left) and a stone chopper used by Peking man (right).

Below: An Acheulean hand axe was an all purpose tool. It had a point for digging, a sharp edge for cutting (shown on the left) and a butt that could be used for hammering.

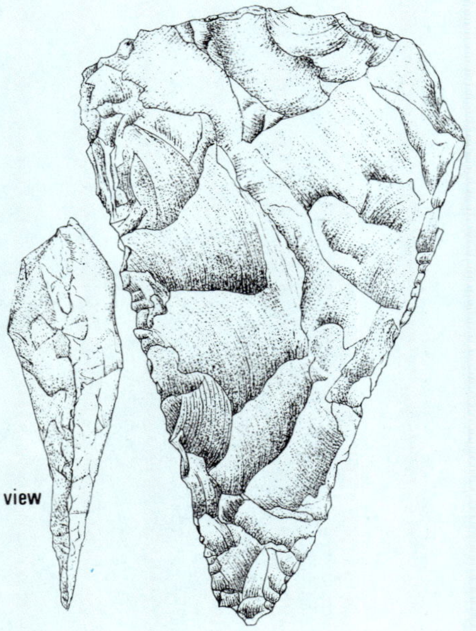

side view

Below: A Mousterian point (left) and scraper (right). The point may have been used as a spearhead. The scraper was used for cleaning animal hides.

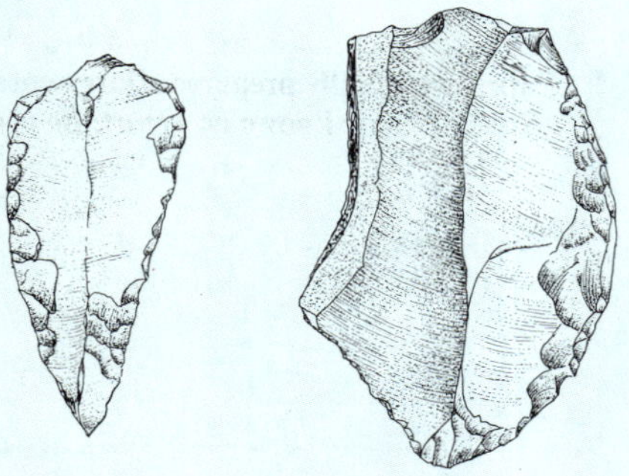

The ability to make things distinguishes man from other animals. Chimpanzees sometimes use small sticks to pry termites out of holes. But only man actually makes tools.

Toolmaking and weapon-making was an important part of man's evolution. Being an unspecialized animal, man has no claws, fearsome teeth or great size and strength. His only advantage is his large brain and greater intelligence. Without weapons, therefore, man is weak and defenceless. With weapons and tools man became a formidable and feared hunter.

The early hominids learned how to use tools before they learned how to make them. Pieces of broken bone were probably used for digging up roots. Stone flints may have been used for sharpening wooden spears.

Gradually, however, man learned that he could improve on natural stones. He could shape them by striking off flakes. Such shaped tools can be recognized by modern scientists.

The progress of toolmaking can be traced through a series of industries or cultures. These are named after the sites where particular kinds of tools were first found. For example, the earliest known toolmaking industry is known as the Oldowan industry, after Olduvai gorge in Tanzania. Here, scientists have found many pebble tools. Flakes were chipped off the ends of the pebbles to make choppers for cutting meat and wood.

These early tools are often called chopper-core tools—simply because choppers were made from the core of the flint. To produce such tools flakes were removed by striking with a stone. More advanced chopper-core tools were made by *Homo erectus* in Africa, Asia and Europe. About 500,000 years ago Peking man used chopper-cores; and he also used the waste flakes. In Europe the first hand axes were made 450,000 years ago and in Britain about 300,000 years ago.

Meanwhile, other *Homo erectus* groups were starting to produce much finer hand axes. The Acheulian hand axe industry is named after St Acheul in France, where such tools were made over 200,000 years ago. But they originally developed in Africa at places like Olduvai and Ternifine.

Acheulian hand axes were pear-shaped. Some had points, others had cutting edges. Acheulian flint workers probably used a pointed, wooden flaking tool instead of striking the flint directly with a stone. As a result they could remove smaller flakes and produce much finer tools.

Until about 100,000 years ago chipped off flakes had either been thrown away or used as they were. But now people began to work the flakes themselves. The Mousterian industry is associated with the Neanderthals. These people worked thick flakes into scraping tools that had a sharp blade on one side. At about the same time the Levalloisian toolmakers were producing flake knives from prepared flint cores (see panel below).

The late Palaeolithic toolmaking industries are all associated with modern man. The Aurignacian and Gravettian toolmakers made blades and scrapers from long, thin flakes. The Solutreans perfected the technique of pressure flaking. This involves removing tiny flakes by pressing the point of a wooden tool against the flint workpiece. The Solutreans produced precision-made, leaf-shaped spear tips up to 18 centimetres long.

The last of the Palaeolithic toolmakers were the Magdalenians. They produced stone tools for carving and engraving weapons and implements from wood, bone and antlers. The Magdalenians were also cave painters and some of their tools were used for engraving pictures on cave walls.

The Mesolithic cultures are noted for their use of tiny flints, or microliths, as arrow heads. During the Neolithic period, as people began to take up farming, they also learned how to fashion stone tools by grinding and polishing.

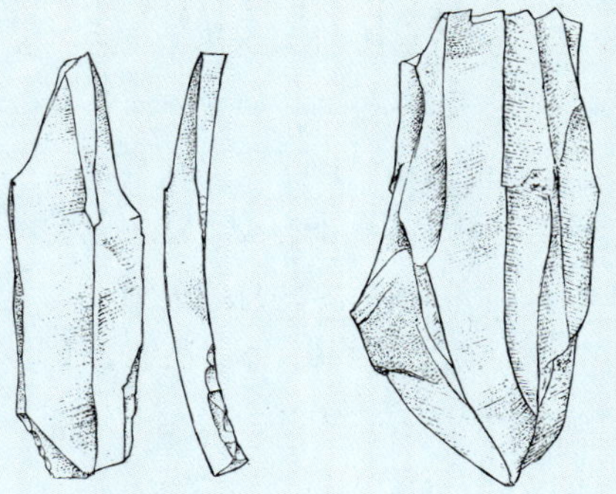

Above: Two views of a Magdalenian engraving tool (left). The point, shaped like the end of a screwdriver, could be sharpened with a single blow. The Magdalenians also made flint blades. These were flakes taken from a long, flint core (right).

MAKING A FLAKE KNIFE

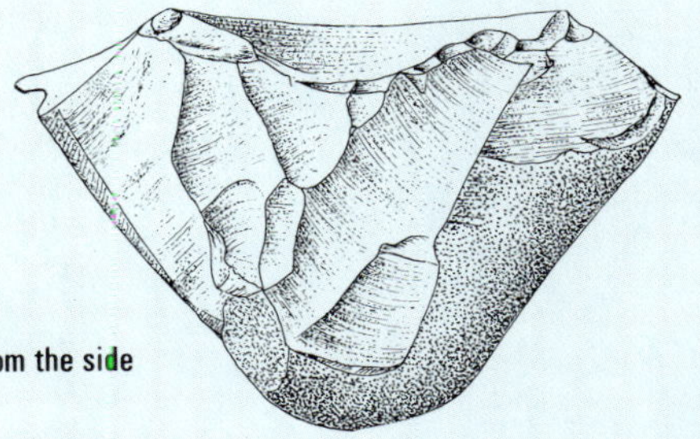

core, from the side

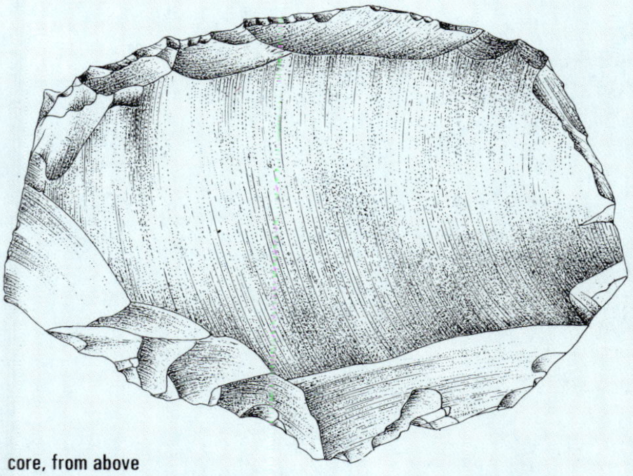

core, from above

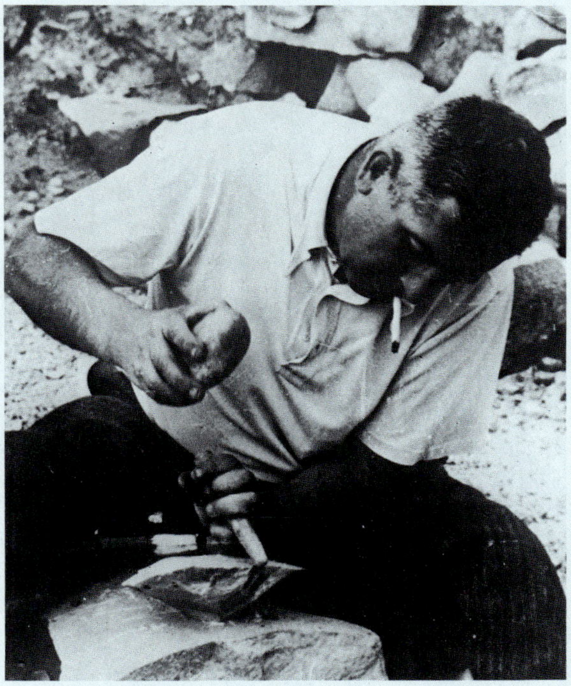

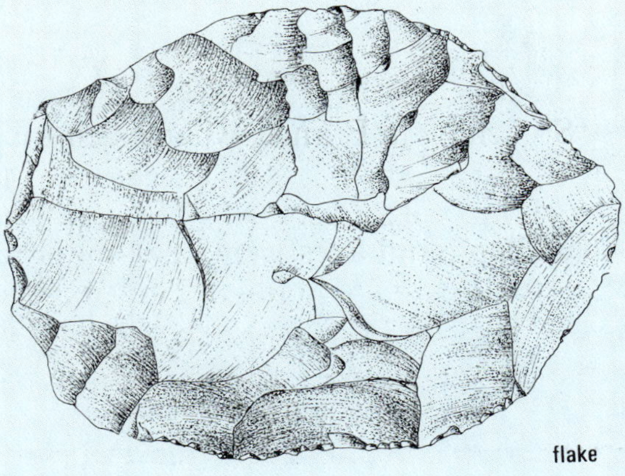

flake

The Levalloisian culture produced thin, oval-shaped flake knives. The flint worker carefully prepared a large core so that one side was as flat as possible. Such a core is known as a 'tortoise core' because it resembles a tortoise lying on its back. Using a hammer stone and a pointed wooden tool, the worker then carefully aimed a blow at the edge of the core, as shown in the photograph. A single, thin flake became detached. A flake produced in this way needed very little work before it was ready for use.

Time Chart of fossil Man

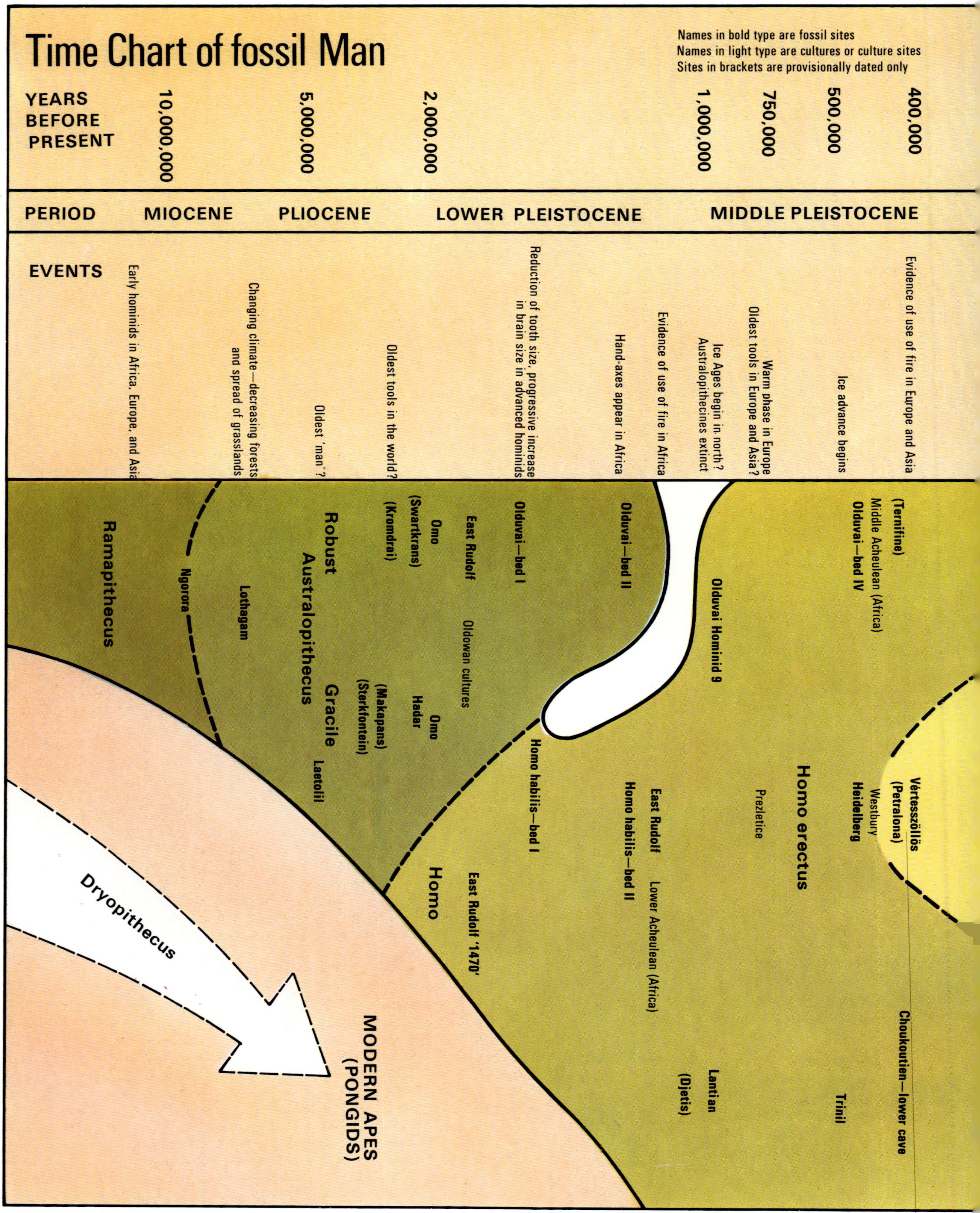

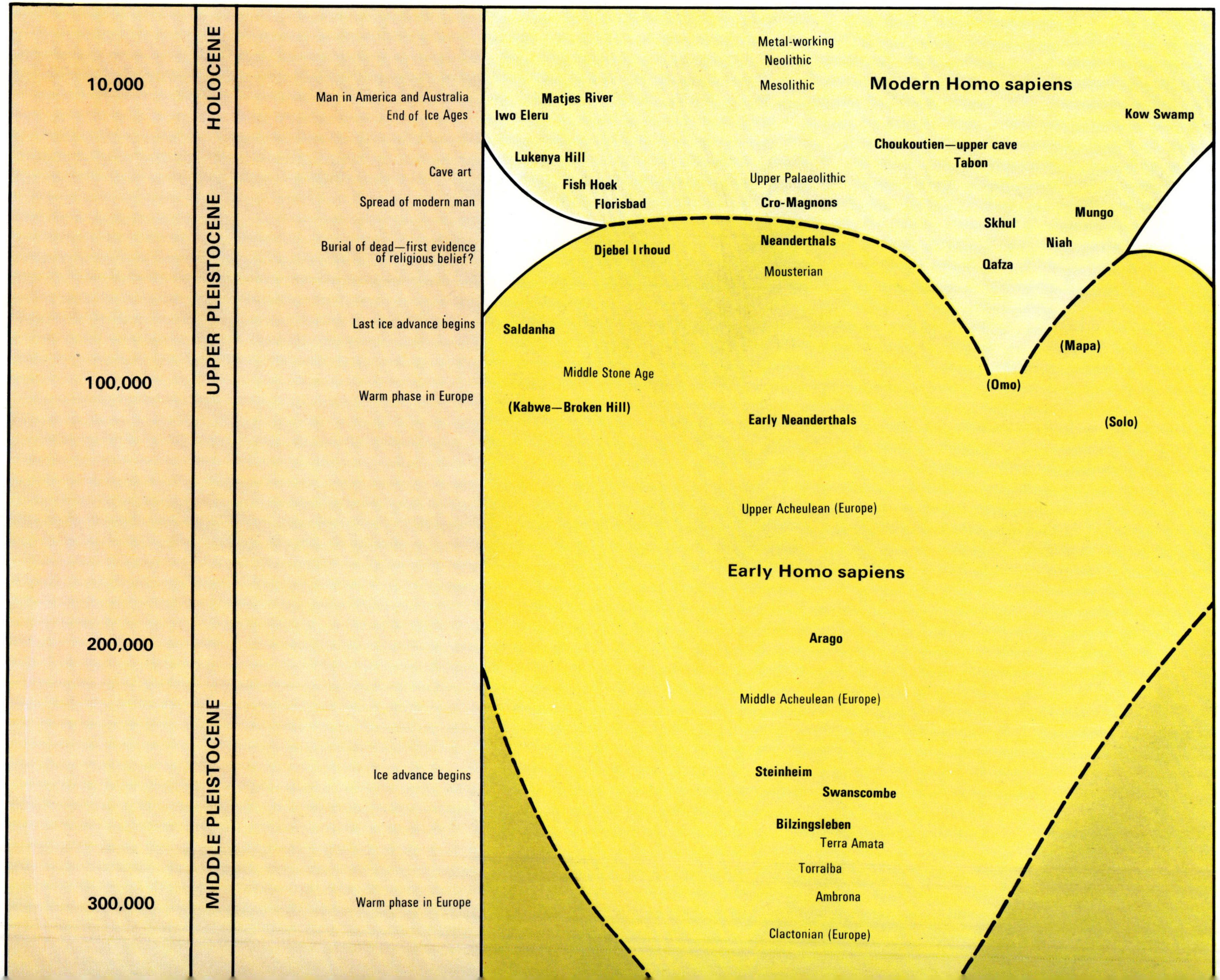

10,000
100,000
200,000
300,000
HOLOCENE
UPPER PLEISTOCENE
MIDDLE PLEISTOCENE
Man in America and Australia
End of Ice Ages
Cave art
Spread of modern man
Burial of dead—first evidence of religious belief?
Last ice advance begins
Warm phase in Europe
Ice advance begins
Warm phase in Europe
Modern Homo sapiens
Metal-working
Neolithic
Mesolithic
Matjes River
Iwo Eleru
Kow Swamp
Choukoutien—upper cave
Tabon
Lukenya Hill
Fish Hoek
Florisbad
Upper Palaeolithic
Cro-Magnons
Skhul
Mungo
Niah
Qafza
Neanderthals
Mousterian
Djebel Irhoud
Saldanha
(Mapa)
Middle Stone Age
(Omo)
(Kabwe—Broken Hill)
Early Neanderthals
(Solo)
Upper Acheulean (Europe)
Early Homo sapiens
Arago
Middle Acheulean (Europe)
Steinheim
Swanscombe
Bilzingsleben
Terra Amata
Torralba
Ambrona
Clactonian (Europe)

GLOSSARY

Acheulian industry A human toolmaking industry characterized by fine hand axes. These tools have been found in Africa and Europe, often with the fossil remains of *Homo erectus* and early *Homo sapiens,* such as Swanscombe man.

Algae Simple plants without stems, leaves or roots. Some are single-celled; others are many celled, e.g. seaweeds.

Amino acid Complicated chemical compound of carbon, hydrogen, oxygen and nitrogen. Amino acids are the 'building blocks' of PROTEINS.

Arthropod An INVERTEBRATE with a hard outer skeleton and jointed legs. Arthropods include insects, spiders, scorpions, trilobites, crabs and lobsters.

Aurignacian culture The first of the late PALAEOLITHIC human cultures. Dating from about 30,000 years ago, it spread from Africa into the Middle East and Europe. Stone tools include long, thin flakes used as blades and scrapers. The Aurignacians also made ornaments and jewellery from bone, ivory and stone and were the first cave artists.

Bacteria Microscopic living organisms whose NUCLEIC ACIDS are not contained within a nucleus.

Binocular vision Type of vision achieved when both eyes are focussed on an object at the same time. Because each eye sees the object from a slightly different angle, the brain receives a stereoscopic (three-dimensional) picture with an impression of depth and distance. All primates and some other VERTEBRATES have binocular vision.

Biology The study of living organisms.

Bipedalism Walking on two legs as opposed to four legs (quadripedalism). Bipedal animals include man, birds and many dinosaurs.

Bivalve A MOLLUSC, such as a mussel, that has its shell in two parts linked by a hinge.

Bone The hard material that makes up the skeletons of most VERTEBRATES.

Bovids A group of artiodactyls (even-toed hooved mammals) that include antelope, bison, cattle, sheep and goats.

Brachiopod An INVERTEBRATE with a shell in two parts linked by a hinge. Brachiopods differ from BIVALVES in that they have symmetrical shells and one part is larger than the other. Their internal structure is also different.

Canine teeth Pointed 'dog' teeth, or 'eye' teeth, found in mammals and some mammal-like reptiles. There are two canine teeth in each jaw, just behind the INCISOR TEETH.

Carnivore 1. A meat-eating animal. **2.** A member of the mammal ORDER Carnivora, which includes the cats, bears, dogs, weasels and seals.

Cartilage The material softer than BONE, that makes up the skeletons of sharks and rays. It is also found in various parts of the skeletons of other VERTEBRATES.

Cephalopod A MOLLUSC with tentacles projecting from its head. Cephalopods include nautiloids, ammonites, belemnites, squid and octopuses.

Chlorophyll The green pigment found in plants. It absorbs light energy from the Sun and this energy is used in PHOTO-SYNTHESIS.

Clactonian industry A human toolmaking industry that existed in Clacton-on-Sea in Britain about 300,000 years ago. Stone tools include choppers and flake blades.

Clay A sediment of very fine particles.

Deposit *See* SEDIMENTARY ROCK.

Echinoderms A group of 'spiny skinned' INVERTEBRATES that include starfish, sea urchins, sea lilies and sea cucumbers.

Edentates A group of mammals that includes anteaters, sloths and armadillos. The name literally means 'without teeth'. Members of this group have few teeth or none at all.

Evolution The gradual process of change that produces new groups of animals and plants.

Flint A pebble or nodule of hard rock composed of the chemical silicon dioxide. Flints are usually found in Cretaceous and Tertiary chalk deposits.

Fossil The remains or evidence of an ancient living organism preserved in rock or some other material.

Gastropods A MOLLUSC group that includes snails and slugs.

Genus *(plural:* genera) A term used in the classification of animals and plants. A genus may include several SPECIES. And several genera may make up an ORDER.

Geology The study of the Earth, its history and its rocks.

Gondwanaland The name given to the large southern continent that formed during the Silurian period. It consisted of Africa, India, South America, Antarctica and Australia. Gondwanaland began to break up into these continents during the Jurassic period. *See also* PANGAEA.

Gravettian industry A human toolmaking industry, dating from about 25,000 years ago and named after La Gravette in France. Stone tools included long knife blades with blunt backs and sharp points.

Herbivore A plant-eating animal.

Hominid A member of the family Hominidae. This group includes all members of the GENUS *Homo* and the australopithecines.

Incisor teeth The cutting teeth found at the front of the jaws of mammals and some mammal-like reptiles.

Index fossil A fossil used to identify and date a rock layer, or stratum.

Insectivore 1. An animal that feeds on insects. **2.** A member of the mammal ORDER Insectivora, which includes shrews, moles and hedgehogs.

Invertebrate An animal without a backbone.

Ironstone A rock containing large amounts of iron-bearing minerals. Ironstone is often found in the form of rounded lumps, or nodules.

Laurasia The name given to the northern part of PANGAEA that broke away from GONDWANALAND during the Triassic period. Laurasia began to split up into North America and Eurasia (Europe and Asia) during the late Cretaceous and early Tertiary periods.

Levalloisian industry A human toolmaking industry, dating from about 70,000 years ago and named after the Levallois suburb of Paris. Stone tools include oval flake knives.

Magdalenian culture Human toolmaking and artistic culture, dating from about 15,000 years ago and named after La Madeleine in France. Tools and weapons from this period include barbed harpoons and spear points, carved spear throwers and eyed needles. Many tools were carved from bone or antler. The Magdalenians were the finest cave painters.

Mesolithic Middle Stone Age. The general name given to the human cultures that date from about 10,000 years ago. Mesolithic peoples were hunters and fishermen.

Molar teeth The crushing back teeth of a mammal.

Molluscs A large group of INVERTEBRATES that includes such animals as snails, mussels and squid. They are all soft-bodied animals, but their bodies are often protected by a shell.

Mousterian industry A human toolmaking industry, dating from about 70,000 years ago and associated with Neanderthal man. Stone tools include scrapers, knives and points.

Mudstone A rock formed from hardened and compressed CLAY.

Neolithic New Stone Age. The name given to Stone Age farming cultures. These date from about 9,000 years ago until the start of the metal age about 5,000 years ago.

Nucleic acids Long chain molecules known as DNA and RNA. These are found in the nucleus of a cell and provide instructions for making proteins and other cell activities. DNA is the material that passes on characteristics from one generation to the next.

Oldowan industry A human toolmaking industry, dating from about two million years ago and named after Olduvai in Tanzania. The stone tools are known as pebble tools.

Palaeolithic Old Stone Age. The name used to describe all the human toolmaking industries and cultures up to about 10,000 years ago.

Palaeontology The study of fossils.

Pangaea The name given to the supercontinent that formed from GONDWANALAND and the northern continents during the Permian period. During the Triassic period it began to split up into Gondwanaland and LAURASIA.

Photosynthesis The process in which a plant converts carbon dioxide and water into oxygen and sugar, using sunlight as a source of energy. The plant uses the sugar to make new plant material.

Premolar teeth The crushing teeth of mammals found just in front of the MOLAR TEETH.

Protein A complicated chemical compound made up of many different AMINO ACIDS. Proteins form an essential part of every living cell.

Protozoan A single-celled animal, such as an amoeba.

Sandstone A rock formed from sand (medium-sized particles mostly consisting of quartz).

Sedimentary rock A rock formed from particles that have been compressed. The particles are either eroded rock particles deposited in water or the remains of once-living animals. A sedimentary rock is sometimes known as a deposit, particularly if the sediment is young and not completely compressed into rock.

Shale Thin layers of rock formed from CLAY.

Solutrean industry A human toolmaking industry, dating from about 20,000 years ago and named after Solutre in France. Stone tools include beautifully-worked, long, laurel-leaf spear points.

Species The smallest group used in the classification of animals and plants. Several species may belong to a GENUS. Members of the same species can breed successfully with each other, but they cannot breed with members of another species.

Vertebrate A backboned animal.

Index